Jocks and Burnouts

Social Categories and Identity in the High School

PENELOPE ECKERT

Teachers College, Columbia University
New York and London

Published by Teachers College Press, 1234 Amsterdam Avenue, New York, NY 10027

Library of Congress Cataloging-in-Publication Data

Eckert, Penelope.
   Jocks and burnouts: social categories and identity in high school
  /Penelope Eckert.
     p. cm.
  Bibliography: p.
  Includes index.
  ISBN 0-8077-2964-7.—ISBN 0-8077-2963-9 (pbk.)
   1. High school students—Michigan—Social conditions—Case
studies.   2. Social structure—Michigan—Case studies.
3. Socialization—Case studies.   4. Peer pressure—Michigan—Case
studies.   I. Title.
LC205.5.M5E34   1989
373.18'09774—dc20

89-33266
CIP

Manufactured in the United States of America

95 94 93 92 91 90 89   1 2 3 4 5 6 7 8

This book is dedicated to my mother,
Dorothy Applegate Eckert,
who helped me maintain perspective
during my own adolescence.

Contents

Preface

The ethnography reported in this book grew out of a study of the social motivations of linguistic change. The linguistic work focused on the "northern cities chain shift," a series of vowel changes currently taking place in the area around the northern cities of Detroit, Chicago, Cleveland, and Buffalo (Labov, Yaeger, & Steiner, 1973), and that constitute what some people may hear as a midwestern accent. Linguistic change is a constant and regular process, which gives rise over the short term to regional dialects or accents, and over the long term to language families (this is how Latin changed into the modern Romance languages). The forces behind linguistic change are to be found both in the linguistic system itself and in the social dynamics that determine the spread of individual changes from speaker to speaker and from community to community. Sound changes have been found to spread outward from urban centers through working class social networks, and to spread upward through the socioeconomic hierarchy within communities. Much of the work in sociolinguistics has been devoted to the study of the social patterns of linguistic variation that represent the spread of changes in progress, in order to uncover the social dynamics of this spread.

Sound changes have social symbolic significance, and thus they are used in connection with the expression of social identity. It is not surprising, therefore, that it is adolescents who lead their communities in sound change in our society. Adolescents are engaged in the development of social identity, and of a sense of community structure outside the family. Their use of social symbols such as dress, territory, cars, music, and language is an important part of the process of manipulating and signaling this developing identity and of marking social differences within their evolving communities. It is for this reason that I chose the high school as the locus of my study of sound change, since it is the high school that brings together adolescents from a variety of social backgrounds in such a way as to force them to interact with, and react to, each other.

The field work for this study took place between 1980 and 1984. At the time, since I was teaching in the Department of Anthropology at the University of Michigan, I located the study in the Detroit area. The study is limited to the suburbs for linguistic reasons. I was primarily interested in the dynamics of socioeconomic class in the spread of change, and I was studying a sound change that is largely limited to the dialects of white speakers. Therefore, I had to find ethnically homogeneous communities, where class was the primary social variable and where the northern cities chain shift was affecting the entire population. Unfortunately, such communities are all too easy to find in the Detroit area, where a very racist climate has created an all-white suburban area. I spent a little over two years doing participant observation in one suburban high school, which I call Belten High in this book, and an additional year of field work in four other Detroit suburban high schools that differed significantly among themselves and from Belten in size and in socioeconomic makeup. Despite these differences, the phenomena described in this book, which focuses on Belten, are repeated in all the other schools. I cannot overemphasize the fact that the dynamics to be described in the following pages are society-wide and not specific to any one school or district.

The field work for this study was primarily ethnographic, with the collection of linguistic data woven into the normal pursuit of participant observation. The taped ethnographic interviews quoted in this book have also been used for linguistic analysis, as have recorded speeches and other public events, and formal word lists that I recorded after the ethnographic work was completed. The linguistic results have so far been reported at a number of conferences and in several articles (see the References). The major linguistic findings will appear in a book to follow this one.

Although this research originated in linguistic issues, it was, from the beginning, as much an ethnographic study as a linguistic one. While deep and detailed ethnography is a requirement of my linguistic work, part of my motivation for this particular study was a separate and long-standing interest in, and commitment to, adolescents. This interest and commitment led me to choose to study the sociolinguistic dynamics of this age group rather than some other, and to devote a separate book to the social dynamics of the high school.

My work in the school was aimed to explore the many aspects of social identity in the adolescent community, and to examine the social significance of socioeconomic class to that age group. I came, eventually, to focus on the social polarization between the class-based social categories, the Jocks and the Burnouts. While these two categories only account for part of the school's student population, they emerged in the course of field work as the basis of the social organization of the high school community and of individuals' sense of identity within that community. The importance of these categories has been underscored in my linguistic findings (Eckert 1987, 1988, in press). Category affiliation, social network orientation, and gender have turned out to be the major, and intricately interacting, social parameters that determine participation in sound change in the adolescent community. There is a shocking lack of literature on adolescent social categories like Jocks and Burnouts, despite the fact that these categories are a fact of life in public schools across the country. And most work on social categories focuses on categories like the Burnouts, as "deviant" and as representing acute problems, not recognizing that Burnouts and Jocks alike are normal, abiding, conservative—and mutually defining—forces in the school institution. What is deviant about the Burnouts is the active neglect that they receive in their society's schools.

Acknowledgments

Because this book has been long in the making, and because the linguistic and ethnographic work are so intertwined, the list of people who have had an influence on it is long and diverse. I miss the community of research assistants at the University of Michigan who not only did so much work, but kept me company when it was time to do the tedious part and kept track of my hours in the video arcade. Lynne Robins assisted me in the earliest stages of the field work at Belten, and Michael Jody assisted me in the other four schools; Marcia Salomon, Lynne Robins, and Mary Steedley transcribed the interviews; Susan Blum, Jane Covent, Larry Diemer, Alison Edwards, and Becky Knack did the phonetic transcription; and the most accurate typist of all time, Leanne Tyler, shared her own adolescent afternoons to do the deadly work of data entry.

Three graduate students, Lynne Robins, Alison Edwards, and Becky Knack, independent of their official employment, played a special role in this work. They were involved from the very start and stayed around for the good parts and the bad parts. The same is true of Steve Novak, who listened to it all and always asked the foreigner's questions. I feel a great debt to my colleagues and faithful friends Robbins Burling, Conrad Kottak, and Roy Rappaport for providing encouragement, support, and intellectual insight at all stages of this work; and to my colleague and husband, Ivan Sag, for his appreciation of my research and his eagerness for me to get it out the door. Finally, and as usual, I must express my gratitude to William Labov, this time for having taught me that one scholar can do many things.

While colleagues, friends, and family provide intellectual, social, and emotional support, this work would have been very hard to do without the help of funding agencies. This research was funded by grants from the Rackham School of Graduate Studies at the University of Michigan, the Spencer Foundation, and the National Science Foundation (BNS 8023291).

I was fortunate in this field work to come across a school system that was open and cooperative, that shared my interests in adolescent social structure in the school, and that did not feel threatened by not having control over my findings. Considerations of confidentiality prevent me from naming this school district, which I refer to in this book as Neartown, but I will remain ever grateful and full of admiration for people I encountered in every capacity in this school system. I am also grateful to the four other nameless school districts for opening their schools to me, and to the Neartown school administrators for helping me convince them that they should.

I would like to thank the Neartown administrators for their practical, expeditious, and frank administrative style; the leaders at Neartown's alternative program for their warmth and judiciousness; the teachers who put up with me, which was all I asked, and those who offered their help, which was more than I had hoped for; the head custodian for all the coffee and a warm place to drink it, and the other custodians for their friendly presence as I met them time and again in the most improbable corners of the school; the principal's secretary, who provided a constantly friendly demeanor and the most invaluable practical help; and the librarians, who treated me as if they had been put on this earth to help me.

Thanks and gratitude are not adequate words to express my feelings for the hundreds upon hundreds of students who gave this work its life. Every single one of them has influenced me, from those who sought me out repeatedly to tell me their thoughts to those who just passed me in the hall. The students at Belten were continually amazed that I remembered all their names, and considering that names are normally my worst downfall, this should be an indication of the unbelievable importance of each of these individuals to my thought and to my life. I only wish that these names could appear here, but, like "Neartown," all the names in the quotes throughout this book are substitutions for real names that I will probably never forget. A large proportion of the students I interviewed thanked me at the end, before I had a chance to thank them. Some thanked me for getting them out of study hall; some thanked me for a thought-provoking discussion; and some thanked me for giving them the chance to speak out to the world. For all, I am glad to have given something in return for what only they could have given me. I feel a special responsibility to that last group, and it is my greatest hope that I have not let them down.

1

Introduction

SO WHAT IS A JOCK THEN?

Someone who gets into school, who does her homework, who, uh, goes to all the activities, who's in Concert Choir, who has her whole day surrounded by school. You know, "tonight I'm gonna go to concert choir practice and today maybe I'll go watch track, and then early this morning maybe, oh, I'll go help a teacher or something." You know.[1]

In the center of Belten High School there is a courtyard: an attractive space with grass, trees, and shrubs, protected from the wind, but not from the Michigan cold, by the hallways and classrooms that surround it. Between classes and during lunch hour, the courtyard comes to life. There are boys wearing flared or bell-bottomed jeans, running shoes, rock concert T-shirts, parkas, jeans jackets. A few have chains attaching their wallets to a belt loop; a few wear black jackets with DETROIT on the back. Many of them have long hair, and stand slightly stooped, leaning somewhat confidentially toward their companions. Many hold cigarettes in their mouths, or cupped in hands held slightly behind their thighs. There are girls with virtually the same clothes, a number with long straight hair, darkly made-up eyes. Many of them stand slightly stoop-shouldered, toes pointed inward, holding cigarettes before them between extended fingers.

For all the activity, the atmosphere in the courtyard is subdued: Faces are serious; talk is quiet, earnest, confidential. Occasionally someone shouts something, laughs aloud, gestures extravagantly. Once in a while there is a small scuffle. Occasionally a hit changes hands, or a joint

---

[1] The quotations are from tape-recorded interviews, with the author's questions, where applicable, in uppercase. The quotations have been edited somewhat to remove false starts and hesitations. The occasional removal of extraneous material is signalled by dots (. . .); dashes (—) signal hesitation. Clarifying material has been added in brackets. All names are fictitious. Many of the interviewer's frequent "back channel" remarks ("yeah," "mm hmm") have been omitted.

passes through a group, casually shielded from that second story window where a certain teacher is said to lurk with his television camera (courtyard rumor has it that the teacher who makes the most busts will win a color TV). In the hall along one side of the courtyard, an occasional assistant principal, hall monitor, or teacher strolls by or pauses, looking out the windows into the courtyard. Sometimes the principal walks through the courtyard, stopping to chat with a group or two of students. Groups spread out and lounge on the grass in good weather; when the weather is particularly cold or wet, they huddle near the doorway or crowd around the radiator just inside the hall.

Just 50 feet from that radiator, around the corner in front of the cafeteria, people who look quite different pack into a small area waiting for the bell to ring. The area roars with conversation, eyes dart across the surrounding crowd, shouts and greetings fly between groups. These people are wearing slacks or jeans with the currently more fashionable pegged or straight-legged cut. Some of the girls are wearing dresses or skirts. Many sport designer labels, carefully feathered hairdos, and perfectly made-up pastel faces. Voices are high pitched, and bodies agitate and jostle in the small space. Postures are straight and open, faces are smiling. The hall is as crowded and agitated as the courtyard is spacious and subdued.

The school as a whole is not overcrowded: Even the short stretch between the radiator and the cafeteria hall is sparsely populated. If the cafeteria crowd were to spread out into the courtyard, there would be plenty of space. But most of the cafeteria people have never been— would never dream of going—into the courtyard. It is not the winter cold that keeps them indoors: The courtyard is Burnout territory, and the cafeteria people are Jocks.

SOCIAL CATEGORIES IN THE HIGH SCHOOL

There is nothing new or exotic about Jocks and Burnouts. Most of us who have attended an American public school recognize the opposition between a "leading crowd" (Coleman, 1961), who enthusiastically participate in, and receive the sponsorship of, the school; and a "rebellious crowd," who reject the hegemony of the school and in turn feel largely rejected by the school. In other places and other times, the Burnouts may have been called "Hoods" or "Greasers," and the Jocks may have been "Soc's" (short for "Socialites" and pronounced *soshes*) or "Collegiates." With modifications to allow for local and historical differences, the stereotypic Jock and Burnout represent categories that are almost universal in American public high schools. In the early 1980s, the stereotypic Belten High Burnout came from a working class home, enrolled primarily in general and vocational courses, smoked tobacco and pot, took chemicals, drank beer and hard liquor, skipped classes, and may have had occasional run-ins with the police; the Jock was middle class and college bound, played sports for the school, participated in school activities, got respectable grades, and drank beer on weekends. The Jock had a cooperative, the Burnout an adversarial, relationship with the school. These stereotypes contain grains of truth but belie a complex reality. While differences in activities and aspirations are clear, there are deeper differences in values and norms that are themselves more important than substance use or choice of leisure activities.

Although Jocks and Burnouts take their names from athletics and drugs, respectively, these are neither necessary nor sufficient criteria for category membership. The term *Jock* originated in sports, which are so central to the high school culture. Indeed, varsity athletes are seen as serving the interests of the school and the community, representing the school in the most visible arena, and symbolizing all that is thought to be healthy and vigorous in American culture. (See Henry, 1965, for a thorough discussion of the role of sports in the American school.) Most important school activities center around sports events, and in common usage the term *Jock* has extended beyond athletes to all students who make those activities run. Although Jock is a common term for "athlete" in our culture, it is generally applied to people for whom athletics is a way of life. A Jock may be simply a person who engages regularly in some sport, but in general usage the term is used for someone whose life-style embraces a broader ideal associated in American culture with sports. The ideal Jock is good at more than one sport, trains regularly, follows the "clean" life-style considered necessary for maintaining physical fitness, and generally embraces American ideals of athletic fair play and competition. In the high school, this ideal of the squeaky-clean, all-American individual is given an even broader interpretation. The high school Jock embodies an attitude—an acceptance of the school and its institutions as an all-encompassing social context, and an unflagging enthusiasm and energy for working within those institutions. An individual who never plays sports, but who participates enthusiastically in activities associated with student government, unquestioningly may be referred to by all in the school as a Jock.

Another name in Belten High for Burnouts is "Jells," shortened from "Jello Brains" and alluding to the degenerative effects of drugs. But just as there are Jocks who are not athletes, there are Burnouts who do not do drugs. Drugs are this generation's most frightening form of rebellion, and as such they are taken as a symbol by and for the school's alienated category. One might more properly consider that these alienated adolescents are "burned out" from long years of frustration encountered in an institution that rejects and stigmatizes them as it fails to recognize and meet their needs. The complexity of the connotations of the category names is reflected in their use. Although the terms *Jock* and *Burnout* are used in certain unambiguous contexts to refer to an athlete or a "druggie," they frequently must be disambiguated through compounding. Thus, such terms as "Jock-Jock," "Sports-Jock," and "Burned-out Burnout" are commonly used to refer to an athlete or a habitual drug user.

The names, and even the stereotypes, of the Jock and Burnout categories belie a broader distinction and a profound cultural split, which reflects in turn the split between the adult middle and working classes. This does not mean that category membership is strictly determined by class, or that all differences between the categories arise directly from class differences. However, the considerable extent to which class is salient to these categories conspires to elevate the category stereotypes to class stereotypes, to produce a polarization of attitudes toward class characteristics associated with either category within the value-laden atmosphere of the school, and hence to force a corresponding polarization of behavioral choice. In this way, the Jock and Burnout categories come to mediate adult social class within the adolescent context. This book, based on three years of participant observation in Belten High and in four other high schools in the suburban Detroit area, will describe the role of the Jock and Burnout categories in the reproduction of adult social class. It will show how an adolescent social structure characterized by an opposition between Jocks and Burnouts integrates the forces of neighborhood and family experience, the structure and norms of the school, and peer social interaction in such a way as to polarize attitudes and behavior along class lines. While class differences may also have a subtler role in the life of the adolescent community, it is largely in reference to the Jock–Burnout opposition that this community perceives and experiences these differences.

Perhaps the greatest difference between this and other books on adolescents and adolescent social categories is its focus on the Jock and Burnout categories as the stable and conservative foundations of adolescent society. Studies of adolescent social categories are usually problem-oriented and focus on deviant groups. The Jock and Burnout categories are not deviant, nor are they strictly products of the times, acute problems, or reactions to temporary conditions in the adult world. On the contrary, they are the essence of continuity. It is these two categories, and the oppositional relation between them, that mediate social class and control change in the adolescent world as their members cooperate, through their competition, to control and interpret the world around them. The Jocks and Burnouts are adolescent embodiments of the middle and working class, respectively; their two separate cultures are in many ways class cultures; and opposition and conflict between them define and exercise class relations and differences. However, they do not exist separately as inward-looking categories, but in a state of intense mutual awareness and thus of continual mutual influence: each category defines itself very consciously as what the other is not. Through their competition and the relative universality of their social differences, the Jocks and Burnouts cooperate to maintain the hegemony of the American class system in the school. The important facts about Jocks and Burnouts are not to be found simply in their reactions to adults or in how they are influenced by adults, but in the mutual reactions and influence of the two categories of adolescents. However much the adult world may influence these categories, the force of the category system resides in social dynamics among the adolescents themselves. The resulting Jock–Burnout split is a function of competition among adolescents for control over the definition, norms, and values of their life-stage cohort.

Just as adult class differences involve differences in orientation to society's institutions, the Jock and Burnout categories reflect opposing relations to the school, the single institution that dominates the life of the adolescent age group. Their mutual differences are defined in terms of the fundamental issue of rejection or acceptance of specific values and interests of that institution, yielding a set of clear binary oppositions. By virtue of their binary interpretation of values, the two categories together achieve hegemony in the social structure of the school, so that the set of choices that represents affiliation with the Jocks on the one hand or with the Burnouts on the other is recognized by the high school community as defining the individual as a social being. It is not the categories themselves, but the opposition between them that is hegemonic. Thus although the majority of high school students are not members of one category or the other, an important part of most adolescents' social identity is dominated by the opposition between the two categories. The oppositional social structure, based on the extremes of school orientation, focuses adolescent attention on the narrow set of choices that define the differences between the Jock and Burnout categories. As a result, the considerable number of high school students who are not affiliated with either category are referred to, and refer to themselves, as "In-betweens" and tend to describe their social identity in terms of traits shared with each of the categories, sometimes even indicating their place in terms of linear distance between the two.

Belten High is a suburban school with no ethnic divisions to speak of. Like the community it serves, the school is virtually all white, all English speaking. While a variety of groups from Eastern and Western Europe and the Middle East are represented in the population, ethnicity is downplayed and does not determine social networks in Belten High. In those schools where ethnic categories crosscut social class, they also crosscut the Jock and Burnout categories, with alliances shifting on the basis of ethnicity or category affiliation according to the issue and the occasion. In other schools, ethnic and class boundaries coincide, and ethnicity is apt to become the more salient issue in the Jock–Burnout split. In Belten High, even the class differences that come into play are not extreme. There are no very rich and no very poor people in Belten: The polarization between the Jocks and the Burnouts is played out in a community that is frequently invoked as Detroit's homogeneous suburban stereotype. It is significant that relatively small differences, given the whole of American society, can be exaggerated in such a way as to create an immense and limiting polarization.

The individual, face-to-face experiences that inhabit social process veil the class origins of many of the needs and attitudes that participate in polarization, particularly in a young population that is just learning to think abstractly about its relation to society. It is the possibility and the fear of social mobility through individual action that makes the categories what they are. The choice of social identity is there to be made, but a choice to cross boundaries—to leave a Burnout neighborhood for a Jock network or vice versa—brings with it the dangers of an unknown culture and of personal rejection. It is the day-to-day cultural differences, and the possibilities of acceptance and rejection, that fill in the class outlines of life in the high school. While many of the origins of the Jock–Burnout split are in the adult economy, that split is made real through adolescent social dynamics. Adults do not impose their class system and ideologies on adolescents; they provide the means by which adolescents can do it themselves.

THE REPRODUCTION OF SOCIAL INEQUALITY IN THE SCHOOLS

The relation between class and the Jock–Burnout split is apparent to most people in the school. Nonetheless, school ideology views category affiliation as a matter of individual choice. Although members of the school community acknowledge that neighborhood and upbringing "predispose" individuals to choose certain social groups, to develop certain interests, and to "like" or "not like" school, there is an implicit understanding that the school itself provides individuals with the means to make choices, and that the maturity of adolescence entails the responsibility to make the "right" choice regardless of childhood experience. The prevailing attitude in the school is that Jocks become involved in school because their families have instilled in them confidence, ambition, and academic skills, while Burnouts become alienated from school because their families have failed them. Burnouts' rebelliousness is seen as resulting from problems at home and from frustration at their lack of academic ability. In other words, the theory of cultural deprivation so popular in the 1950s and 1960s has found its place in the social ideology of Belten High School. In actuality, the years that lead up to secondary school witness a multifaceted process of separation of children on the basis of class and (in many schools) ethnicity, in which children's beliefs are built on adults' beliefs, and in which individual beliefs are built into group beliefs. At no stage can one realistically talk about children's or adolescents' choice without understanding the dynamics of schooling and of the relation between schooling and children's and adolescents' social groups. Although school ideology would have all students be Jocks, it plays a clear role in creating Burnouts.

Schooling around the world is designed to perpetuate cultural and social systems through the preparation of young people for roles in those systems (Carnoy, 1974). Studies ranging from broad examinations of demographic patterns to detailed scrutiny of classroom interaction have demonstrated the role of American education in preparing young people for participation in capitalist society (Bowles & Gintis, 1976). These studies focus on two main mechanisms for the reproduction of the class hierarchy—the perpetuation of class inequalities through the funnelling of children into their parents' place in society, and the enculturation of children into hierarchical social forms through explicit and implicit educational practices. Through the inequality of resources and practices in schools serving communities of different regions, ethnic groups, and socioeconomic levels, and through the unequal treatment of children of varying backgrounds within the same schools, schooling teaches children both their place in society and how to behave in that place. The gradual accumulation of differential experience in the early years of schooling leads mainstream children to believe that education will ultimately bring rewards and success, while non-mainstream children frequently come to view education as a humiliating and fruitless pursuit. I use "mainstream" here in the sense adopted by Heath: "literate, school-oriented, aspiring to upward mobility through success in formal institutions, and looking beyond the primary networks of family and community for behavioral models and value orientations" (1983, pp. 391–392).

Of course, schools do not create these distinctions in a vacuum—their ideology, structure, and practices reflect the society that supports and controls them. And children do not have to go to school to learn what society expects of them. Individuals', families', and communities' perceptions of the ultimate yield of education in employment opportunities lead to differential perceptions of the educational system as a means to advancement. Ogbu (1974, 1978) maintains that the lack of educational motivation among children of subordinate minorities—those "who were incorporated into the United States more or less against their will" (1974, p. 2)—corresponds to a realistic assessment of their opportunities in the employment market. The fact that equal skills and qualifications do not lead to equal employment and income opportunities in our society clearly reduces subordinate minorities' belief in the value of education, regardless of the quality of education that may be available to them. Non-minority groups at the lower end of the economic hierarchy, who are not subject to discrimination on the basis of ethnicity, are in a position to see the limitation of opportunity in an economy that depends on low-priced labor. The schools do not introduce, but validate and reinforce, low expectations that many children acquire in society at large. The means by which children reproduce the experience of their parents are intricately woven into the fabric of society and thus of the school. The outcome is a strong correlation, independent of ability, between educational attainment and home socioeconomic status, with a greater class differential for members of subordinate minorities (Bowles & Gintis, 1976; Coleman, 1966).

A long line of researchers have claimed that children reproduce their parents' experiences in school, under the influence of differences in parental attitudes and tutelage. It is commonly believed that mainstream parents, with their own higher academic attainment and more positive experiences in school, are more inclined to instill greater ambition and more positive attitudes toward school, to help and encourage their children in the actual performance of schoolwork, and to provide conditions and facilities at home that are more conducive to the academic success that is believed to bring broader success in adulthood. (See, for instance, Sewel & Shah, 1967; Strodtbeck, 1958; Rosen, 1956; Davis, 1951; Davis & Havighurst, 1948.) Currently, the evidence is snowballing that the effects of society's, and thus of the schools', differential treatment of mainstream and non-mainstream students overshadow any differences that might be attributed to parental style. It is also becoming clear that while parents in all segments of society may provide help and support for their children's school success, the kinds of parental activities found in the mainstream home match more closely those expected in the school.

While American public schools are intended to provide equal educational opportunity to children of all backgrounds, they base their practices on only one background—that of the white middle class Anglo-American. They assume that parents "who care" will send their children to school with the same set of mainstream assumptions, skills, and modes of behavior and interaction. An array of studies on preschool and early school experience provides dramatic evidence that the smallest components of the schools' cultural assumptions are false. Heath (1983) shows in great detail that children from working class black, working class white, and middle class white homes come to school with well-developed verbal and literacy skills, but based on different orientations to the spoken and written word. The fact that only those of the latter group correspond to those of the school leads to differentiated adjustment to classroom methods. Ethnic differences in communication patterns lead to differences in children's interpretation of a variety of everyday school verbal events, such as "show and tell," classroom participation, reading groups, and counseling sessions (Erickson & Schultz, 1981; Michaels, 1981; Philips, 1972; Scollon & Scollon, 1981). Teachers' ethnocentric interpretation of students' performance in these events leads to an increasingly negative evaluation of non-mainstream students, which is at the same time transmitted to the students themselves.

Dialect characteristics of many non-mainstream students also play an important role in the schools' misjudgment of students' abilities and attitudes. That role has been most thoroughly studied in relation to the Black English Vernacular. Perhaps the most dramatic official acceptance of the purely social role of dialect differences in the school was Judge Charles W. Joiner's decision in the much-publicized "Ann Arbor Black English Case" (1979). Joiner ruled that it is the schools' and teachers' responsibility to recognize and understand the differences between their own dialect of English and that of their students, not simply because these differences cause interference in communication, but because the misinterpretation of these differences can be a source of prejudice against students.

The hegemony of white middle class culture in the schools led educators in the late 1950s and early 1960s to label as "cultural deprivation" differences in early training that are maladaptive to the schools' teaching and evaluative techniques. This notion of "cultural deprivation," which has given rise to both societal complacency about failure and a frenzied development of compensatory programs, is embedded in the attitudes of many teachers of non-mainstream children. Leacock (1969) found that teachers in a low-income black elementary school accounted for student behavior in terms of "deprived home-life" stereotypes that directly contradicted their actual knowledge of these children's homes. It has been found more generally that teachers' classroom expectations for non-mainstream children are lower, leading to a tendency to underencourage and underevaluate their work, and to steer them into general and vocational programs (Becker, 1952; Cicourel & Kitsuse, 1963; Rist, 1970). Furthermore, a variety of factors apparently dispose teachers to respond differently to ability and achievement in children from different backgrounds. Such responses are no doubt a complex combination of ideas about what different children most need to learn in school and differential comfort with the kind of behavior that tends to come with ability and achievement in children from different backgrounds. A broad range of classroom values and strategies combine to socialize middle class children to lead others (in a limited way), and lower-income children to be respectful and obedient. Both are clear preparation for different societal roles later in life.

The 1950s and 1960s brought increased awareness of the overwhelming mainstream bias of classroom materials—not only curricular materials but even such details as the materials made available for classroom decoration (Klineberg, 1963; Larrick, 1965; Marcus, 1961). School materials traditionally portray relatively affluent white middle class families in innocuous and cheerful situations. These materials not only devalue the homes and experience of those from other kinds of backgrounds, but they also fail to provide and promote discussion of the kinds of situations that such children might benefit from in their day-to-day lives. Teachers' responses to children's own life experiences can show the same bias toward mainstream culture, as teachers accept and build preferentially on mainstream children's personal knowledge. The schools' attitude toward children's life experiences is mirrored in parental involvement in the schools. The relative social statuses of parents and teachers is an important factor in the degree and kind of parental involvement in schools, and resistance to community control of lower-income and minority schools stands in contrast to the schools' acceptance, however reluctant, of such control in mainstream communities.

PEER GROUPS, THE SCHOOL, AND SOCIAL REPRODUCTION

There is apparently no end to the subtle and not-so-subtle ways in which schools direct children into their parents' niche in society. But the relation between the individual student and the school does not simply develop through one-on-one interactions between children and adults in and out of school; instead, it is mediated by an emerging peer culture that develops, both in and out of school, from common experience with adults and adult institutions. Children come to elementary school with residentially based peer groups, which are commonly continued in the academic tracking patterns that tend to group non-mainstream children in "lower," and mainstream children in "higher" classes. These school groupings, themselves prejudiced by the kinds of dynamics discussed above, build differential school treatment into peer group identities. A child is labelled not simply as "low-achieving" or "high-achieving," but as a member of a low- or high-achieving peer group. The group no doubt comes, as a result, to base its identity and interactions on mutual achievement status and to develop group strategies of adaptation to this status. Thus school practices come to be embedded in the age-group cultures of children experiencing similar treatment in the schools. It is no doubt this incorporation of children's individual experiences with school into group identities that accounts for the intensification of the class differentiation of school performance in the higher grades of elementary school, when peer group structure begins to exert its full influence.

This book begins where elementary school leaves off. A student population gradually differentiated through the years of elementary school arrives in a new educational context in which "choice" is the key word. The elementary school's evaluation and ability grouping suddenly becomes the student's responsibility, to be internalized by the individual in the construction of a secondary curriculum. While they are steered into classes on the basis of their elementary school experience, students are expected to view their curriculum as the product of their own choice. At the same time, the question of adult occupation becomes more concrete and directly dependent on curriculum, and the "choice" of occupation, or at least occupational level, is made almost simultaneously with the "choice" of curriculum. Peer groups now incorporate concrete aspirations into their identities, and the differences between groups take on a clear relevance to future adult status. A childhood dislike for schooling is elaborated by an adolescent belief that school is unnecessary for the job that looms ahead; childhood success in school becomes clear preparation for college.

At the same time, peer groups become more tightly embedded into school experience, as the cohort emerges into an institution in which the informal social sphere is incorporated into the formal sphere of schooling. Now, in addition to classroom activities, students are expected to participate in a range of extracurricular activities predominantly in the social, political, athletic, and artistic spheres. These activities, in which adults allow students a degree of control not encountered in the classroom, are expected to merge with the informal social structure of the student population. At this point, the disaffection of non-mainstream students attains a new high, as extracurricular activities become the exclusive domain of mainstream students (Coleman, 1961, 1966; Coster, 1959; Smith, 1962; Wilson, 1963).

The responsibilities of adulthood are quickly imposed on students as they arrive in secondary school. Although they have had little control over the choices made for them in elementary school, they are expected to assume full responsibility for the outcome. And in fact, as elementary school decisions have been incorporated into their emerging social identities, the individual now may enjoy even less choice. In secondary school, where the social structure of the student cohort dominates virtually all aspects of life in the institution, choices in all domains are restricted not so clearly by adult judgment as by peer social boundaries. And because adolescents make many important and lasting decisions on the basis of considerations within their peer society, adults who choose to ignore their own role in the development and sponsorship of this society can throw up their hands in helplessness.

Although adolescents' overwhelming peer involvement has surfaced in the literature as a source of influence in individual behavior, this influence has been most commonly treated as a function of pressure and interaction in groups and cliques. While it is true that adolescents adopt attitudes and behavior to fit in with their close friends, peer influence also functions on a more abstract, cultural level. The culture of the peer group takes over where the individual student–school dynamics leave off. The variety of means by which classroom methods teach children their (or, more accurately, their parents') place in the world are gradually incorporated into interactions among the children themselves. This occurs both through adaptive strategies within homogeneous groups and in the dynamics between different groups. As childhood groups emerge into the politicized atmosphere of the secondary school, they take on differential roles in a highly structured peer society. Students who enjoyed the favor of their teachers in elementary school are now in a position to enjoy ascendancy over their peers in the control of many aspects of the social life of the institution. In this way, the power relations of class take hold within the cohort itself. Mainstream children who have been socialized for limited leadership in the elementary school classroom look forward to applying these skills in the more student-dominated atmosphere of the high school. It is no wonder that those who stand to lose power in this new comprehensive school context react swiftly to reject the context itself.

ADOLESCENT CULTURE, SUBCULTURES, GROUPS, AND CLIQUES

The relation between adolescent social categories and socioeconomic class has been an issue in the literature on adolescent social structure since Parsons first used the term "youth culture" in 1942. As Murdock and McCron (1976) point out in a brief sketch of the history of thought on adolescent subcultures, early writings in the United States posited a relatively classless adolescent culture. They single out particularly Parsons (1942), Coleman (1961), and Douvan and Adelson (1966) as presenting a classless adolescent society. While these studies did not deny differential experience, they tended to downplay regional, ethnic, and class differences by stressing the common experience of adolescents imposed by the place of their age group in society. However, Murdock and McCron (1976) also note the clear evidence in early studies that adolescents from different backgrounds experience their life stage very differently. Beginning with Thrasher (1927), studies such as Hollingshead (1949), and even Coleman's 1961 study, showed significant class differences among adolescent groups and "subcultures." Smith (1962) defined "American Youth Culture" in terms of the withdrawal of adolescents of all social backgrounds from adult socializing institutions, claiming that all adolescents are united in a youth culture by "a series of informal socializing institutions, initiated and perpetuated by youth, which form a dominant part of the process of socialization of American youth" (p. 38). Smith did not ignore social differences within the age group, but claimed that the specific characteristics of adolescent "informal institutions" vary with social milieu. He maintained that such things as the dating patterns of middle class adolescents and the "anti-social" behavior of gang youths, for instance, served equivalent functions. The fact that the differences between middle class and gang youths reflect, among other things, differences in relations with adult society and adult institutions casts doubt on this functional analysis. Smith himself observed that gang youths are integrated into adult criminal society, and certainly middle class participation in school reflects a qualitatively different orientation to formal socializing institutions from gang youths' categorical rejection of school. Allen (1973) raised the issue, which will recur in the chapters to follow, that the adolescent life stage is not equally salient to diverse groups in our society. Although Smith's emphasis on the commonalities of adolescent reaction to adult institutions is important, it gives the impression that class and ethnic differences among adolescents are somehow secondary to the more fundamental age split in society.

More recent work has emphasized the class basis of adolescent subcultures (Berger 1971; Clark, 1962; Cohen, 1955; Miller, 1958; Sebald, 1960). Most notable in this context is work coming out of, and influenced by, the University of Birmingham Centre for Contemporary Cultural Studies.[2] A number of studies view British adolescent subcultures such as "Teddy Boys," "Mods," "Skinheads," and "Punks" as complex manifestations of the place of the working class in British society. These are not simplistic representations of adolescents "reacting" to adult society, but meticulously contextualized examinations of working class adolescents' place and potential in, perceptions of, and reactions to the evolving class system in a changing economy.

All of these studies focus on the relation between adolescent subcultures and the broader society, with relatively little attention to the relations among the subcultures. To a certain extent, this is a function of the use of the notion of "subculture," which presumes deviation from mainstream culture. Brake (1985) defines subcultures as

> meaning systems, modes of expression or life styles developed by groups in subordinate structural positions in response to dominant meaning systems, and which reflect their attempt to solve structural contradictions arising from the wider societal context. (p. 8)

Accordingly, an adolescent culture as proposed by Parsons (1942) and Smith (1962) forms a broad subculture in response to the place of the age group in general to adult society in general, with differences among members of this subculture representing subordinate variants of a common age-group experience. More recent writings, particularly those coming out of Birmingham, portray youthful class and ethnic groupings as forming subcultures in response to a mainstream culture. Here age is salient insofar as it structures the subculture's relation to the economy, but it does not set youth apart on the basis of their relation to adult society as such.

There appears to be no objective basis on which to assign relative importance to age-group, ethnic, and class differences, particularly since

---

[2]See, for example, Mungham and Pearson (1976). Hebdige's study of British subcultural style (1979) is a semiotic work in this tradition. See also Willis (1977, 1978), Hebdige (1976), Hiro (1972), Jenkins (1983), and Brake (1985).

all equally owe their salience to the economic structure of society. Adolescents, like adult members of minority and lower socioeconomic groups, are isolated in society and play marginal roles in the economy. It is the isolation of adolescents in age-segregated institutions, and the concomitant exclusion from meaningful roles in the community and the economy, that is regularly cited as the cause of many adolescent and societal problems (Boyer, 1983; Schwendinger & Schwendinger, 1976).[3] Whether on the basis of age, ethnicity, or class, isolation and economic subordination encourage the development and maintenance of distinct subcultures. It is significant that the acceptance of age segregation is greatest among mainstream adolescents. These adolescents can accept economic marginalization because their parents provide more adequately for their material needs, and they anticipate that greater rewards in adulthood will compensate for temporary segregation in the institutions designed for their age group. Non-mainstream adolescents, on the other hand, who must rely more on their own material resources, are more eager to integrate themselves immediately into the adult economy. At the same time, because their own adult communities do not benefit fully from participation in the economy, these young people anticipate no great benefit from temporary segregation and thus reject society's age-group institutions. Thus while mainstream youngsters are segregated from society largely on the basis of age, non-mainstream youngsters try to minimize this particular segregation, but share their parents' and communities' long-term segregation. The degree of isolation of various groups of adolescents may be similar, but the balance of age and social status as factors in this isolation varies.

The notion of subculture presents a structural difficulty in a study such as the present one, since it implies clear boundaries between the individual subculture and whatever is taken as the mainstream culture to which it reacts. To the extent that the Jocks are adolescent representatives of the adult mainstream, the Burnouts could be seen as a deviant subculture reacting to adults and Jocks in the same way. Both the Jock and Burnout categories, however, are clearly subordinate to adult society, and view themselves as competing with each other to define an age-based community. The school may consider the Burnouts to be residual insofar as they do not participate in what the school defines as the school culture, but they are a structurally equivalent force within the age cohort, and the entire cohort, including the Jocks, recognizes them as such.

---

[3]Eisenstadt (1956) gives the most frequently cited argument that the exclusion of youth from meaningful roles in the wider community is conducive to the development of separate youth cultures.

The mutual definitions of the Jock and Burnout categories dictate that they be taken as opposed categories rather than simply as a dominant culture and a counter- or subculture. As discussed by Clarke (1974), a notion of overlapping subcultures (such as youth vs. adults, Jocks vs. Burnouts) weakens the notion of culture intended in the term, but may in fact be the most accurate portrayal of the relations among the various groupings. The notion of subculture, on the other hand, has the advantage of emphasizing the cultural component of adolescent groupings, and of recognizing an abstract level of social organization beyond the groups and cliques that dominate many sociological studies. For present purposes, I prefer to use the more neutral term *category* to describe Jocks, Burnouts, and other groupings in Belten High, with the understanding that these categories are in many ways culturally distinct.

Structural Relations Among Categories

The apparently endless variety of colorful adolescent categories should not be taken as evidence that adolescents respond somewhat randomly to a wide variety of influences. In fact, it is more striking that they respond to so few. The apparently large number of American adolescent categories represented by such names as "Freaks," "Hoods," "Punks," "New Wavers," "Mods," "Jocks," "Stoners," "Burnouts," "Rednecks," and "Grits," and the distinctive dress and other symbolic manifestations associated with each of these categories, suggests to the casual observer that adolescents are insatiable in their search for new styles and cultural forms. However, each of these categories, and many more, fills one of a small number of slots in the structure of any given community at a given time. Whereas studies of adolescent subcultures "at large" tend to focus on extreme and colorful styles, school studies continually come up with two relatively conservative categories. A number of American school studies have discussed divisions similar to that between the Jocks and the Burnouts. Clark (1962) distinguished a "fun" subculture characterized by involvement in school activities, and a "delinquent" subculture characterized by reaction against the school.

Researchers dissatisfied with the dual category analysis have focused on a greater multiplicity of subcultures, some positing a third, "academic," subculture, and some (such as Buff, 1970) isolating such subcategorizations as the "Hippy" and "Greaser" branches of the "delinquent" subculture. One problem with this multiplication of categories is that subcategorizations will occur wherever the researcher has greater experience. Cohen (1979), for instance, isolated three subcultures: the "fun" subculture, the "academic" subculture, and the "delinquent" subculture. However, his distinction between the "fun" and the "academic" subculture is based on factor analysis of distinctions made at the "Jock" end of the social spectrum, ignoring those made at the Burnout end. All of these differences exist, and one could factor out any number of valid constellations within any school. However, these analyses ignore the participants' view of hierarchies of difference. Differences between "Brains" and "Rahrahs" (Larkin, 1979) on the one hand, and between "Troublemakers" and "Normal Burnouts" on the other, are structurally subordinate to overarching differences that unite the first two as involved in, and the latter two as alienated from, the school. This overarching, structurally primary opposition is not simply a product of analysis, but is to be found in high school students' descriptions of their social systems across the country.

Willis's (1977) particularly profound examination of the mechanisms of working class alienation in an English vocational school focuses on two opposed categories, the "Lads" and the "Ear 'Oles," which are strikingly similar to the Burnouts and Jocks of American schools. I am not familiar enough with British adolescent society to be able to speculate about the relation between Willis's "Lads" and "Ear 'Oles" and British Punks. Therefore, the following discussion is based entirely on American schools. While extreme categories such as "Punks" play an important role in American schools, they are not structurally equivalent to Jocks and Burnouts. It is also clear that American Punks are highly derivative, and thus not strictly equivalent to British Punks. Nonetheless, the role of Jocks and Burnouts in American schools cannot be fully understood without consideration of the more spectacular categories. While some categories appear to come and go, reflecting historically specific styles and issues, the Jocks and Burnouts endure by virtue of their conservative role in relation to the more fleeting and radical manifestations that attract media attention.

The "Beatniks" of the 1950s, the "Freaks" of the 1960s, and the "Punks" of the 1980s represent dramatic new forms in contrast to the stable, enduring, and conservative Jock and Burnout categories. Within the American context, "progressive" categories such as Beatniks, Freaks, and Punks present a challenge to the hegemony of the stable class system represented by the Jocks and Burnouts. In the nonconfrontational style of class differences in American society, the Jocks and Burnouts, modelling themselves on their immediate local predecessors, represent stable continuations of their parents' roles in society, and see themselves as America's "typical teen-agers." Their age-group identity is based on the differences between their own behavior and that of adults and adults' own past adolescent behavior. When categories such as the Beatniks, Freaks, and Punks emerge, their more spectacular behavior poses a threat to this age-group identity. While Jocks and Burnouts are continuations of local stable categories, the radical categories respond to influence outside the local context—frequently through contacts with college students—and represent a "progressive" force in the school. This outside influence is important for the Punks I have encountered in the 1980s in several schools, and corresponds to reports and recollections of Beatniks and Freaks.

The progressive groups consciously rebel against the Jock and Burnout categories, and particularly against the social separation that they represent. Thus the progressive groups pose a threat to the Jock–Burnout hegemony, not only because of their "unpredictable" style but because of their opposition to the category system itself. This threat accounts for the intensity of their hostile reception—in the early 1980s, the mutual hostility between Belten's Jocks and Burnouts was exceeded only by both categories' hostility toward the emerging Punks. Once the progressive category attracts sufficient media attention to threaten the Jocks' and Burnouts' age-group hegemony, or their status as "typical teen-agers," these conservative categories are forced to take the progressive category more seriously. By absorbing elements of the more radical category, the Jocks and Burnouts defuse its potential for serious influence. The Jocks and Burnouts in effect divide up and adopt enough of the new category's symbols to render it ineffectual; sometimes they even take on its name. Thus the "Greasers" in some schools gradually acquired the name "Freaks" in the 1970s, along with bell-bottomed jeans and the "drug culture." In this way, the opposition between the Jocks and the Burnouts preserves the adolescent (and thus the adult) social order, keeping attention focused on limited issues and reinterpreting and controlling change.

All adolescents, whether they attend school or not, are subject to national norms for their age group. Insofar as the educational institutions that American society has created for adolescents are relatively uniform in their goals of instilling specific American cultural forms, all those attending school must function in some relation to the norms and values of the school. If one wishes to talk about an adolescent culture, such a culture can be said to reside in the relatedness, rather than similarity, of the responses of diverse adolescents to these norms.

It is important to distinguish categories from cliques, which are the predominant unit of analysis in some American studies of adolescent social structure (see, for example, Gordon, 1957). As well-defined, bounded groups, cliques have clear memberships. Categories do not have memberships per se, but represent ideologies and cultural forms that are variously adhered to by individuals and groups. It is for this reason that In-betweens may refer to themselves as "part Jock, part Burnout," or may shift their affiliation according to the situation without changing their friendship group. Individuals' occasional indecisiveness about affiliation reflects a struggle with the Jock–Burnout split, and with the apparent necessity of aligning oneself in relation to it. Because he was looking for cliques, this indecisiveness led Varenne (1982), in his study of an American high school, to reject the concrete existence of "Jocks" and "Freaks." Finding that the adolescents he talked with tended to avoid categorizing themselves, and were ambiguous both in their use of the terms in referring to others and in their attitude toward categorizing at all, Varenne concluded that the constructs "Jocks" and "Freaks" represented a part of the symbolic process of the community rather than actual groups of people.

Although students in my experience, at Belten High and elsewhere, identify far more readily with one category or the other than those in Varenne's experience, most individuals do express discomfort with the system of classification and distance themselves from the process of categorization in their talk. The Jock and Burnout categories are, as Varenne (1982) says, part of students' "way of talking" about their social structure, and their frequent reference to categories may exaggerate the importance of these categories. It is also true that the ethnographer's assumption of the existence of these categories can elicit more talk about them than might otherwise occur. On the other hand, it should not be ignored that the avoidance of category references can stem from the fact that adolescents know that adults do not approve of categorizing people. Moreover, many adolescents do not approve of their own tendency to categorize and would generally prefer to appear not to take such constructs altogether seriously. But in my interviews, the names "Jock" and "Burnout" came up regularly in response to a request simply to describe their group of friends. It was also common for an individual who had told me that he or she did not categorize people to explain in other circumstances—or simply later in the same interaction—some fact of social life in terms of these very categories.

Adolescents' ambiguous and ambivalent participation in the system of categories is a reflection of the tension between a need for clarity of choice and identity, and a need for individuality, freedom, and change. This fluidity of viewpoint, which makes adolescents unclear in their references and vaguely self-contradictory in their talk about these categories, is not specific to this age group or this context. It is important to most social beings to retain a certain amount of flexibility of self-definition in interacting with a variety of people and in a variety of contexts, and adolescents are perhaps more extreme in this because they are just learning. The experimentation with social identities character-istic of the adolescent period requires the individual to step in and out of roles and identities and to develop strategies for resolving apparent personal contradictions.

Thus Jocks and Burnouts do not constitute clear groups or cliques; they are cultural categories, which define and unify collections of groups and cliques. The Jock and Burnout categories organize the ide-ologies of the groups within the social network of the school, aligning groups at different parts of the network according to key issues in the adolescent society. They are cultural foci rather than clearly defined groups, and their differences are organizing principles within the com-munity rather than definitions of individuals or groups of individuals. Some cliques may evolve into categories. The Punk category of the 1980s in Belten began as a group, and rose to cultural prominence as other groups and individuals adopted its style. In contrast, a small group of low visibility in Belten, who referred to themselves as "Cow-boys" because of their involvement with horses, came and went in the school unnoticed by the school society. A small group of girls in a Cali-fornia high school, referring to themselves as "Duranies," remain a clique united by their devotion to the rock group Duran-Duran. The Cowboys and the Duranies failed to become categories by virtue of their specificity. The very localized and limited interests that set these groups apart did not represent important cultural issues that could be general-ized to the rest of their age group. The significance of a category is precisely that it exists on a higher level of abstraction than the social groups that compose it. Social groups orient themselves to the category in individualized ways, but recognize a cultural connection with other groups that affiliate with the same category.

JOCKS, BURNOUTS, AND THE SCHOOL

In accepting the necessity of high school graduation for entrance into the working class, and in participating in a school-based social op-position to the Jocks, the Burnouts, like the Jocks, endorse the impor-tance of the school. Their alienation from the school is based not on the feeling that school is altogether irrelevant to their lives and aspirations, but on the feeling that the school could be but is not serving their needs. The Jocks and the Burnouts represent opposing ways of existing within the school, and thus the Burnouts should not be equated with subcul-tures that are more effectively separated from the school, such as

Thrasher's (1927) gang culture. Contrasts between extreme groups, such as Jocks and gangs, cannot illustrate the effects of close contact among adolescents of differing backgrounds on the development of class identity. In general, the work on adolescent class cultures that concentrates on socioeconomic groups in isolation emphasizes the relation between adolescents and the society at large, or between adolescents and the school institution. The emphasis in this book is on the relation between contrasting adolescent populations within one community. The purpose is to show how divisions emerge in day-to-day interaction within the one institution that is intended to, but does not, serve all social groups equally.

Certain commonalities arise from the adolescent need for autonomy and the uniformity of the institutions that appear to deny them this autonomy. What is specifically adolescent about adolescent culture is the negotiation of this autonomy not only between adolescents and adults, but among adolescents. The contrast between diverse groups of adolescents in the face of adult institutions is as much a part of adolescent culture as whatever is common in their reactions to these institutions. Whereas Smith (1962) located an adolescent culture in the commonalities of various adolescents' reactions to the adult world, I would argue that such a culture resides in the structuring of their differences. A culture marks and elaborates certain internal differences, and it is the recognition and interpretation of these differences that is shared by members of the culture. For there to be an adolescent culture that subsumes the categories of school-oriented middle class white students and gang youths, for instance, this culture must define their differences. By virtue of their status at two extremes, middle class and gang youths do not frequently come into contact. However, each of them does interact regularly with intermediate groups as if they, too, were at an extreme; the contrast of each extreme to these intermediate groups provides the focus for a process of social differentiation that is fundamental to the development of categories.

Studies of adolescents in school frequently isolate as two dominant categories those who share the goals of the school and those who form a counter-school culture, as discussed earlier. This basic division into pro- and anti-school categories is a social process common to virtually all public schools, and it generates and institutionalizes differences among adolescents on the basis of responses to the school. The nation-wide structure of schooling imposes a common social context, therefore, which gives rise to common generalized responses not simply to the school but among its student population. Adolescents who come into regular contact in school are united by a set of assumptions that interpret and structure differences among adolescents at the same time that they articulate the age group as a whole with adult society. One could say, therefore, that there is an overarching school culture, which generates categories defined by differences in orientation to the school. These categories reflect larger socioeconomic and ethnic groupings in the society, which affect (however indirectly) school orientation. While the specific characteristics of any given set of categories in a school will depend on the regional, ethnic, and socioeconomic characteristics of the community, the social processes involved in institutionalizing differences between the categories are inherent in the national institution of the school.

This book is not just about the differences between Jocks and Burnouts; it is also about how these differences tie them together in mutual definition and in competition and cooperation to define their community and their age group. The book is about schools too, because they are the institutions that provide the context for these dynamics. The school assembles people from diverse segments of the community that might otherwise remain separate and engages them in a competition to control their environment, to define their age group, and to set norms for interaction among themselves and with adults. Both the Jocks and the Burnouts are eager and frightened to grow up. Both categories seek and fear the autonomy that qualifies them for and signals adulthood. The Jock and Burnout ways of life comprise different ways of fulfilling the need for autonomy: the Jocks through cooperation with adults in the fulfillment of adult-like roles in a limited environment, and the Burnouts through coping with the dangers and opportunities of the world beyond the school and community. A Burnout's confrontation with the police and a Jock's conference with the student activities director represent to each, respectively, participation in the adult world. Perhaps it is the classic ambivalence of adolescents toward autonomy that makes its pursuit such a hot issue—but above all, Jocks and Burnouts accuse each other of not facing up to the responsibilities of adulthood.

Although the school serves as the context for the differentiation between Jocks and Burnouts, the elaboration of the two categories through the years of secondary school yields differences that transcend responses to that institution. The Jock category, based on participation in school activities and closely articulated with the adult power structure of the school, develops a corporate orientation that yields hierarchical social networks and instills corporate values in personal relations. The Burnout category, focusing on the more immediate development of adult status as defined in the working class world, develops egalitarian social networks focused on transcending the school context. The two categories represent alternative and, within the confines of the school, opposite adaptations to the demands that our society makes on adolescents. Responding to different, yet specifically adolescent, needs, each category provides a cultural milieu within which its members can negotiate their way through the difficult period of adolescence, and into their adult social statuses. Participation in either of these cultures represents a very particular way of being an adolescent and serves as training for corresponding adult roles. The following chapters will show how these categories develop, how they mediate social identity within the adolescent community, and how they function to continue the enculturation of adolescents into the adult class system.

The Jocks and Burnouts do not represent static categories, but a means of organizing the cohort's evolving sense of social structure. An adolescent age group does not simply merge with the adult world, but takes into adulthood the attitudes and styles of interaction learned during adolescence. It is during adolescence that the cohort becomes conscious of itself, and that individuals' relations with age-mates and with members of surrounding age groups evolve, along with the cohort's continual reevaluation of itself in relation to its surroundings. Thus adolescent society represents the foundation of the cohort's permanent social organization and consciousness. As one of the few settings in which contrasting social segments of a local population are brought into regular intensive contact, the school provides the main context within which the cohort develops a sense of ethnic and socioeconomic identity. Although the participants in this adolescent society are aware of the class basis of the Jock and Burnout categories, they do not experience their differences in purely social class terms. Their adolescent experience with different local social categories will fill out their characterizations of and attitudes toward what they will later come to recognize as different classes.

It would be a mistake to equate the Jocks and Burnouts simply as opposing embodiments of conflicting norms or as opposing means of achieving class identity. What makes them equivalent is their mutual opposition within the school, and the power of this opposition to incorporate independently motivated characteristics into overwhelming stereotypes, which in turn dominate the evaluation and treatment of individuals of all kinds. Within the context of the school, which mediates between adolescents and adult society, the corporate norms associated with Jocks are positively evaluated and rewarded, while the noncooperative norms associated with Burnouts are stigmatized and discouraged. As a result, the school provides not an open community in which individuals can explore their values and pursue their interests, but a social regimentation in which particular values and interests restrict each individual to a well-defined place in the institution and in the adolescent community.

It is obviously difficult to arrive at a perfectly balanced view of the role of class in the development and preservation of high school social categories. Many of the characteristics of either category reflect very clear class differences, but each individual's affiliation is bound to be more complex, because each category offers attractions to certain individuals independent of the class origins or outcomes associated with these attractions. But just as it would be a mistake to be overly simplistic and deterministic, it would be a mistake to deny the overwhelming salience of class and class conflict in the category system, and the ultimate power of this system to lock individuals into life patterns. The discussion in this book, therefore, will present the relation between adolescent social category and class, while trying not to neglect the independent factors that may lead to individual affiliation.

2

Field Work in the High School

Okay, what I'm going to say doesn't go any farther than this room, right?

When I began studying adolescents, I felt a certain amount of pressure from my age peers to be "in" with adolescents and to know what was cool. And I found myself instantly transformed into an expert on adolescents, consulted by parents and, even more embarrassingly, presented to their adolescent children as an expert on adolescents. I frequently felt that a performance was expected—that I should give a field work demonstration, or perhaps the audience was waiting to see if the adolescent would recognize me as "one of them" and say something to me in a language that only we two could understand. This is not an indication of the silliness of my acquaintances, but of the puzzlement our society feels about adolescents, which colors expectations about work with adolescents. Adolescents are seen as living in their own world—as unreachable to the average adult—which no doubt explains why so many non-anthropologists asked me if I was passing as a teenager in order to do my work.

Books and articles have been written about adults posing as high school students and getting the "scoop" on adolescents. There is a certain amount of romanticism about being "one of the kids." I was 38 years old when I began the field work for this book, and although I didn't look quite my age, there was certainly no question of passing for under 20. Nor is there much chance that the average American anthropologist could pass for Sherpa. In the end, the challenges and responsibilities of doing participant-observation in an American high school are not very different from those facing an ethnographer working in any other culture or age group. I was an outsider trying to get to know and understand a community. I needed to gain the confidence and trust of the members of the community so that they would allow me access to their activities and knowledge, and I needed to become sufficiently part of the local woodwork to be able to observe activities without producing a distraction. I needed to be sufficiently aware of my native cultural assumptions to monitor their effect on my observations and perceptions. And I needed to overcome the mistrust of a subordinate community towards me as a member of a dominant power group. Like any other anthropologist, I had the minimum responsibility of leaving no ill effects from my visit and no regrets on the part of those who participated in my work. I needed to respect the privacy and the wishes of the people who helped me with my work, not simply to inspire trust but to honor it as well. The fact that the people I was studying were white American adolescents in a formal institution changed nothing in terms of what I owed the members of the community or in terms of how much I could learn from them. I do not claim to have been completely successful in all of these aims; indeed, all ethnographers come away from the field full of regrets and unanswered questions.

PROBLEMS OF THE NATIVE ANTHROPOLOGIST

Doing ethnography in one's own culture brings obvious problems, and an American doing ethnography in an American high school certainly stretches the limits of ethnographic method. My challenge, in doing this work, was not to pretend to be a complete outsider to the community, but to assess the real nature of my status. While I was not a member of the Belten high school community, I was an ex-member of an earlier high school community. I might have been shocked by the changes that time and distance had brought to the high school or by the timelessness of the high school. Either way, I entered the school with a largely unarticulated social model of high school. The nature of my own high school, the roles I played in it as an adolescent, and the range of my social and institutional contacts all provided me with one story about high school. My high school experience has been reworked and reinterpreted over the years, so that my memories at the age of 38 bore an exceedingly complex relation to what was, in 1959, already a complex reality.

I came from an upper middle class mainstream home in New Jersey and attended a high school of fewer than 1000 students, where I was a Jock and a stubborn underachiever. Probably because of the small size of the school, there was less need to identify people by category membership, and the polarization between the equivalents of Jocks and Burnouts was smaller than in any of the schools I have observed in my work. In fact, there was a name for the equivalent of Burnouts, "Hoods," but there was no common name for the equivalent of Jocks aside from "the popular crowd," although there was an adjective, "collegiate," used to refer to their style. Both terms were infrequently used, and when they were used they referred more to style than to a category of individual. But the opposition was nevertheless there, and its consequences were undoubtedly greater than my Jock awareness allowed me to see. The fact that my own background gave me native knowledge of something resembling the Jocks, but not the Burnouts, posed a complex problem. On the one hand, the Jocks were more familiar to me than the Burnouts; on the other, I believed that I knew things about the Jocks that I knew I did not know about the Burnouts. There is no special way to deal with the potential interference of personal experience. My responsibility as an ethnographer was not to forget my own story, but to know it well and to refer to it constantly to make sure that it was not blinding me to what I saw or focusing my attention on only some of what I saw. Careful articulation of my previous beliefs about school and adolescence was interleaved with a constant questioning of every observation and every interpretation.

ESTABLISHING A SITE

I attribute a good deal of my success in this field work to the arrangement that I was able to develop with Belten High. As I gained experience with school districts in subsequent years, I realized how much I owed to the sheer luck of having at the outset sought the cooperation of a very open district administration. At the time I began looking for a field site, I had no ties with the schools or with the School of Education at my university. I selected Neartown on the basis of its demographic characteristics and its location in the Detroit suburbs and sent a brief research proposal to the Neartown district administration. I went to my first meeting with district administrators feeling embarrassed and defensive about the intrusion I was proposing. My relief knew no bounds when they began that meeting by saying that they were inclined to like my proposal if only because I was the first researcher in their memory who wanted to talk to students rather than administer tests or questionnaires.

Unlike most communities that ethnographers study, the school district has a formal procedure for deciding whether to provide access and the means to monitor the person's activities once access has been given. In addition, the people making the decision in this case were not those to be studied, but were legally responsible for their safety and their interests. If I had been a survey researcher, they could have reviewed my "instruments" and allocated specific times and places for my interactions with students. What I was asking for, however, was virtually unlimited access to a school and to the students when they were not in class. With such an open-ended agenda, the administrators could only base their decision on a judgment about my aims, my methods, and my character. Our final understanding grew out of discussions of such things as how I would handle hypothetical situations, the general kinds of things I was going to discuss with the students, and how I would go about protecting their rights in the course of field work. In the end, the only formal limitation that they imposed on my behavior was necessitated by questions of liability—that I would never be the only adult present in a building with any students. They then helped me choose from among their several high schools by providing information not only about the demographics of the student body but also about things that would affect my functioning in the school, such as the principal's governing style.

The principal of Belten High turned out to be as sensitive to my research interests and needs as the district administrators had been. I was given free access to the school for an indefinite period of time, with the understanding that I would avoid being disruptive and that the principal would let me know if my activities ever became a problem. This never happened. The principal introduced me to the faculty at a faculty meeting, briefly saying that I was an anthropologist doing a study of adolescent social networks, that I would be "around" for some time, and that I would be glad to discuss what I was doing at any time. The teachers' reactions were varied but mild, and once it was clear that I was interested in the students rather than them and that I was not going to disrupt their teaching, we settled into a relatively comfortable and orthogonal coexistence.

LIFE IN THE SCHOOL

I spent two years at Belten. The first year I went regularly, and the second year I went more occasionally. At the time of this field work, I was an assistant professor at the University of Michigan and commuted to Neartown—about a 40-minute drive. Part of the time, I was on leave so that I could devote full time to the field work. The rest of the time, I arranged my schedule so that I did my teaching in the late afternoon or evening. My normal schedule was about the same as a Jock's—I arrived in school at the beginning of the day and stayed until there was nothing going on any more. Occasionally I hung out at the fast-food restaurants where students went to skip class, or wandered around the streets with someone who was "blowing off" school. Sometimes after school I went along to parks, homes, or hangouts, and sometimes I came back in the evening for a game, dance, concert, or other activity. But while I did see students outside of the school, most of my work took place in and around the school during school hours.

My aim in this work was to be relatively low-keyed and informal and to interest students sufficiently in what I was doing that they would accept my constant presence. I dressed more or less like the average Belten In-between—jeans or cords, sweaters, ski jacket. This was not dressing "down"—if anything, my dress was slightly more respectable when I went to Belten than when I went to the university. I introduced myself as "Penny Eckert," a person who was writing a book about teen-agers, social life, and the school. In spite of society's preoccupation with age, adolescents generally have only the vaguest sense of what happens beyond 25, and the students at Belten were generally not concerned with my age. It would be a mistake to assume that youth—particularly extreme youth—is an advantage in working with young people. I have noticed, in having college classes do field work, that adolescents can be extremely wary of field workers too close to their own age. This makes perfect sense when one considers that someone who has recently left the adolescent life stage may be reacting against the culture and behavior so recently left behind and can be expected to judge adolescents rather harshly by the new standards of the next life stage. An obviously older person is a member of an entirely different social world and hence poses no significant social threat. Inasmuch as many of the students at Belten were concerned with the fruits of my work, they certainly preferred to believe that I had not only adult competence but adult credibility. The only potential threat that I as an older person could pose would lie in my ties to the generation of their parents and teachers, and in any generational social norms I might judge them by. My main job in impression management, therefore, was maintaining a separation from the norms and the authority structure of the school, and establishing a role for myself in the school that did not resemble any previously existing institutional roles.

"No, I'm Not a Hall Monitor"

The one part of the school that I assiduously avoided was just that part that most school studies focus on—the classroom. I did this in order to avoid being associated with the official functions of the school or with the authority of teachers or administrators. I also preferred to limit my interaction as much as possible to students, so as not to raise questions about my allegiances. I spent most of my time in the "public" areas of the school, such as the halls, the cafeteria, the library, the courtyard, the stairways. There are clearly things that I did not observe about the social dynamics of this cohort because I did not attend classes, but there is no question that the disadvantages of involving myself in any way with the formal educational process would have far outweighed the advantages.

I had no office or hangout in the school because I did not want any of the implications of having my own space. I preferred to remain an outsider with no great status—someone who was tolerated in the school but not associated with the functioning of the institution. I was like a nomad, therefore, and spent a lot of time just wandering around, dropping in, and chatting with people I met on the way. I knew which rooms were empty when, as did many of the students, so any time I needed a place to talk to someone, we simply looked around until we found some privacy. My homelessness and my concern for not annoying the teachers no doubt enhanced my credibility as an independent operator. A new person in any community is quickly assigned a place, and my constant wandering in the halls led many students to assume that I was a new hall monitor. But since I greeted the students I met rather than challenging their right to be in the hall, they doubted this assignment as soon as they had made it. As one student pointed out, I couldn't have lasted that long in the job without busting somebody.

There was one context in which I did come into regular contact with teachers. There are no student lounges in the school, and when I was tired from running around I occasionally repaired to one or another of the faculty lounges. In addition, my constant need for coffee led me to join the head custodian's coffee pool, which attracted a clique of teachers and administrators to hang out in his back room. At these times, I was privy to a certain amount of gossip about students as well as personnel, but I was grateful that those present rarely asked me more about my work than a general inquiry about how "it" was going. The ethnography of the teachers' world, their social networks and their hangouts, is an extremely important aspect of the education of adolescents, but beyond my own realistic expectations. This obviously did occur to more than one of the teachers, and I was occasionally teased about my alleged spying activities as well as about my "easy life" on a government grant.

Another place where I spent some time was in the district's alternative program, in another building a half mile or so from Belten. This program was compulsory for students with chronic attendance or discipline problems, but could also be attended by any student who chose to do so. Students spent several hours every day in this program and the rest of the day at their regular high school. The people in charge of the alternative program were a close team of skilled, dedicated, and sensitive teachers, who provided their students with an important sense of belonging and who dealt quite directly, fearlessly, and constructively with many of their problems. There were many Burnouts in this program, and I discovered it to be one place where I could get to know a variety of students in a more open setting than the regular school.

Getting Around

Although the principal offered to make some introductions, I preferred to make my way into the student population on my own. My first day in the school, there were auditions going on in the auditorium, and I went along and started talking to an idle spectator. He turned out to be the proverbial "marginal individual" that anthropologists must look out for, and put himself entirely and invaluably at my service. His marginality stemmed from the fact that he was quite sophisticated and politically involved, and prided himself in being the school's gadfly. He knew people of all descriptions, worked hard to defy stereotypes, and was one of the few volunteers attending the alternative school. Initial contacts with a marginal community member present a variety of dangers—that individual may monopolize the ethnographer, act as gatekeeper, and in a variety of other ways limit the field worker's view of and access to the community. My first marginal contact presented no such problem, primarily because his need for me was quite small, and because he dropped out of school soon thereafter. He rushed me over to the alternative school, and later into the courtyard, to make sure that I didn't get taken over by the Jocks. He need not have feared, but his early introduction to Burnout territory smoothed my way.

As one develops a life in a new community, a certain amount of routine evolves that tends to lead one in some directions more than others. It is this routine that makes the field worker accountable to the community, providing the kind of predictability necessary to render the outsider tolerable. Indeed, the community renders newcomers accountable by easing them into some kind of routine and assigning them some kind of role, and it is part of the ethnographer's challenge to maintain independence and flexibility in spite of this routine. This was less of a problem for me in the large institution of the school than it had been in my previous work in a Pyreneen village of 80 people. However, in the village I knew when I was falling into small patterns, whereas it was easier to be fooled in the school. I used checks of various sorts, therefore, particularly to ensure that I was not concentrating too closely on certain networks or certain areas. While some of my hanging out was dictated by circumstances, I devised a schedule so that I spent blocks of time at all times of the day and the week in each area of the school. This means that I spent hours sitting in back halls and odd corners, observing activity or its lack, and getting to know some people who rarely surfaced in other areas of the school.

My progress through the social networks of the student body involved a similar combination of informal interaction and formal procedures. The school provides numerous settings where students are forced to sit around and entertain themselves quietly. Some of these, such as home room, were not available to me. Others, though, such as waiting for school to start, waiting for activities to begin, and waiting for the bus, were public situations. At these times, students frequently welcome some diversion, and I took advantage of this to introduce myself to people and strike up desultory conversation. This proved problematic only on one occasion. Over a period of several days, a group of public health nurses showed up in the auditorium to give tetanus shots to students who had not provided proof of vaccination. After I had been hanging around the auditorium for 45 minutes or so, taking advantage of this occasion to talk to those who were waiting their turn at the needle, one of the nurses ordered me up to the table in no uncertain terms. Once she saw me up close, she good-naturedly offered me one "on the county," and after calculating the number of years since my last tetanus booster I went ahead.

As in any social situation, making new contacts became easier as time went on. Students introduced me to their friends, and as my reputation spread, some came and introduced themselves to me on their own. But just as I methodically sampled the physical areas in the school, I kept track of and controlled my progress through the social network that constituted the graduating class that I was focusing on. In order to make sure that my networking technique did not limit my efforts to a fixed segment of the population, I kept a list of a random sample of the class members. I consulted this list regularly to make sure that I had touched on these individuals in the course of my work, and went in search of one of them to start making contacts from a new location in the network.

I gathered information through observation of normal activities and interaction, through participation in independently occurring activities and interactions, and through brief encounters and long and short discussions with groups and individuals that either I or they initiated. I spent many hours noting down what people were wearing; what they were doing, where, and with whom; seating arrangements in the cafeteria; and anything else that would provide a formal check of my less formal observations and conversations. And throughout my time in the school I did tape-recorded interviews with both individuals and groups. The quotations found throughout this book are from these interviews.

The individual interviews, which took place after school or during students' free periods, were designed to gather a fairly fixed range of information in the context of free-flowing conversation about the individual's personal history, friendships, social networks, stories and feelings about school, social norms, and personal aspirations. I normally began these interviews, which lasted between one and two hours, by asking the interviewee to trace his or her friendships from childhood through to the present. It is important to note that interviewees overwhelmingly introduced the categories of Jocks and Burnouts during this recounting, as they explained what had happened to their elementary school groups when they reached junior high school. I also elicited a range of demographic information during these interviews, about their parents' education, profession, and so forth. In all, I conducted tape-recorded individual interviews with 118 students in Belten High (these form the basis of some of the demographic statistics in Chapter 3) and another 100 in other schools in the area.

The group interviews were also tape-recorded and lasted anywhere from one to four hours. Almost all of these interviews took place after school in order to allow plenty of time. Each group was recruited by some student, whom I had asked to get together a bunch of friends to talk about "stuff." The group sessions were free flowing, with my asking questions only to get the discussion going, and covered whatever topics the group considered interesting or important. The understanding in these group sessions was that in just shooting the breeze among themselves, things might come up that I should know about, but that neither they nor I would have thought of otherwise. Sometimes the discussion centered on social issues in the school, on problems and interpersonal relations, or on gossip. One turned into a dirty joke session.

Tape-recorded interviews were an important source of data, and they were a good way of establishing a fairly strong relationship with the students. I was surprised at the number of people who thanked me for their interviews, saying that they appreciated the opportunity to think and talk in a structured way about themselves and about high school social issues. However, formal interviews were only one way of learning about people and the community, and although I needed a good deal of recorded material, I did not stress interviews as my main means of getting to know individuals. Many discussions took place in halls, in the cafeteria, in the library, outdoors, in restaurants—wherever I found myself with people with time on their hands who felt like talking. No doubt

I owe a good deal of my time with students to the fact that they are always eager to get out of study hall. The fact that I did not have the power to get them out of math or English was always a disappointment, but probably enhanced my treasured "nobody" image.

RELATIONS WITH ADOLESCENTS

After people ask me if I had to pass as an adolescent, they ask me how I got "them" to trust me. As in any field work, different members of the community liked me, trusted me, and interacted with me to different degrees. What I was not prepared for when I began this field work was the number of adolescents who desperately need an adult to talk to. The problem, as far as I could see, was not how to gain people's trust, but how to deal with it when it came. A nonjudgmental and confidential adult looking for people to tell her all about themselves is a rare and seductive thing in a school. An ethnographer is not an everyday occurrence in the life of an adolescent (or anyone else for that matter), and for most it is not a known occupational category. On the basis of my behavior and interests, the closest such category that they might have associated with me was social worker or psychologist. It was extremely important, therefore, to make sure that they, as well as I, knew my goals and the limits of my powers and abilities. If I were to point to the one area in which I was the least prepared for this work, it was in knowing where to send people when I could not fulfill their expectations. I needed to know the full range of resources available to adolescents, in particular, the adolescents in this school.

The greatest pitfall for field workers is the desire not just for acceptance, but for manifestations of acceptance that one can bring back and display to friends and colleagues. Our ability to gain acceptance in field work is part of our professional success, but it satisfies simultaneously our own personal social needs. This is an extremely dangerous area. Most people enjoy being interviewed, frequently because most of us rarely get a chance to talk about ourselves for long periods of time to someone who seems genuinely interested. It is not that difficult, as a result, for a reasonably attentive person to get people to tell all kinds of things about themselves. But we frequently do not know, once we have gone away, the kinds of regrets they may have for having told us these things. During my work in the Pyrenees, I once had occasion to interview a normally quite reticent person, who "opened up" during the interview and left me feeling rewarded and fulfilled. She, however, suffered a week of sleepless nights worrying about her indiscretion. As far as I could see, she had not been indiscreet—she had not told me any-thing that was not common knowledge. But to this day, some 15 years later, I believe that she feels a tug of regret every time she sees me.

Adults are inveterate voyeurs where adolescents are concerned, and I was repeatedly asked if people told me about their sex lives. I decided before I entered Belten that I would never initiate the topics of sex or of drugs. I did not ask about sex because of an acute feeling that adolescents' private lives are frequently considered free territory, and experts of all kinds explore their most personal behavior. I did not ask about drugs because I did not want anyone to walk away and wonder why I had. Drugs are the one thing that many adolescents have to feel para-noid about, and the danger of being suspected of being a narc is real and great. Almost all students brought up the subject of drugs them-selves, and some of them brought up the subject of sex. I suppose I might have felt as if their willingness to discuss these topics with me was a measure of my success at winning their confidence. However, forcing such discussion should not be mistaken for the establishment of confi-dence.

3

The Setting of Belten High

I guess the thing about the different schools that—only thing different I guess is that Casper thinks of Belten as a punk rock school, and Simmons I guess they have—they're all Beatlemaniacs over there. Belten thinks that Casper people are stuck up . . . stuff like that. Other than that, the people are the same, really, the ones that I know.

Opened in the 1950s, Belten is the oldest of several high schools in Neartown, a suburb of Detroit. Belten's approximately 2000 students come from families ranging from solid working class through upper middle class. Part of Detroit's urban sprawl, Neartown is one section of a vast geographic and socioeconomic continuum. In the Detroit suburban area, geography and class are clearly tied along the north–south and east–west axes. With the notable exception of some wealthy waterfront areas east of the city, socioeconomic status rises as one moves north and west from the primarily black and poor inner city. Neartown's northwest corner, the farthest from Detroit, is the most rural, most recently developed, and wealthiest. This pattern is repeated by and large within the sections of the town served by its several high schools.

The students of Belten High generally point to the less affluent eastern end of Neartown as "Burnout" neighborhoods, particularly those at the more densely populated southeast end. In fact, these neighborhoods yield Jocks, Burnouts, and In-betweens, but there are certain factors that make them "Burnout" neighborhoods. First, there is somewhat of a concentration of Burnouts living in the southeast corner of town. In addition, the main local Burnout hangouts are in the eastern neighborhoods, particularly in the southeast: the parks and school yards where many Burnouts organize pickup games or hang out in good weather. The socioeconomic makeup of each category is not homogeneous, but the socioeconomic balance of the categories reflects clear differentiation. Table 3.1 shows the percentages of members of the central Jock and Burnout clusters, as well as of a range of In-between clusters, from three socioeconomic strata. These percentages are based on stu-

TABLE 3.1 Socioeconomic Class Makeup (in percentages) of Each Social Category

	JOCKS	IN-BETWEENS	BURNOUTS
Working class	16	16	50
Lower middle class	34	42	22
Upper middle class	50	42	23

dents' reports, in the 118 tape-recorded interviews of Belten students, of their parents' education and occupation. It should be noted that the percentages did not change significantly when the determination of class was based on information about a working mother, a working father, or both. The percentages show a clear difference in the overall socioeconomic makeup of the polarized categories and suggest an intermediate status for the In-Betweens.

The Jock and Burnout categories are more than a simple reflection of parents' socioeconomic identity; they are pivotal in the transition from childhood to adult status, and both upward and downward mobility are achieved through the mediation of these categories. Of course there will be changes once the cohort has graduated from high school, but the current aspirations of the members of each category are more closely related to class than to actual origins. While almost all of the Jocks intend to go on to college, only 10 percent of the Burnouts expressed interest in college, and a number of them were not enrolled in college preparatory curricula. As Table 3.2 shows, the balance of choice of curriculum reflects these differences in aspiration. This table is based on school records of second semester junior year enrollments for 102 students clearly belonging to Jock and Burnout network clusters.

TABLE 3.2 Course Enrollments (in percentages) Within Each Social Category

	ACADEMIC COURSES				VOCATIONAL COURSES			
	AP	A–B	C	R	M–A	VOC	BUS	F–L
Male Jocks	5	71	12	0	4	5	3	0
Male Burnouts	0	36	14	9	6	33	3	0
Female Jocks	11	70	7	0	7	0	2	4
Female Burnouts	0	19	28	7	11	9	5	21

AP	Advanced placement courses	M–A	Music and art
A–B–C	Letters refer, in descending order, to the level of difficulty as listed in the school catalog	BUS	Business courses
		F–L	Family life (traditional home economics courses and courses in child care)
R	Remedial	VOC	Other vocational courses

THE LOCAL ENVIRONMENT

Neartown itself is a continuum: There is no town center, only inter-spersed industrial, commercial, and residential areas, with scattered shopping centers. Hangouts are fast-food restaurants and shopping centers, parks, and roller-skating rinks. Some of the most salient differ-ences between social categories in Belten are closely involved with dif-ferences in geographic orientation and in the exploitation of local re-sources. The adolescent population must carve a relatively uninteresting geographic continuum into a world with significant areas, and they do this as part of the expression of their social identities.

As the following chapters will show, one of the important differ-ences between Jocks and Burnouts is geographic orientation. Both cat-egories use restaurants, and particularly fast-food restaurants. But while the Burnouts make regular use of other local public space—parks, streets, skating rinks, pool halls—the Jocks confine their activities largely to movie theatres, homes, and the school. To a great extent, the Jocks' small use of local geography is a function of their intense involve-ment in school, which serves as the center of most of their leisure activ-ities. Mobility beyond Neartown is equally telling. Most middle class Neartowners have turned their backs on Detroit and discourage their children from visiting or taking an interest in the city. The parental up-ward mobility that brought people from Detroit to Neartown dictates the abandonment of urban orientation and ties. To a great extent, Jocks visit other towns only in connection with sports events and to go to shop-ping malls and restaurants. The latter two take them not east to Detroit, but generally to more affluent suburban areas. Most Jocks rarely go to Detroit; of those who do, most limit their use of the city to public facili-ties, particularly sports arenas. A few go to museums and concerts, Greektown, and the Renaissance Center. Burnouts, on the other hand, cautiously extend their activities beyond Neartown toward Detroit. As they get older and more mobile, Burnouts expand their use of public space into the suburbs closer to Detroit, and into Detroit itself, gravitat-ing to areas that provide contact with people from other towns.

This difference in geographic orientation stems from a variety of factors. Perhaps the clearest of these is the large number of Burnouts that have moved recently to the suburbs from Detroit. Some of them still have friends in Detroit and still visit their old neighborhoods. The urban migration that creates suburban populations plays a clear role in the Jock–Burnout split, even in schools such as Belten, much of whose population moved there at one time or another from Detroit or its closer suburbs. More than half of Belten's students were born outside of Near-town, most of them in Detroit. Based on the reports of 94 students, 40 percent began school before coming to Neartown, and about 24 percent moved to Neartown after the fifth grade. These numbers are not evenly distributed between the social categories: 17 percent of the Jocks, 23 percent of the In-betweens, and 36 percent of the Burnouts moved after fifth grade.

A further aspect of the differential geographic orientation of Jocks and Burnouts is adaptive. While most of the Jocks' next life stage will be in an isolated and specialized institution similar to the high school, most Burnouts will leave school and directly begin to compete with adults in the workplace. While the high school negotiates the next life stage for its Jocks, it is of little use to the Burnouts in finding a place in the job market. Participation in school activities is an important qualification for college admission, but it does little to enhance an individual's qualification for a blue-collar job, and while the school plays an active role in advising about college admission, it does little toward placing students in blue-collar jobs. In finding employment, most Burnouts expect to rely on contacts outside of school, particularly on relatives and friends already in the work force. Therefore, it is not in a Burnout's interests to pursue social activities in school; it is in his or her interests to pursue activities and contacts that provide access to the local work force. This work force is centered not in the affluent suburbs, but in the urban center and the closer, more urban suburbs. A work force orientation, therefore, is in many ways an urban orientation.

Finally, the Burnouts look at Detroit as a source of personal autonomy. While the Jocks seek autonomy in the occupation of institutional roles, the Burnouts seek it in the personal freedoms associated with adult status and in an independent relation with the larger environment. To some extent this can be linked to the difference in the salience of the adolescent life stage between those who will remain in educational institutions and those who are emerging into the work force. With adult responsibilities looming in the near future, the Burnouts can see no reason to postpone the pleasures of adult status. Adult status represents both personal freedom and interaction in the "real world," both of which are highly circumscribed in the school. Finally there is the simple love of freedom, excitement, and, for some, danger. These various factors weigh differently for different Burnouts, but ultimately they all conspire to lead Burnouts into the urban area.

The sociogeographic continuum of the metropolitan area provides adolescents with a clear perspective on their place in the world. Belten

High School lies squarely in the average socioeconomic range in American society. When individuals compare themselves with those surrounding communities, they develop more of a perspective on their "real-world" social status. Burnouts can look to the relative poverty of friends in Detroit, with their greater problems and lower aspirations; Jocks can look to those in more westerly and northerly suburbs who do not have jobs, who drive fancy cars and wear designer clothes, and who may even plan to go out of state to college. The local environment polarizes Jocks and Burnouts, but at the same time it protects them from the threat of comparison with those in surrounding communities who represent greater socioeconomic and behavioral extremes. Within the limitations of the local context, Jocks can avoid feeling poor and unsophisticated in comparison with their more affluent neighbors in suburbs to the north and west, and Burnouts can feel independent and rebellious without facing the dangers and insecurities of those living closer to Detroit. During high school, the confrontation with the world outside the community is still mitigated by the familiar and relatively safe context of the school. For this reason, many of those who hate school most are nonetheless loyal to their school. In part, this is a loyalty to what the students see as the school's socioeconomic mean, as reflected in one student's discussion of Neartown's wealthier school:

> They're a lot richer and they're really stuck up and they are better at a lot of things, but I'd rather be worse and proud of Belten than go to Simpson.

Each school seems to pride itself on its socioeconomic characteristics—Belten staff and students alike quote the broad socioeconomic range of its student body as its main advantage and as accounting for what they consider to be the school's very special character.

Just as the opposition between Jocks and Burnouts organizes social identity within the school, it mediates differences among schools. Within the school, socioeconomic class has a relative rather than an absolute relation to orientation to school. A variety of studies of adolescent society have shown that the "leading crowds" that dominate school activities come from the upper end of the local socioeconomic hierarchy, and that those from the lower end are by and large alienated from curricular and extracurricular activities. More specifically, Coleman (1961) demonstrated that the leading crowd comes not from the top of the socioeconomic hierarchy, but from the highest significant mass. The leading crowd, therefore, represents norms of the dominant upper socioeconomic level rather than socioeconomic status as such, making it incumbent upon the wealthier extremes to assimilate downward to local norms if they wish to fit in. In this way, class within the school is interpreted in the framework of the local context, and relation to the school is not simply a matter of objective socioeconomic class.

Within the Detroit suburban area, each school has a characteristic socioeconomic makeup, and each school's identity in relation to other schools is based on the absolute socioeconomic characteristics of its dominant population. But within each school, the Jocks and the Burnouts stand in a constant mutual relation and represent the relatively more and less affluent segments of the local population. Since each population is limited to its local resources, the Jocks in a school ranging from lower working class to middle class will look and behave somewhat differently from those in a school ranging from lower middle class to upper middle class. And Jocks from the former school will look somewhat like Burnouts to those from the latter. As the socioeconomic milieu changes significantly, the social categories build around different social content and even have different names: Jocks in a richer town may be called "Preppies," and Burnouts closer to the city may be called "Hoods." In one famously affluent Detroit suburb, the Jocks sport the name "Cake-Eaters." Chances are that a Jock moving from the poorer to the richer school would have difficulty "making it" as a Jock, not so much because of his or her own socioeconomic status as because of the different Jock style learned in the previous school. One boy who moved from a suburb adjacent to Detroit into a Jock group in Neartown remembers changing his clothes fast:

WHAT WAS YOUR IMPRESSION?

All these short-haired kids. My hair was long, it was really long, you know, and these people were, "well, get your hair cut," you know. And they all had these Nike tennis shoes on, and that's what I remember. Nike tennis shoes. So I went home and said, "Mom, screw these Trax tennis shoes, I got to get some Nikes," you know, "We're moving up in the world." So I had to get Nike tennis shoes like the rest of them. You know, that's about the thing—they all dressed like way nicer than in Garden City. Garden City was strictly jeans and T-shirts, you know. That's what I remember.

In this way, socioeconomic class is mediated by the social context of the school. This suggests that the individual's social identity may depend to some extent on the socioeconomic characteristics of the school he or she attends and on his or her relative socioeconomic status within that school.

All this is not to say that the category breakdown and characteristics are the same regardless of the school's overall socioeconomic level. Since·category affiliation is to a great extent linked with aspirations, schools in lower socioeconomic communities may have fewer Jocks, and schools in upper socioeconomic communities may have fewer Burnouts. Burnouts ("Stoners") in one uniformly affluent California high school account for less than 5 percent of the school population, as do Jocks in one uniformly working class suburban Detroit high school. In the latter school, furthermore, the Jocks do not function in the same way as the Jocks in Belten. Because their numbers and constituency are smaller, their activities are far more modest and their political organization is less elaborate. One Jock in this school, who was planning to go to college, expressed concern that her high school preparation was inadequate for the leadership roles she was hoping to acquire in college. Her experience at regional leadership camps and meetings had impressed upon her the greater sophistication and experience of people from wealthier schools.

PHYSICAL ARRANGEMENT OF THE SCHOOL

The physical layout of Belten High is shown in Figure 3.1. The school forms a B, with two open courtyards at the center. The top and bottom (north and south ends) of the B contain specialized rooms—the auditorium and classrooms for theatre, music, industrial arts, and family life (home economics) at the top; the cafeteria, physical education, and custodial facilities at the bottom. The center wing of the B, cutting across the open center of the building, contains the library and greenhouse. The center and west wings have second floors containing classrooms and a storage area. The center wing cuts the school's open court into two: The part to the north is relatively small and unused, while the part to the south is larger and elaborated with paths, benches, and landscaping, and is referred to as "the courtyard." The courtyard is the school's main lounge area, with entrances at each corner making it convenient to classrooms and to the cafeteria and gym area. There is also an entrance at each of the four corners of the building, with those at the front (west) leading into large lobbies. The main, but largely unused, lobby at the northwest end has entrances to the main office and auditorium. The southwest lobby contains entrances to the cafeteria, gym, and student store. The ethnographer trying to keep regular tabs on the day-to-day goings-on in Belten High walks around this B countless times. Track teams and a group of women employees trying to keep in shape

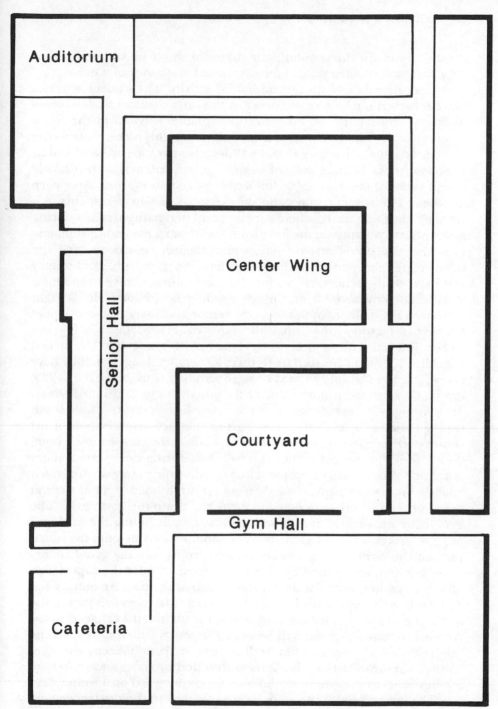

Figure 3.1. Belten High.

during winter do the ground floor circuit of the main rectangle regularly after school. One tour of the first floor is a quarter of a mile.

The cafeteria lobby is a main hub of activity. The student activities
office is carved out of a front corner of the cafeteria, and student organizations occasionally set up tables to promote activities in the lobby
across from it. The center of activities planning, this office contains the
student activities director's desk and files, the paraphernalia of public
relations (racks holding rolls of colored paper, cabinets with masking
tape, markers, paint), a table for meetings and work, and a popcorn
machine. The student store, also off the lobby, is where students in a
retailing class sell candy, school supplies, and pep paraphernalia during
lunch hours. Walking up the long front hall toward the auditorium, one
passes several administrative offices and English classrooms, and the
school paper and yearbook offices. This hall, the most visible and heavily
trafficked of the school, is "Senior Hall," containing most of the senior
lockers. Directly above it on the second floor is "Junior Hall." A right
turn from the main lobby at the top of Senior Hall takes one into a quiet
hall across the top of the B, past the industrial arts rooms. Ninth-grade
lockers line this hall, and between classes ninth-graders with hunched
shoulders and bent heads dart to their lockers, making sure they have
everything needed for the next class. (Beginning with the class of 1983,
the ninth grade was moved out of the junior highs and into Belten.)
Turning right at the east end of this hall, one begins the long walk south
through the back (east) hall, passing the subdued conversation of art
classes and snippets of science and math talk through the mostly open
doors. Tenth-grade lockers line this hall, and during class periods there
is a steady thin stream of people self-assuredly going after the forgotten
book or homework paper. One then goes down a small flight of steps at
the south end of the back hall and turns right into the "gym hall." The
gym hall runs slightly uphill, past the blank walls hiding the pool and
the gym on the left, and a long bank of windows looking onto the courtyard on the right. One has to be careful turning into the gym hall, because it is frequently used by girls doing sprints under the supervision
of a gym teacher seated at the top (west end) of the hall. An entrance at
each end of this hall leads into the courtyard. The gym hall jogs to the
left by the west courtyard entrance and spills out into the cafeteria lobby.
A radiator runs along the wall between the courtyard entrance and the
cafeteria lobby. This radiator (called "the radiator") keeps the gym
teacher warm as she times her girls' sprints and provides a warm refuge
for Burnouts as they move in and out of the courtyard on a winter day.

The geography of the school is meaningless to the newcomer, who
may need a few days to get his or her bearings. To each member of the

school community, the school has a special shape and each of its areas has a special significance. For each person, there are parts of the school that remain mysteries, parts that are taboo, parts that are simply insignificant, and parts that are imbued with magic, terror, delight, purpose, boredom. The Jocks and the Burnouts, on the whole, live in very different parts of the school; to a certain extent, this is a function of the courses they attend. The Burnout boys know the nooks and crannies of the vocational areas—the machine shop, the auto shop, the welding shop, and the woodworking shop at the top of the B, and the back halls and doorways that connect them. The Burnout girls may know these areas distantly from meeting their boyfriends or buddies there, but many of them also know the family life rooms, particularly the child care room, and the business rooms on the second floor. The Jock boys and girls know the student activities room and the athletic facilities; many of them know the music and theatre facilities and the journalism offices. Both Jocks and Burnouts know the administrative areas, but play different roles when they are there. Each individual's knowledge of the building is different, but there is a systematic complementarity in the parts of the building regularly used by Jocks and Burnouts. Jocks and Burnouts pursue activities and curricula that utilize different parts of the building, but, in addition, the maintenance of the opposition between the categories elevates routine building use to the status of territorial claims. Those parts of the building that are not clearly associated with curricular areas, but that are loci of social interaction, are even more strictly divided between the categories than is much of the classroom space.

DAILY ROUTINES

Use of the building is closely tied to the daily schedule. The class schedule outlines a routine for each student, organizing encounters with other students as well as movements into and through various parts of the building. The school day is divided into three 54-minute class periods in the morning, a noon period of approximately 1½ hours, and two 54-minute class periods in the afternoon. Six minutes are allowed between classes for changing rooms. The fourth (lunch) period is divided into three half-hour segments, two of which are spent in class and one at lunch. Fourth-hour classes are staggered so that some meet during the first two segments, some during the last two, and some during the first and third, with the lunch segment in the middle. Following disturbances in the school parking lot in the late 1970s, the administration imposed a "closed campus" policy, forcing students to remain in the school building during school hours except for authorized travel to curricular programs in other schools. Although students may not leave the building during the lunch hour, they are free to gather in the south wing and the courtyard, and with permission they may go to the library. The intersections between the south wing and the north–south halls are monitored during this time, as are the north, south, and middle (leading to the library) exits from the back hall.

Students work their social routines around their class schedules. They also work their class schedules around their social lives, by trying to get into classes with their friends. Thus classes are not simply part of the educational routine, but strategic points in the students' daily social encounters. Changing classes is punctuated with routine social encounters at designated places—in the hall, in the courtyard, at the lockers. Students know whom they can expect to pass in the hall on the way from one class to the next and can adjust their route or speed to guarantee meeting those they particularly wish to see. Depending on the period, individuals may rush to a designated spot for a quick encounter with a group, a friend, or a boyfriend/girlfriend; or they may do their route slowly, greeting a variety of people on the way. One particular class change might be the highpoint of a student's day. By and large, groups meet at set times and places before and after school, and virtually all students have a lunchtime routine, going to the same place with the same people, sometimes migrating at an appointed time to another place to wait for the bell to ring at the end of the period.

To a great extent, the individual's enjoyment of school routine is a function of the size of his or her social network. Those who have only a small group of friends are limited in their encounters to times of mutual availability. Some students have no group of school friends and must move through their day in isolation. Changing classes is not much of a problem for people with limited networks, since they can move with purpose through a crowd, but lunchtime can be a difficult and painful time. The smaller one's social network, the smaller are one's chances of having the same lunch period as one's friends, and the individual who eats alone or walks in the halls alone during this period of heightened visibility is stigmatized. Those who find themselves alone manage as best they can by making themselves inconspicuous, drifting as an unwelcome guest among established groups, or simply hiding. They do not, however, escape notice:

> We'd make fun of people that walked too close to the wall. We'd always call them "wall huggers." Because they didn't, they wouldn't walk down the middle of the hall. If they were walking by them-

selves, they walked by the wall, like it was their friend. . . . It just seems like anybody who's alone usually stands right next to the wall. Just a little thing we noticed.

Loners can protect themselves by adopting a philosophical attitude, as the following girl who recognizes that people notice her solitude:

They always have to be with someone because they're worried about what other people would think if they were walking down the hall alone, which is no big deal. It doesn't hurt.

But it does hurt, as one girl who finds lunch company by imposing on relatively inhospitable groups poignantly described:

I just have friends that I say "hello" to and are acquaintances, but I don't have any best friends. . . . I just see them a lot in school, because like they're, they got their own very good friends. I'm just, you know, like to the people I know, I'm just a friend. I'm not a person you'd call up and invite to parties and get stoned with, you know. I wish I was, though. I mean I feel, at weekends I feel so left out. I sit there and, you know, "Ma, I'm so depressed, I want friends," you know. But, you know, there are some times, some times I think, uh, I'm better off not having too many friends because one can get just bogged down with all their, "Oh, can you come over my house today"; "No, I'm coming over her house, sorry." You know. I don't know. They just don't like me for what I am.

Lunch the first day of the semester is stressful for most high school students, as they worry about whom they're going to eat with. The degree of stress varies inversely with the extensiveness of one's social networks. "Who has the same lunch" is a major preoccupation that can serve as a factor in choosing classes.

See, this semester I was really bummed out. I wanted to get a change to fourth hour, because there's nobody in my lunch hour that I really know. But I sit, like, at a table with a bunch of girls that I know, but I don't really know. Um, Joan Smith, Judy—I don't know her last name, shows how well I know her. Those are really the only two that I even know that sit there. The rest of them just . . .

HOW DID YOU START EATING WITH THEM?

Well, I don't know. Um, I went in the first day, and I was going to sit with Daphne Brown. But she was hanging around all the people that are on the swimming team. And like, I don't know them, you know.

The contrast between being a loner and being a member of the vast networks that constitute the Jock and Burnout categories can be the difference between social night and day. By virtue of their extensive networks, the Jocks and the Burnouts suffer the least at lunchtime. Intensive consultation lets Jocks know whom they will be eating with before they arrive in the cafeteria. There is always at least one girl Jock and one boy Jock table in each lunch hour, and Jocks find both security and visibility in their ability to sit at that table.

Well see, well you find out, you know, before you go in there. And it's like, Joe Sloan, he played basketball with us, Alan Marsten did, and Peter Brown. And like I know Dan Jones, and Mark Johnson, I knew them already. So you know, Joe and Alan and those guys that play basketball, I knew what they had, you know, what lunch. So I was, I went in there looking for them. . . . Everyone asks what lunch you eat to find out who they can sit with.

The Burnouts do not even have to find out ahead of time who has the same lunch, since they know that their friends will be in the courtyard.

This book deals more with Jocks and Burnouts than with the people who make up the majority of the student population—the many In-betweens who find their way between and around the categories. It also does not deal with the people who never find their niche in the high school—people who don't fit in and who feel lucky if they can remain sufficiently invisible to escape community ridicule. While this book never describes social isolation, it describes social dynamics that make extreme isolation possible. If a Jock is the opposite of a Burnout, a nerd is the opposite of both. While the Jocks and the Burnouts are no more interesting than the rest of the student body, the concentration of social energy in the maintenance of their oppositional identities not only limits their own freedom but that of everyone else in the school.

4

Symbols of Category Membership

WHAT MAKES SOMEBODY A BURNOUT?
You know, maybe somebody who smokes all the time, you know, smokes marijuana and stuff, but you know, everybody does that. You could call me a Burnout. You know, I've did that . . . maybe, maybe it's the way they dress. It's a lot of things, I think. Your look, you can wear these leather—and these wallets with chains and look really bad, you know—lot of people say, "Oh, that guy's got to be a Burnout."

The Jock and Burnout categories emerge upon entrance to junior high school, where they develop in mutual opposition through a rapid fore-grounding and differentiation of selected values, behavior, and symbols. Unstructured differences that have developed through elementary school are imbued with significance as they are thrown into opposition, and the opposition itself gains hegemony as it absorbs more and more aspects of everyday life. In an effort to differentiate themselves, the two categories progressively separate their worlds, developing opposing ter-ritories, appearances, demeanors, and activities. The underlying ideol-ogies that separate Jocks and Burnouts are in turn strengthened by the increasing range of external manifestations associated with them.

The differences between Jock and Burnout social structure and norms are not very apparent in the daily business of life. In fact, by the time the cohort reaches graduation, Jocks and Burnouts know precious little about each other. What everyone knows of their differences is what shows—the symbolic manifestations of category affiliation. Ask high school students or recent graduates about the social categories in their school, and they will begin with how they dress, where they hang out, or what substances they use. Clothing and other forms of adornment, ways of speaking, territory, and even substance use and school perfor-mance all have symbolic value in the adolescent context. However sub-consciously, they all stand for deeper cultural differences that may them-selves not be accessible to all who participate in the symbolic system. Differences in symbolic behavior are commonly taken as the only differences between the categories—and such things as clothing differences are regarded as if they had social value in themselves rather than simply in association with an evaluation of the people who wear them. Category symbols attain their value from association with clear differences in both form and content, developing around salient social differences between the categories and maximizing distinctness in visible form.

Clothing and adornment is perhaps the most powerful symbolic subsystem in the Jock–Burnout opposition. An individual's bodily adornment is seen simultaneously with the individual and thus provides the guarantee that the individual will not be separated from his or her social identity. To the extent that they are inseparable from the person, other portable symbols, such as books, radios, cigarettes, and sports paraphernalia, are also effective indicators of social identity, as are cars. Musical taste can be unambiguously displayed through the use of radios. Styles of demeanor and movement rely to a great extent on action and interaction, as does language. Finally, territorial and activity displays are limited to specific settings. All of these areas of behavior are fully exploited to express social category affiliation, and because adornment is the only ever-present symbolic subsystem, it is manipulated to incorporate as many of the elements of other subsystems as possible. Musical tastes can be displayed on T-shirts; activities, on activity-specific clothing (such as motorcycle boots or football jerseys); language style and demeanor, in action and in messages on buttons and T-shirts; territory, on jackets (such as the DETROIT jackets worn by some Burnouts).

Just as the Jock and Burnout categories develop in mutual opposition, so do their symbols. Elements of behavior that come to represent one category will be rejected by the other, and they may be exploited by the other category through the development of a clearly opposed element. Thus the Burnouts not only avoid the pastel colors that characterize Jock clothing, but they consistently wear dark colors. (This opposition could, of course, be expressed in reverse—the Jocks avoid dark colors and consistently wear pastels.) At the same time, these colors have positive significance: Pastel colors are associated in our society with youth, innocence, and gaiety, while dark colors are associated with sombreness, age, and sophistication—all qualities that are associated with the categories that wear them.

Many Jock and Burnout symbols stand above all for differences in economic means, perception of life stage and adult domination, and school and local orientation. Jocks are locally oriented both to the school and to the local community, while Burnouts are oriented away from the school, toward the neighborhood, and toward Detroit. Jocks embrace adult norms for the adolescent life stage, while Burnouts constantly lay claim to adult status. Finally, Jocks associate themselves with the middle class and its relative affluence, while Burnouts associate themselves with the working class and its relatively limited material means.

SCHOOL TERRITORIES

Jock and Burnout use of school facilities is symbolic of differences in attitudes toward the school and in orientation to the adolescent life stage. The Jocks accept the facilities provided by the school and use them in rough conformity to school expectations—they store their coats and books in lockers, use the bathrooms for their intended purpose, and eat in the cafeteria. Burnouts, on the other hand, express their counter-cultural position in the school by transforming the school facilities to suit their needs and identities (See Willis, 1977, for a discussion of such transformation.) To a certain extent, their use of the school is built around cigarette smoking, which, as will be discussed later, is a key symbol in the Jock–Burnout split. In schools across the country, Burnouts' smoking leads them to hang out in doorways and stairwells, parking lots, bathrooms, breezeways, and loading docks. This use of marginal areas has added significance in its representation of Burnouts' more generally marginal place in the school. This marginalization not only is imposed through the school's rejection of Burnout values, but is embraced by Burnouts in their rejection of the school as a comprehensive social institution. While the Jocks center their social lives in the school and accept the school as a "home away from home," the Burnouts energetically deny any such function of the school. The Jocks embrace whatever facilities the school offers them. In contrast, the Burnouts pick and choose. They use facilities that reflect recognition of their adult status and needs—the courtyard, vocational classrooms, parking lot. They shun those that reflect the school's parental role of providing food and living space, namely, lockers and the cafeteria. Those they cannot shun—the bathrooms—they transform into alternative smoking areas.

Lunchtime Territories

In addition to seeking marginal spaces, Burnouts reject school facilities that represent the school's in loco parentis role. One such facility is the cafeteria. Although the food in the Belten cafeteria is quite good, the Burnouts are overwhelmingly critical of it. The common Burnout claim that cafeteria food has made people sick implies a rejection of not only the school's right but its ability to assume a parental role. The few

Burnouts who do eat in the cafeteria occupy the most marginal table in the room—a table off to the side and next to the rear exit, where they can be "half in and half out" of the cafeteria and separate from the main cafeteria activity.

DO YOU EAT IN THE CAFETERIA?

Sometimes. . . . When it looks edible. When it doesn't look like it's moving around at you.

OH GOD. WHO DO YOU EAT WITH USUALLY?

All the Burnouts, you know, just anybody who comes along and sits at the table . . . right next to the first line. We just sit there and chow down, and talk.

Many Burnouts do not eat lunch at all, and of those who do the overwhelming majority limit themselves to packaged food, which they can carry out to the courtyard. The Belten cafeteria provides two hot food lines leading from the main entrance and a fast-food line leading from a side hall (and emptying near the Burnout table referred to above), where Burnouts buy their cookies or potato chips. One Burnout demonstrated the norm against eating in the cafeteria, in her reaction to a friend's insistence that she did eat there, and her proud denial of engaging in legitimate transactions with the school.

DO YOU EVER EAT IN THE CAFETERIA?

In there? Huh-uh.
[friend speaking] Yeah, you do.
Bullshit. I never eat in there.
[friend] Come on.

NOT EVEN WHEN THE WEATHER IS REAL BAD?

No, I used to chow in the hall. Or I don't eat at all.

BUT DO YOU EVER, LIKE, BUY FOOD THERE AND THEN GO OUT INTO THE COURTYARD?

Yeah. Well, I don't buy food. . . . Everybody rips off from them. I remember one time I went up to the chip rack, you know. I had Linda and them stand behind me, and when they weren't looking I'd whip chip bags back there. And they're cramming them in their purse. We'd walk out, we were munching down.

High school cafeterias everywhere show strict territorial specialization. A high school in a neighboring town shows a stratified use of the cafeteria, with the Burnouts (called "Freaks" in this school) eating near the outside doors at the bottom of the cafeteria so they can slip out for a smoke, and the Jocks at the top of the cafeteria—an area actually elevated above the rest. The "In-betweens" occupy the middle area. The Belten cafeteria is set up with long tables along three walls and round tables in the middle. The human geography of the cafeteria varies between lunch periods and semesters, but by and large the Jocks occupy the tables on the west wall and an occasional round table, while the fast-food line and the Burnout table are on the east wall. Some people refer to the tables along the west wall as the "Jock tables."

Burnouts are not the only ones who eat elsewhere than in the cafeteria. Members of the choir, which rehearses before and after lunch, frequently eat in the choir room; those who work in the student store sometimes eat in the room behind the store; many on the yearbook staff eat in the yearbook room; ROTC members sometimes eat in the ROTC room; and a few people eat in various classrooms and faculty spaces. Lunch periods are so routinized that I knew exactly where to find most people during that time. People always eat in the same place with the same people, and if they don't stay there for the whole period, they retire to a specific place to wait for the bell to ring. In-between people who smoke may go to the courtyard, a few go to the library or to the room where their next class meets (if they can get past the hall monitors), and many stand, always in the same place, in the cafeteria lobby and the gym hall. The Jocks who are not in any of the specialized areas stand directly in front of the main entrance to the cafeteria and in front of the student store opposite, the Burnouts who are not in the courtyard stand in thc hall by the radiator at the courtyard's main entrance, and the In-betweens congregate between the two areas. Students clearly see this after-lunch standing around as a significant activity, and some remain in the cafeteria expressly to avoid it.

AFTER LUNCH, DO YOU STAY IN THE LUNCHROOM?

Mm hmm. I hate standing out in the hall. I feel like I'm on exhibit. Bothers me. You just stand there, and everybody else looks around, it's all crowded. Don't like it. I'd rather just sit.

The Courtyard

The locus of Jock–Burnout territorial separation is the courtyard. Whereas the cafeteria is in the public domain, the courtyard is Burnout territory by virtue of its designation as the authorized smoking area. The close association between Burnouts and the courtyard comes out repeatedly in conversation, as Burnouts are commonly described as "the people who smoke" and "the people in the courtyard." One Jock accounted for his split-up with several junior high friends in the following way:

> Like there's a few others . . . who also go here who I don't hang around with at all any more, I mean, not that I, you know, wouldn't want to, it's just, we just went different ways in tenth grade and ever since.
>
> HOW DID YOU GO DIFFERENT WAYS?
>
> They went into the courtyard and I went into the student government.

Burnouts who do not smoke go regularly to the courtyard, but few other nonsmokers do, since smoking is the only legitimate excuse for a non-Burnout to be in Burnout territory. Those non-Burnouts who do go into the courtyard are apt to be labelled as Burnouts by many of the people in the school, both because of their use of the courtyard and because they smoke. These people stick to the southwest corner of the courtyard, which is recognized among those in the courtyard as neutral—a distinction not recognized by those who do not frequent the courtyard. The courtyard is the one place in the school that the Burnouts consider their own, and their care for the courtyard contrasts with the graffiti found on the walls that lead to it. This care was described by one In-between smoker who frequents the southwest corner of the courtyard.

> I've always, I've always liked it out here. It's just, just, besides the litter. But there's not really that much, because, um, like people, you know, a lot of, most of the Burns come out here, you know, the Burnouts that think they're real cool and stuff. They come out here and, um, and, you know, if they see litter, believe it or not, they'll pick it up. Because, you know, like they, they, this is the one part they can say is theirs, you know, because all the really popular people really don't come out here. . . . It, it really is nice, you know, it's big, and, I don't know, it's nice. They have, they have flowers, and people really don't pick the flowers and stuff, you know, like, and they don't step on the little, like we plant trees in here sometimes, and they don't pick them and everything, you know, and throw them away, and just. . . . I think a lot of people

take care of it because they look, they look at other high schools, and, you know, like they have nothing at all.

Smoking and the courtyard (probably because of its association with smoking) are the most widely recognized Burnout symbols and are therefore the most carefully maintained areas of differentiation. Presence in the courtyard is recognized as an unambiguous social statement. One In-between gave the following explanation for why she and her best friend do not go into the courtyard:

DO YOU EVER GO IN THE COURTYARD?

No.

ANY PARTICULAR REASON?

I've well, let's see. Julie and I are, you might say we party. I mean, there's Jocks and Jells like that. But we don't smoke cigarettes. And I think—I don't know—I get the impression that if people who don't smoke cigarettes go out there, everybody automatically thinks, "Oh, they want to be a Jell." So I wouldn't want everybody saying, "Oh, what are you, um, trying to be a Jell now?" or something.

Avoidance of the courtyard incurs considerable inconvenience, because the courtyard provides a shortcut between classes and from classes to the cafeteria. Some In-betweens will use this shortcut between classes but will not go there during lunch:

I don't go out in the courtyard because [of] all the smokers and stuff. . . . I'll go outside and walk through it, probably, but I won't stay out there.

Most Jocks go through their high school years without ever setting foot in the courtyard. Some say this is because of the smoke, although in a large outdoor area like the courtyard, it is easy to avoid other people's smoke.

AND WHEN YOU'RE CHANGING CLASSES, DO YOU EVER WALK THROUGH THE COURTYARD TO TAKE A SHORTCUT?

No. No, I don't . . . even if it were longer inside, I'd stay inside. Because there's a lot of that smoke, you know, and stuff, especially near the areas where people are allowed to smoke. And it gets in my hair and I have to wash it. That's the only reason. It smells bad, it really reeks.

Others cite the Burnouts themselves as a reason not to go into the courtyard.

DO YOU EVER GO INTO THE COURTYARD?

Hm mm. Something might bite us. . . . They're dangerous animals. They're so funny. It's like watching prehistoric man out there. It's so funny, because one time we saw, these two guys were acting like "Kung Foo Joe" you know, and me and Sally were, "I don't believe it."

Many cite fear of ridicule as the main reason for avoiding the courtyard. A few say that because presence in the courtyard implies smoking, they would run the risk of expulsion from a team if they were seen there. The following Jock, who prides himself on his ability to get along with Burnouts, evoked the more general significance of territory in his account of why he never goes into the courtyard. The confusion of his account reflects the fact that his behavior toward the courtyard has been so strongly dictated by social norms that he has not incorporated it into his personal ideology.

I think I've walked through the courtyard twice, and both the times, it was like after school and nobody was around. I never walk through the courtyard.

EVEN TO CHANGE CLASSES AND STUFF, YOU DON'T DO THAT?

Nope.

HOW COME?

Well, for one thing, there's other ways to get around, you know, if you want to walk through. And when it's cold, I can't see people standing out in the courtyard, that doesn't make sense. But just being out in the courtyard has a lot of significance. When people see you out there, even if you're out there just to walk by and everything, if somebody walks by, you catch their attention, if you've never been out there before, and, you know, somebody sees you, they might think something. I think, you know. But it—that's not why. Because I really, I really don't care what people think about me, as long as, you know, I do what I think is right. But it's just the idea of having—having to walk through there. It doesn't, you know, it doesn't make sense. If you want to get somewhere, you don't have to walk through the courtyard. It's—I don't know, I don't know how to explain it. It's like, it's territory which you don't have to go through. If it's going to cause problems, why—you know, avoid it. . . . I think it—I think when you walk through the courtyard, you're easily—it's easy to get a label . . . and if you talk to the people out there that have the reputation of, you know, always around drugs, or, you know, having any kind of influence with drugs, then you're going to get labelled that way. I mean, if you're inside the building, that's a different story, you know, if somebody walks by and sees you talking to somebody that, you know, is around drugs, they're not going to think too much about it because they'll say, "Well, maybe they're just talking about a class or something." They don't know what you're talking about. But once you're outside, it's like, you're in his shop. He can tell—you know, it's like you're working with him on his type of you know, his thing, so, I don't know.

Because cigarette smoking is a universal Burnout symbol, Burnouts across the country occupy high school smoking areas: In one California high school, the Burnouts are called "Sectioners" by virtue of the fact that they hang out in the smoking "section." Most schools that permit smoking designate unattractive outdoor areas in the back for this purpose, and one school in the Detroit area co-opted the Burnouts' choice of territory by tearing out the fixtures and stalls from one boys' and one girls' bathroom and designating them as sex-segregated smoking areas. The central location and attractiveness of the courtyard in Belten provides an unusually habitable and nonmarginal Burnout territory. I have been told by students from the wealthier Neartown high school that the proof that Belten has a "Burnout problem" is that it allows this category its own territory. However, while the courtyard is Burnout territory, almost the entire rest of the school is Jock territory. As a number of Burnouts have pointed out, "the Jocks own the school." The Jocks can afford to have their territory defined residually in relation to the Burnouts', because they dominate so much of the functional area of the school. They can regularly be found during their free time in the student activities office, in the various areas of the athletic department (gym, multipurpose room, faculty offices), in the music rooms, and in classrooms and teachers' offices. Territorial disputes do not arise in Belten, probably because there is adequate territory for both categories. In a nearby town, where Burnouts hang out in stairwells and vestibules, the "Freaks" occasionally invade the opulent central lounge that is known as Jock territory. The invasions have taken place on boys' varsity game days, when symbolism is at its height and Jocks are wearing their game day "uniforms": uniforms for cheerleaders and pompom girls, jackets and ties for players.

Lockers

Just as the courtyard is home base for the Burnouts, the Jocks' home base is their lockers. Each class is assigned lockers in a specific area of the school, and with seniority each class graduates from the least to the most prominent location in the school—freshman and sophomore lockers in the back halls, junior lockers in the upstairs front hall, and senior lockers in the front hall on the main floor. Lockers serve as age-segregated gathering places, each area named for the class it houses: "Senior Hall," "Junior Hall," "Sophomore Hall." It is significant that Burnouts do not acknowledge these names. Two people are assigned to a locker at the beginning of the school year. Jocks generally visit their lockers between classes and spend a lot of time "fooling around" at their lockers before and after school. One peripheral junior Jock described her feelings about Junior Hall in much the same way that Burnouts describe the courtyard:

> I like that hall too, because I know everybody. Junior Hall. I can say "Hi" to everybody. I don't feel left out.

In one school in the Detroit area, the senior Jocks are particularly territorial about Senior Hall, and most underclasspeople take detours rather than risk harassment by walking down it. The lockers in this hall are elaborately decorated—some Jock boys have carpeted the insides of their lockers, and joke about installing stereos. They spend long periods of time sitting against the wall opposite their opened and impressively adorned lockers. At Belten, Jocks decorate the outsides of locker doors for important events: birthdays, performances, and games. For Valentine's day, girls anonymously decorate the lockers of the boys' starting varsity basketball team. The location of prominent people's lockers is important information and is frequently essential to the interpretation of the signs that appear on them, such as "Nice going, Joe!"

Locker sharing, virtually always among members of the same sex, is as close as Jocks can come to living together and as such is an important sign of friendship. People frequently affirm the importance of a friendship by pointing out that the friend is their "locker partner." In keeping with the Jock norm against limiting themselves to a "best friend" (this will be discussed in Chapter 6), many share a locker with as many as five people.

> And now it's like all three of us, and Laurie Smith is good friends with us too. We all share a locker. All four of us. It doesn't have a lock on it either.

> DO THEY USUALLY ASSIGN LOCKERS TO FOUR PEOPLE OR DO YOU JUST—
> THEY ASSIGN IT TO A COUPLE OF PEOPLE AND EVERYBODY ELSE MOVES IN?

> Two. Two people for each locker, and like we, "this isn't even anybody's locker, I don't think." We just kind of, "Oop, no one's in this locker."

> IS THAT REALLY IMPORTANT, WHO YOUR LOCKER PARTNER IS?

> It is, because I wouldn't see Alice during the day if we weren't locker partners. I wouldn't—I'd see Laurie a couple of times, but not, you know, I wouldn't see Alice at all. Because we don't have any classes or even lunch or anything.

This girl's pride at not having a lock on the locker is reminiscent of pride at living in a "good neighborhood," and contrasts with the Burnouts' claim that stuff gets stolen from lockers.

The first week of school brings almost a total reshuffling of lockers, as people move into lockers with their friends and as rows of lockers are taken over by networks. By virtue of this reshuffling, the Jocks in each grade occupy a specific area of lockers in their hall. The locker houses not only school paraphernalia, but personal effects. The insides of lockers are frequently decorated with signs and pictures.

Burnouts do not keep much in their lockers, rarely visit them, and never "fool around" at them. Because they go into the courtyard between classes, Burnouts do not have time to go to their lockers, and scorn those who do. But they also claim that lockers are unsafe, that the locks never work, and that things get stolen from them. This claim, along with their claim that cafeteria food is bad for you, amounts to a denial of the adequacy of the school's parental ability, further justifying their rejection of the school's claim to a parental role. Adding to the Burnouts' hostility toward lockers is the school's reservation of the right to examine lockers for drugs—a right that Burnouts argue against strongly, claiming that lockers should be private space and inviolable. Since the lockers are not to be treated as adult living space but as the living space of a child subject to parental supervision, the Burnouts will not use them.

LOOKING AND ACTING DIFFERENT

Smoking

Drugs and alcohol have come and gone as symbols of rebellion for adolescents, but the one classic and enduring magical substance is tobacco. While the Burnouts may be named for drug use, their key symbol is—as it was for the hoods of the 1950s and the greasers of the 1960s—the cigarette. Cigarette smoking is the pivotal issue in the beginning of seventh grade and remains the key symbol (Ortner, 1973) of the Burnout category throughout high school, even after more potent symbols of rebellion, such as drugs, became part of the opposition. The Burnouts are most frequently described as "the people who smoke," and Jocks continue to shun cigarettes, even after a number of them begin to smoke pot covertly. The cigarette's symbolic value within the adolescent culture undoubtedly arises from its condensation of referents and its portable, displayable, consumable, and quasi-illicit properties. The cigarette is most commonly interpreted as a symbol of adulthood, but is also associated with rebellion, machismo, sophistication or "coolness," independence, and vice. Burnouts display cigarette packages rolled in T-shirt sleeves or protruding from shirt pockets or purses, and requests for cigarettes or elaborate craving gestures are common forms of greeting. In keeping with the Burnouts' norms of sharing (to be discussed in Chapter 7), cigarette sharing with an extended network serves to solidify social relations. Cigarettes are the ideal commodity for such a system of exchange, since they are relatively inexpensive and carry additional value in themselves as a symbol of Burnout identity. Several Burnouts report having used cigarette exchange as a way of making friends when they first arrived at Belten.

HOW DID YOU MEET?

She comes up to me, "Got a smoke?" I go, "Yeah." And then, then the other day, "You got a smoke?" And then, and one day, a couple days later, I go, "Hey, you," because I didn't have no smokes, I go, "You, you owe me a couple smokes." She goes, she goes, "Oh, really?" Then I don't know, I don't know how I got to know her.

*   *   *

I usually, when I come into a new school, I've learned to make friends real quick because I've moved so many times, so I just walk up to someone, you know, "You want a cigarette?" "Yeah," and start talking, and "yeah, check out that girl over there," or something, you know, just get something going.

The symbolic status of smoking for the Burnouts is reflected in and matched by the Jocks' vocal and passionate opposition to smoking. Jocks overwhelmingly do not smoke: Of 49 Jocks asked, only 2 reported being smokers, and neither smokes at or near the school or at school functions; of 38 Burnouts, 35 reported being smokers. Of 20 In-betweens, 9 reported being smokers. Opposition to smoking is an important Jock norm, and Jocks join the school in its campaign against smoking. One of the prestigious extracurricular activities at Belten is the "Smoking Committee," a group that gives anti-smoking presentations in elementary schools around the area. The status of this committee and other anti-smoking activities as part of the institutional structure of the school brings the Jock alliance with the school squarely into the Jock–Burnout opposition (Eckert, 1983). The Jocks and the school, together, condemn and oppose the Burnouts in this "unhealthy," "smelly," and "self-destructive" behavior. One girl's account of how one of her teachers helped shepherd her back into the fold illustrates the symbolic value of smoking.

> In junior high I was really bored with like, you probably experienced this too, it just, you just get really bored with the whole situation . . . and, um, and like the Burnouts always seemed like they were, they had so much fun, you know, they were always the neat people to be with, so I started getting mixed up with them a little bit. And so, um, I got my first D that I ever got in math. And my math teacher always like teased me in front of the class, you know. And like we'd draw like, um, geometric figures, and one time there was one like this, I'll never forget, like a, a cigarette box with a, a cigarette sticking out, and he said, "Denise, what does that look like to you?", you know. And then this one guy said, "A pack of cigarettes," and like they'd always, like, because they were all like really straight kids in AP math. And so I think that helped me a lot, though, to have all of that, because it, it made me, I don't know, it just kind of made me realize what was going on.

Clothing

The stranger to the high school notices a variety of clothing, but just as the geography of the school becomes meaningful only when one begins to see how various people use the building, the clothing styles take on meaning as one begins to notice that certain patterns of clothing appear in certain parts of the school, and eventually as one comes to know the social significance of these patterns. Clothing is a particularly powerful social marker because it is regularly renewed and never separated from the individual in public situations. Just about every component of external clothing has indexical or symbolic value in the category system.

Throughout society, clothing style signals economic means, access to information, and specific group identity. Economic means are reflected both in a rapid turnover of clothing—exhibited through wardrobe size and swift style changes—and in the quality and expense of individual items. Within any social group, the specific items and combinations of items one chooses reflect group consensus. These subtler differences, which can be achieved only through private information, are the ultimate indication of group membership. The relative paucity of an outsider's or a marginal individual's information may prevent that individual from even knowing that he or she is not completely "in style" with the target group. Each group's style is thus a function of specific identity, information (including both verbal information and exposure), economic means, practical needs, and an ideology based on all of these. As a social marker of group membership, clothing style is closely associated with the social and cultural characteristics of groups and can elicit powerful emotional reactions. Style is not interpreted simply as an indication of social affiliation but as a direct and intentional expression of group values, a marker of group boundaries, and thus a rejection of alternative values. Failure to conform to group style, therefore, is taken to signal lack of solidarity.

The significance of clothing is not equal for men and women. In American society, women are expected to pay more attention than men to clothing style. Women's style encompasses a wider range than men's, and even includes much of men's style. In general, women wear more accessories than men, and their clothes include a wider range of colors and of cuts. The difference between women's informal and formal wear is greater, and women's adornment extends beyond clothing and accessories to cosmetics and labor-intensive hair styles. Differences in adornment serve as simple gender markers, but women's greater stylistic elaboration is also an indication of their greater reliance on symbolic means of signalling social status in a society that denies them equal access to social mobility through action. Adolescent girls have to work harder to achieve social status and are far more constrained by physical attractiveness than boys. In addition, girls are more constrained by social distinctions than are boys and must take greater care to signal the appropriate identity through the full range of symbolic means. Just as boys are freer than girls to cross category boundaries, they are less bound by category-specific clothing styles.

Jock and Burnout clothing is clearly differentiated on the basis of cost. Jocks, particularly girls, strive for a good number of outfits and consciously avoid wearing the same thing too closely in succession. Expense of clothing is apparent in the quality of cut, fit, and fabric, and in the more obvious designer labels. Most Belten Jock girls shop, frequently in pairs or groups, in the mid- to somewhat higher-priced stores in major shopping malls in the Detroit suburban area. Burnouts, much of whose solidarity is based on relative lack of economic means, pride themselves on not being concerned with clothing as a status symbol and maintain somewhat more limited and inexpensive wardrobes. Even those Burnouts who can afford to dress on a Jock scale tend not to, as an expression of solidarity with those who cannot. Lack of means is in itself a positive value, and Burnouts criticize Jocks for what they see as unnecessarily expensive and competitive dressing. The Burnout taboo on competitive dressing reflects not only solidarity in lack of means, but the more general disapproval of social competition, as will be discussed in Chapter 7.

Many Jocks' enhanced economic status is indeed reflected in their ability to follow the fashions and in their emphasis on "designer" clothing, particularly Calvin Klein jeans and Izod shirts. The economic aspects of Jock clothing, like the social value of economics in general, are not absolute but geared to the dominant means of the main Jock group. While in some wealthier schools around the Detroit area, Jocks wear entire Izod outfits, it is frowned upon in Belten to wear more than one Izod item at a time or even to own more than one or two. The preppy look, therefore, is not adopted with abandon at Belten. The stigmatization of "preppy Jocks" as conspicuously wealthy extends to the entire preppy look, as reflected in one Jock boy's strong reaction to one group of girls' habit of wearing their collars up.

> Like some of the people are wealthy, you know, and I hate Preppies, I mean, I hate people who wear their collar up and stuff, like, you know, that's totally stupid, I mean, if so many people do it, I guess it's not stupid, but it looks dumb, I don't know why they do it. And there's one girl . . . she'll ah, wear her collar up, and whenever you say anything, or happen to mention "Preppy," she'll make sure it's up—you know, make sure it's really good and up there.

Burnout fashion includes some elements that spread from working class urban areas and some outmoded elements of Jock style. In the early 1980s, Burnouts were wearing the bell-bottomed jeans popular among Jocks five years before, and Burnouts boys' long hair styles are another throwback to that era. In 1986, Burnout girls were wearing the straight-legged jeans and feathered hair style fashionable among Jocks in the early 1980s, while Jocks had moved on to short, pegged jeans and permed hair styles. The chronological relation between certain Jock and Burnout styles is not an indication that fashions simply pass from Jocks to Burnouts, for Burnouts' current jeans and hair styles correspond also to current young adult working class fashion and to the fashions currently worn by certain hard rock and country music stars. Just as Jocks follow mainstream adult influence in clothing, Burnouts follow the fashions of working class adults and the entertainers that appeal to them. Certain elements of style never adopted by Jocks reflect "country" influence, such as the buckskin "squaw boots" popular among Burnouts in the early 1980s and still popular today.

Bell-bottoms were a particularly strong Burnout index in the early 1980s and, of all the Burnout indices, the greatest object of disparagement among Jocks. Bell-bottoms are the most salient, and the first mentioned, item of Burnout fashion at Belten. This is reflected in one In-between's characterization of the lower socioeconomic school in Neartown as a place where "they wear bell-bottoms 10 feet wide." This reference to the specific width of the bell-bottoms reflects the significance of the width continuum. Jeans in the early 1980s ranged all the way from the wide bells of the early 1970s through the slightly more conservative flares, to the mainstream straight legs, and finally to the new and very fashionable pegged baggies. Among the latter two cuts, the prestige hierarchy of designer names had become an additional element of style. Even ignoring brand name, the casual observer could notice before long that jean leg width and school territory were closely related, particularly in the distribution of jeans in after-lunch territories in Belten (see Eckert, 1982). The geographic continuum from the lobby directly in front of the cafeteria (Jock territory), down the gym hall, and into the courtyard (Burnout territory) corresponds to a striking continuum in jean leg width. As one moved from the Jock to the Burnout territory, the average jean width gradually increased.

This distribution reflects not simply an opposition between bells and straight legs, but a width continuum corresponding to the social continuum. Just as the school population boasts a mass of In-betweens in addition to Jocks and Burnouts, the cut of jeans presents in-between alternatives. Not only are there more bells in the courtyard and more straight legs in the cafeteria lobby, but there are more flares in the transitional area. This continuum is repeated in the styles worn by students who spend time together. Quantitative observations of casual groups of students showed that people walking together commonly wear the same cut of jeans. However, pairs and groups also show combinations within a limited range of the jeans continuum: bells with flares, flares with straight legs, straight legs with baggies. Virtually no groups or pairs reflect jumps in the continuum.

While Jocks wear polo shirts, button-down shirts, and crew-neck sweaters, Burnouts overwhelmingly wear rock concert T-shirts. These T-shirts have the double symbolic value of displaying lack of means and of advertising the Burnout taste for hard rock. Burnouts girls wearing sweaters do not sport the "preppy" look of woolen crew necks, but opt for patterned sweaters frequently made of synthetic materials.

The most richly symbolic element of Burnout upper body wear is the jacket. The Burnouts signal their peripheral relation to the school—the fact that they are "just passing through"—by wearing their jackets all day in school. They say that they wear their jackets because they go into the courtyard between classes, because their lockers are not safe to keep anything in, and because it facilitates skipping out on the spur of the moment. The jacket worn in school very closely signals all of these elements of Burnout culture.

Certain elements of Burnout clothing also symbolize urban identification. Some Burnout boys signal their affiliation with Detroit by wearing black jackets with DETROIT written in white on the back. This urban style stands in clear opposition to the frequent Jock letter jacket, which indicates local and school orientation and participation in sports. In the early 1980s, most Burnout boys wore lined jeans jackets, which gradually gave way to the current urban fashion of hooded sweatshirts under unlined jeans jackets. Familiarity with and competence in the tougher and more crime-ridden urban environment is also symbolized by two elements of male style—metal studs, particularly on leather jackets and wrist bands, and chains attaching the wearer's wallet to his belt loop.

Sports

Sports present a complex picture in the Jock–Burnout opposition. Many Burnouts are good athletes and pride themselves on their physical abilities. Their resentment that the Jocks' involvement in school sports implies athletic superiority, and the fact that some good Burnout players defected from school teams, gives rise to considerable competition wherever Jocks and Burnouts come into contact in an athletic context. As one Burnout said:

God, in gym, man, it's Jocks against the Burnouts whatever you're doing, man. That's where, you know, it gets let out a little bit.

During junior high, there was at least one Jock–Burnout game, but, as one Jock describes below, the school tried to discourage such competition:

> Like when we were in Rover we used to have a Jock–Burn football game, Jock–Burn baseball game and stuff, you know. . . . Like they'd come up and ask one of our—you know, one of the guys from the football team, "Hey, you want to have a game?" You know, "You guys think you're so great." They're just, not really mean, they're just, you know, goofing around. Just, you know, for something to do. So, I don't know, it's just anybody, just some— they get an idea or we get an idea and we. . . . Except our coach found out and he goes, "Yeah, I'm gonna be driving down, driving by [the park] today, and if I see any of you guys out there, uh, don't be—don't be coming back to practice" or something.
>
> WHY?
>
> I don't know, it's just, he didn't want no one getting hurt and stuff, you know how that goes, and he just thought it was a dumb thing to do to have a—he just thought it was dumb having a distinction too, you know. But if some of the Burnouts, or whatever, would have just played football, we could have been a lot better, so he was kind of mad because they'd—they'd stay away just because, you know, kind of peer pressure.

While Burnouts were on school teams, particularly football, in junior high, their numbers fell off as they reached high school. Several factors contributed to this disaffection. Since the Jocks' corporate mentality leads them to form social networks around school activities, school sports enhance their social lives. The Burnouts, on the other hand, for whom social networks are primary, found that the time taken up by afternoon practices threatened the solidarity of their peer groups and excluded them from group activities. Coaches' disciplinary actions were another factor: Burnouts who missed practices or were caught using forbidden substances were suspended and dropped from teams. In keeping with their hostility toward the school's parental presumptions, Burnouts came to consider school athletics as a threat to their personal autonomy. One Burnout explained that the coaches' attention to substance use contradicted meritocratic selection—that a coach should be concerned simply with the individual's athletic performance regardless of his or her life-style. Eventually, Burnouts began to feel that they were being discriminated against, in team selections and in interactions with their teammates, on the basis of their category affiliation. As a result of all these factors, most Burnouts confine their athletic activities to city and commercial teams and to informal games.

Co-ed pickup games in neighborhood parks are a common Burnout activity in good weather. These games are as much social activities as athletic events, and all levels of skill are accepted. Particularly significant in these games are the cigarette breaks. On several occasions in games in which I participated, play was interrupted while a "runner" ran onto the field to pass a cigarette around to players stranded on base—a clear affirmation of Burnout solidarity in an activity that might otherwise be identified as "Jock."

Language

Perhaps the strongest evidence of the depth of the difference between Jocks and Burnouts lies in their use of language. There are the obvious, conscious differences—the Burnouts' more frequent and public use of obscenities and of specialized vocabulary such as drug-related slang. On a somewhat less conscious level, there are differences in routine expressions such as greetings. While Jocks tend to use the common short greeting "hi" when they come across a casual acquaintance, Burnouts overwhelmingly use the longer "how 'ya doin'." These particular greeting differences are repeated in the larger society between middle class and working class speakers. While such differences are not consciously maintained, they are recognized when pointed out to speakers.

Grammar is a conscious marker of Jock and Burnout affiliation—both in recognition and in use. The Burnouts are overwhelmingly seen as speaking "ungrammatically," that is, as using nonstandard grammar. Standard grammar is the grammar used by the powerful society's mainstream and embraced by its institutions, including the school. Its forms are not necessarily more conservative historically, nor is it any more systematic, logical, or beautiful. The use of standard grammar simply signals one's membership in and identification with the national mainstream. At times the use of nonstandard grammar may reflect sufficient isolation from the mainstream to prevent significant exposure to standard language, but its more important mechanism is its social symbolic value in the local non-mainstream community. And as with any symbolic material, the use of nonstandard grammar can reflect rejection of mainstream society and identification with the local non-mainstream community.

The multiple negative (such as *I don't know nothing*) is among the most commonly cited features of nonstandard grammar. (Multiple negation has been absurdly associated with a variety of cognitive shortcomings, with which it was never connected in the sixteenth century, when it was standard in English.) All the students in Belten High have access to standard negation; all of them use it at least some of the time, but many of them also use multiple negation. The Burnouts use far more multiple negatives than Jocks. The Burnouts used multiple negation in their tape-recorded speech with a probability of .720, while the Jocks used it with a probability of .280 (sig. = .006). None of the speakers in either category used multiple negatives all the time. The variable use of multiple negation may mean that the speaker uses standard negatives when he or she is speaking carefully but multiple negation is more natural. It may also mean the opposite: that standard negation is more natural but the speaker intentionally uses multiple negation on occasion. Finally, it may mean that the speaker's usage depends on the situation and the kind of impression he or she is trying to make or the connotations he or she wants to give to the utterance. No doubt all of these apply within the community of speakers at Belten. There is certainly no question that much of the Burnouts' use of multiple negation, and the Jocks' use of standard negation, is symbolic of category affiliation and of the relation to schooling associated with that affiliation.

While vocabulary, greetings, and grammatical patterns function on a relatively conscious level, there are also patterns of pronunciation that differ between Jocks and Burnouts. Some of these are used almost entirely unconsciously. One such pattern is in the pronunciation of several vowels that are in the progress of undergoing historical change in the Detroit area, almost entirely without the awareness of the speakers who are actually implementing the change. For example, there is a tendency in the Detroit area for speakers to back the vowel that occurs in *lunch* so that it sounds more like the vowel in *launch* (there are many such pairs—punch/paunch, but/bought, cut/caught). This change is spreading outward from the urban area, and in Neartown as in other suburbs around the Detroit area the Burnouts lead significantly in this change. In a sample that includes only people who grew up in Neartown, not recent arrivals from Detroit, the Burnouts back this vowel with significantly greater frequency than the Jocks. (This change is discussed in detail in Eckert, 1988.)

Together, these kinds of linguistic features differentiate the Jocks and the Burnouts and serve as powerful symbols of category membership. They are not simply class markers picked up in the neighborhood or the home. It is well known that children acquire their dialects from their peers rather than their parents, and that dialects tend to settle in the preadolescent years—in fact, at the very time that the Jock and

Burnout categories are forming. The clearest indication that these linguistic features are acquired as a function of category affiliation, though, is the fact that while they correlate statistically with category affiliation, they do not correlate with parents' socioeconomic class. That is, there is sufficient class crossover in the categories (as shown in Chapter 3) so that the effects of home can be separated from the effects of peer affiliation.

THE GROWTH OF SYMBOLIC OPPOSITIONS

In seventh grade, the Burnouts aggressively display their counter-school values through the adoption of distinct public behavior with clear symbolic value related to claims on adult status and to orientation to the school. Smoking, drinking, occupation of the illicit smoking area adjacent to the school, and gathering outside of dances and roller skating rinks to smoke and drink are unambiguous in their meaning. The Jocks' development of strong and vocal norms against all of these activities, and their central participation in school social activities (as opposed to hanging out at the periphery), comes to signal opposition to the Burnouts' behavior. This symbolic behavior is supplemented as increasing domains of everyday life are incorporated into the set of oppositions. The clear association of any piece of behavior with one category will lead to the adoption of opposing behavior by the other. As more domains and details of behavior are incorporated as category symbols, the oppositions become mutually reinforcing, developing a structured symbolic system with its own impetus. Clothing, territory, substance use, language, demeanor, academic behavior, and activities all ultimately serve as conscious markers of category affiliation. In each of these areas, the behavior of one category is carefully opposed to that of the other, and one can see clearly that the two sets of behavior have grown in relation to each other. This ever-enlarging set of oppositions strengthens the hegemony of the category system in adolescent life and increasingly restricts individual perceptions and choice.

The elaboration of the system of oppositions exerts increasing constraints on individual behavior, narrowing individuals' personal options and view of the world. Since the two categories develop in mutual opposition, behavioral choices are typically binary, offering alternatives that are seen as opposites and excluding other choices altogether from the range of accepted behavior. As rock concert T-shirts and polo shirts become associated with Burnouts and Jocks, respectively, the choice of a third alternative, such as a frilly blouse, becomes anomalous and is taken to indicate that the individual wearing it does not know the adolescent clothing system. The limitation to the binary choices associated with the category system is reinforced by the adolescent need to deny parental domination of personal behavior, particularly behavior, such as clothing choice, that does not have a clear "good" or "bad" association in the real world. This denial must take the form of participation in the system of socially meaningful choices offered within the adolescent community.

The oppositional system also focuses attention on those areas of behavior that it has made salient, making attention to other areas anomalous. Lunch, for instance, is either bought in the cafeteria or brought in an inconspicuous paper bag. An individual who chose to bring lunch to school in a conspicuous and carefully chosen container would be viewed as paying attention to the wrong things and thus as not knowing what is important in adolescent society. It would also suggest that the individual is participating in some system outside the local adolescent community. In the case of the lunch container there might also be a childish connotation carried over from elementary school lunch boxes, while an individual who carried a newspaper in school would be viewed as trying to look excessively adult. The system of oppositions is further strengthened by the links established among the binary choices, encouraging an association among otherwise independent areas of behavior. The value of smoking and rock concert T-shirts as Burnout symbols links them in an implicational relationship, so that the individual who wears rock concert T-shirts will be assumed also to smoke. This is also apt to be true, because those in need of a clear social identity are likely to make the entire range of choices consonant with one or the other category. Thus, in the development of the system of oppositions, individual traits lose their independence and form a network of associations, resulting in an increasingly powerful system. As the system of oppositions develops, each pole becomes increasingly specified and constrained. The consequences can be far-reaching, because the oppositions dominate not only temporary behavior, such as clothing, but choices with lasting implications, such as curriculum choice, academic effort, and substance use.

The Jock and Burnout categories represent the two extremes in relation to adults, and the oppositions associated with each term of the Jock–Burnout split represent choices that adolescents and preadolescents see themselves confronted with in the process of disengagement from the family. Ambivalence over disengagement leads to confusion over a variety of decisions, particularly those that involve the assumption of adult roles and rebellion against parents. These decisions are played out in the continual exercising of oppositions, which set up the social world in terms of binary choices and simplify the appearance of the choices to be made. At the same time, the category system provides group support for these choices: The decision to smoke is no longer an individual transgression, but is condoned and supported not only by individuals in one's group but by the existence of a social category characterized by these choices. The institutionalization of the opposition provides social sanction for either choice. Thus the decision not to smoke, if it appears to be simply obedience to one's parents, is at least as threatening to one's image as the decision to smoke. Status within a category characterized by non-smoking allows the individual to feel independent from the family while choosing parentally approved behavior.

The simplification of choice within the category system leads to oversimplification of values, and the overwhelming judgments of "good" and "bad" associated with the categories prevent individuals from recognizing the independence of many of the decisions they are faced with. The close association of traits within either category is powerful enough to force individual decisions, not on the merits of the issues at hand, but as a simple requirement and expression of category affiliation and participation in adolescent society. Thus a Burnout will find it difficult to avoid smoking or to participate in a school activity, while a Jock will feel pressured to invest in a wardrobe and to participate in activities that he or she may find uninteresting.

Obviously not everyone in Belten High School describes himself or herself as a Jock or a Burnout. In fact, only about 30 percent or 40 percent of them do. But this does not make these categories any less powerful in the social structure of the school. The fundamental status of these categories is underscored by the fact that almost all those who are not professed Jocks or Burnouts describe themselves and are described as "In-betweens."

> When people go into classifying, you know, you got the Jocks and the Jells, and then there's the In-betweeners, or whoever you want to say, you know.

The status of In-between is a by-product of the oppositional system, dominated by the same binary choices that constitute the opposition between Jocks and Burnouts. Most of the In-betweens do not choose alternative behavior, but simply mix Jock and Burnout choices. People who choose alternatives are generally referred to as "weirdos" or "nerds." The In-betweens describe themselves in terms of which choices they share with either category, and sometimes as occupying a place in a continuum between the poles, defined by the number of traits chosen from either pole. As the cohort matures, the population of the school increasingly constitutes such a continuum, but retains a significant cluster of people near each pole. There is continuous feedback of the separation and hostility between the categories and the symbolic oppositions that develop in association with them. This feedback increasingly isolates the members of each category, so that by the time the cohort reaches eleventh grade, they know relatively little about each other. As one Burnout said in his junior year:

> I don't know the Jocks any more. I don't have anything to do with them. It's hard to remember their names.

5

The Development of Social Categories

I guess, you know, we have all gone separate ways. I remember back in sixth grade, I can look back now in sixth grade, and see all of us kids back there so the same, but now we're all different, totally different. Some have gone so stuck up, and some have gone so burned out, and some have just stayed the same.

The entrance into junior high school is a formal transition to teen-age status, and marks a conscious recognition of the need for separation from the family. The issue of independence from the family is fraught with anxiety and ambivalence, and the long process of separation frequently involves emotional upheaval and sporadic regression (Joint Commission on Mental Health of Children, 1973). The intensity of personal conflict involved in separation is reflected in the intensity of the average adolescent's involvement in peer society. This intensity is an indication not only of the regressive compensatory role of peer relations, but of the progress in the nature of relations involved in the move from the family to the peer group. While pre-adolescent and adolescent peer groups compensate for the loss of the approval, security, and intimacy that the child enjoys in the family, it awards these on a new basis. Whereas family acceptance is based on ascriptive (kin) status, the peer group awards acceptance on the basis of the individual's personal qualities. Eisenstadt (1956) describes this function of adolescent groups.

Within these groups, as in the primitive age groups, new types of discipline, effected through the autonomous participation of the group, entirely different from those of family life, are imposed on the individual adolescent. The main difference lies in the fact that any individual is evaluated, as it were, according to his own worth and not according to his place within a given family; he is judged by universalistic criteria. At the same time his (or her) worth is not judged according to any specific achievement (as, to a great extent in school, in anticipation of his adult specialization), but according to his total personality and its harmony with both group values

73

and goals, or according to diffuse and collectivity-oriented criteria. This diffuse image is defined in terms of new status aspirations and evaluations which emphasize the emancipation from family discipline. (pp. 182–183)

The function of adolescent society in moving the individual's identity into the societal sphere is enhanced by the extent to which that society is structured by broad societal values, and thus to which the individual can perceive himself or herself in relation to those values. This transition takes place gradually throughout childhood, as individuals become increasingly involved in peer groups. As childhood friendship groups emerge into the more organized society of secondary school, a new element of independence is added. Childhood friendship groups function within the purview of parental norms and family obligations, and as such are dominated by adult society. Adolescent friendship groups emerge into a society of their own, providing an alternative to the authority structure of the family. The strictures of adolescent social norms replace those of the parents, and the heightened conformity of adolescents to their age-group norms helps compensate for the greater security of norms imposed by parents, who represent, during childhood, the ultimate in security and authority. Some of the intensity of adolescent peer society, therefore, is an indication of the need for structure and regulation to replace that of the family.

As they become aware that they are replacing peer for family society, adolescents develop a new sense of age-group membership. They are no longer members of an age group imposed upon them by the age-graded structure of the family, but of an age group that they have chosen as an alternative to the family. With the development of a sense of membership in an age group separate from, and opposed to, adults, they acquire responsibility for this age group and develop a stake in its structure and norms. As the alternative to the family as a basis of identity, adolescent society must appear to them worthy and reliable. Thus, the means of acquiring independence becomes a communal issue within the age group, and adolescents develop a sense of responsibility not only for their own behavior but for that of their peers. Within this context, the Jocks and the Burnouts become intensely involved in their mutual differences, which are based on their conflicting means of pursuing independence. The Jocks seek independence from the family in intense involvement in adult-sanctioned peer institutions, while the Burnouts seek it in a peer society that rejects the authority of these institutions. This difference cannot be neutral, since the behavior associated with each mode of separation threatens the basis of the other. The Burnouts' rebellious behavior threatens the carefully tended relations with adults necessary for the Jocks to realize their kind of independence, while the Jocks' acknowledgment of adult authority threatens the Burnouts' claims against this authority.

With their heightened sense of age-group membership, adolescents become sensitive to the possibility that the adult world will judge the adolescent cohort on the basis of the behavior of its most visible members. Alliances form among like-minded individuals and groups to control and monitor the behavior of those seen as working against their interests and to increase their own visibility in an effort to define norms for the age group. These alliances elevate to the level of ideology within the cohort differences in behavior that had, during childhood, been a matter between the individual and relevant adults. This ideological level in turn organizes perceptions of individuals and groups and leads to the development of categories.

Once ideology and identity merge in the formation of social categories, these categories can expand to involve increasing numbers of people and can elaborate category-specific cultural forms. In this way, groups unite into categories. The evolution of categories, therefore, involves the development of ideology around the behavior of individuals and groups; the expansion and consolidation of these groups into categories on the basis of shared ideology; and the elaboration of opposed ideologies through association with an increasing variety of membership, through the evolving issues confronting the cohort, and through the sheer force of contrasting ideologies in interpreting and assigning value to otherwise neutral behavior.

Because of the transitional nature of adolescence, an accurate view of the social categories of this period requires examination of the passage of the cohort into and through the period of adolescence. The passage through secondary school is accompanied by physiological, cognitive, and emotional changes that no doubt alter the cohort's ability and need to perceive social identity in abstract and categorical terms. At the same time, the increasing opportunity for participation and responsibility in school institutions creates new material for cultural differences between the categories. Finally, the progress toward graduation brings increasing orientation to the world beyond high school, adding concrete adult aspirations to category differences.

Since my field work was limited to the high school and did not include any direct involvement with students in their elementary school or junior high school years, my discussion of the development of social categories does not have the same empirical basis as my discussion of the end product in high school. The following is based on the reminiscences and reports of high school students about their own earlier experience. (The childhood and junior high school memories of high school students bear the same relation to actual experience as do my own adult memories of high school, as discussed in Chapter 2.) The reports on which this discussion is based are the product of selection, reconstruction, and reinterpretation of memories. But most of this is a reflection of community process, as indicated by the overwhelming agreement among the reports given by students throughout the school. As such, it is a particularly important version of the development of this community's social categories.

JUNIOR HIGH SCHOOL

Most Belten students report that the differentiation between Jocks and Burnouts arose "overnight" upon entrance into junior high. This is supported by a particularly striking piece of evidence of the suddenness of the category split that I encountered while running a workshop for public school teachers in Flint, Michigan, in 1981. When I introduced the subject of Jocks and Burnouts, a number of the teachers said that they had never heard of Jocks or Burnouts and that there were certainly no such categories in their schools. This response in turn evoked loud expressions of incredulity from a number of other teachers. I asked those who did not have such categories in their schools to raise their hands, and about half of those present did so. When I asked all those who were elementary school teachers to lower their hands, all hands went down. Subsequent discussion of these categories led some of those elementary school teachers to turn to the secondary school teachers and demand to know what they had done to the children. "They certainly weren't that way when we sent them to you." So it appears that suddenly, in junior high school, a population differentiated by what had been perceived in elementary school as individual differences became organized into two major categories.

I hate classifying people, even though it's something that's geared into my head.

UH-HUH. WHEN DID IT GET INTO YOUR HEAD?

In junior high.

DO YOU KNOW WHY?

Because it's what everybody else was doing, you know. I hated junior high. I did. I hated it because it was like—it's a total identity crisis, or it was for me, you know. Just trying to figure out where you belong. . . . OK, seventh grade, day one, Jocks and the Burnouts.

BOOM. RIGHT AT THE BEGINNING OF SCHOOL.

That fast. That fast.

A boy who became a Burnout a little later in junior high describes the same suddenness in the emergence of the categories.

CAN YOU REMEMBER WHEN IT STARTED SPLITTING INTO TWO GROUPS?

First day of junior high school.

REALLY? WHY?

Just about. I don't know. I don't even know if all those Burnouts back then got high. I don't know if they were Burnouts or not. But there was two different groups starting out, right in junior high. I don't know how that came about. Just sort of was. I don't know.

Although the categories became manifest in junior high, the underlying social divisions had been developing throughout elementary school. The Burnout category had its origins in social networks based in the lower-income neighborhoods served by Belten, which were reinforced in neighborhood elementary schools. One girl, who claimed that Finley Junior High had more Burnouts than Rover, gave the following explanation:

WHY ARE THERE A LOT OF BURNOUTS AT FINLEY?

I don't know. I really don't know. I guess, well, lots of them come from Hull, and Hull is supposed to be, you know Hull Elementary, and that's supposed to be, you know, like a really bad elementary school. I don't know why, just, you know, lots of kids, I guess, around from that area and stuff, and they just—they just hang around, I guess, lots of them hang around with, like you know, older kids, you know, so they get involved in stuff earlier.

The age-heterogeneity of Burnout networks can be traced to working class neighborhood and family patterns. Working class adults' greater neighborhood orientation and solidarity provide children with ready-made social networks. Children's networks are matched to a great extent to parental networks, within which a certain amount of parenting responsibility can be shared. Social network and neighborhood are frequently synonymous, as reflected in one Burnout's recollection.

SO WHO DID YOU PLAY WITH WHEN YOU WERE A KID?

Oh, everyone on the block pretty much. There were lots of kids on my block—you just went out the door and looked to see who was around and that was who you played with.

Working class parents frequently rely on older children as caretakers for their younger siblings and encourage closeness and nurturance among siblings. Working parents' lack of time at home gives rise to a relatively strong division between child and adult activities, leaving children to develop strong peer groups that foster solidarity in the face of parental authority. Caretakers are frequently expected to include their charges in their peer activities, and neighborhood networks develop that integrate siblings and friends.

HAVE YOU ALWAYS BEEN CLOSE WITH YOUR BROTHER?

Yeah, like you know when we were growing up and that, we hung around in the same crowd in our old neighborhood and the same crowd when we came here. So we have always been really close. I guess closer as you get older.

Greater resources allow middle class parents to provide adult care and adult-led activities for their children when they cannot be around themselves. Students from wealthier neighborhoods complain that there weren't many other kids to play with, and a number of Jocks remember being taken to other neighborhoods to play with children of their parents' friends. This parental supervision guaranteed age-homogeneous friendships, and although Jocks did of course play with kids in their own neighborhoods, these groups did not have the same kind of autonomy as those in Burnout neighborhoods. To a great extent, therefore, Jocks waited until they began elementary school to develop independent peer networks, which, by virtue of the school's institutionalized age-grading, were age-homogeneous.

Under the guidance of older friends and siblings, Burnouts claimed freedom earlier than their age mates in age-homogeneous groups. Behavior such as going out in the evening and cigarette smoking set them at odds with adults well before they arrived in junior high. In elementary school, this behavior was judged as children's "troublemaking" and acquired a structured social evaluation only within the context of the junior high social system.

WERE THERE JOCKS AND BURNOUTS IN SIXTH GRADE?

No. Sixth grade there was cool people and—in sixth grade it was weird. There was people you knew smoked and they thought they were really cool. The guys, it was the guys.

The relatively unstructured sixth-grade cohort did not, of course, suddenly acquire structure spontaneously upon entrance into seventh grade; it merged into a social system already present in the upper grades. The Burnouts' age-heterogeneous networks introduced them not only to precocious behavior but to the school's social system, in advance of the Jocks. Although the majority of the cohort trace category formation to the first day of seventh grade, the earliest Burnouts trace the beginning of their Burnout identity to late sixth grade, and particularly to the summer between sixth and seventh grade. As they approached junior high school, many sixth graders in "Burnout" neighborhoods gained access to evening group activities with the older members of their networks. Most important of these activities for the development of category consciousness were evening gatherings during good weather in neighborhood parks. During these gatherings, the sixth graders were introduced to smoking, marijuana, heterosexual relations, and discussions of adolescent social structure and adolescent problems. By the time they reached junior high in the fall, therefore, they had been introduced to Burnout culture and integrated into the Burnout network existing in the junior high. They knew to go to the "T," which was an illicit smoking area, their first day of junior high, and they knew to regard those who did not as "childish" and less "cool."

> Well, in seventh grade we were allowed to hang out at the T. That's what they called the T—it was right across the driveway in front of the school. And there's a big field, we'd play Frisbee and stuff, and everybody'd go out there and smoke dope or whatever. So that's where I hung out with all my sister's—all the ninth graders and stuff. You know, they all liked me because I was a little kid that they could tease and I wouldn't care and everything. And then, yeah, after they left is when I started making a lot of new friends and stuff. Yeah, then we hung out at the T. Just to hang out at the T. Because there's nothing else to do.

Since Jocks by and large formed their social networks in the school, academic tracking clearly played a role in the development of Jock networks and in the separation between Jock and Burnout networks. One Jock traced some of her network relations to a "gifted" class in elementary school.

> Well, we started out in reading in kindergarten, and there was a certain group of kids that did. And then they kept us together with the same kindergarten teacher in first grade, and they just kept us together. They just did it. . . . There were other kids in the

class, but that was the group that stuck together. We never were broken up. We were a set. It's like they moved us as a whole and they moved us from teacher to teacher as a whole. It was really, it was, maybe it was a trial experiment or something. But I liked it because you developed fast friendships with these, some of these people. Like Joan, who strayed away from the group in tenth grade. You've heard about Joan. And that sort of thing. There's nothing you can do, she still is a friend and she still is friendly. But it's like, Grace is like, you know, I can go up to her and say, "Hey, Grace, I remember what we did with our Barbie dolls" and stuff like that. And just have chuckles in the hall and that sort of thing. And Joe, who proposed to me in first grade and kindergarten, you know. It's like, you know, he's my old knight, old fiancé, and things like that. And so it's close friends, and just old memories that you share, that ties you together. Plus things in the future, you know, just discussing how you feel about each other and that sort of thing, so we're close.

AND THEN WHEN YOU WENT TO JUNIOR HIGH SCHOOL, WHAT HAPPENED?

Mm, we got more friends, but we really didn't break up. It was very clear in ninth grade that we didn't. We had added friends to our group.

UH-HUH, WHO?

Oh, well, just other, like Georgia had come into the group and—so to speak, the group—and that sort of stuff. And we weren't, we weren't so, as one whole group, we had gone into separate ones, but when we came together we were a group. That sort of stuff. And there were more people, but we were still all close. Even, even through ninth grade and especially ninth grade, some of us got even closer. So it was great.

HOW?

Well . . . we worked side by side diligently on the yearbook and on Honors Committee and on this and that and the other thing.

The following recollection about one of the other junior highs gives the non-Jock's view of the Jocks' cohesiveness:

In junior high school you heard about it (school activities) but you didn't go because you didn't belong, you didn't fit in with the people, you know. . . . They were friends ever since you know they were little and they just kind of stuck together, you know, and then they, somewhere along the line they, they thought they were better than the rest of us and kind of made us like outcasts in a way.

WAS THERE A TIME . . . WHEN THEY HUNG TOGETHER BUT THEY STILL WEREN'T LIKE A CLIQUE?

Yeah, in elementary school. But then it seemed like in more, and then when they got in junior high they got more like, sort of independent, in a way, or went about their own way. Kind of left everybody out. . . . Well, they were usually a little bit smarter than the rest of us. And, um, they were teacher's pets. And, um, I don't know, they were always like the captain of the Service Squad Team, or the captain of the Safety, you know.

DO YOU REALLY THINK THEY WERE SMARTER THAN THE REST OF THE PEOPLE?

No, but I think the teachers had a little bit to do with it. You know, I think they were really teacher's pets, you know, and—I think they made them, you know, they, because they would always say, no, you know, they'd say to the rest of the class, "Now look at Joel," you know, "Now look at his—" you know, how he does his paper. "Now isn't this good," you know, and so, you know we think, "Oh, wow, they're a lot smarter than we are," you know, and stuff like that.

Many non-Jocks trace the origins of the Jock category to differential treatment in more heterogeneous elementary school classrooms and on the playground, where teachers control the visibility that is so essential to developing social status.

There's a good percentage [of Jocks] you could pick out [in elementary school].

REALLY? WHAT WOULD BE DIFFERENT ABOUT THEM?

I don't know. Sometimes, um, it seems to me like . . . oh, I can remember when I was little this one girl who I used to think—and she was so popular—but everybody—it was because she had everything. You know what I mean. It was one of those syndromes, like "I want what she's got." And so everybody knew her. . . . Like I remember, you know, show and tell, she'd bring in her . . . awards, and the teacher used to make such, oh, elaborate things, and show—go around showing the teachers. And she had all kinds of clothes, and you know just the very best, and we're just kind of going, "Ooh," you know.

*   *   *

You have the little groups in sixth grade and you begin to form
little groups and stuff and, I don't know if you could even classify
it as popular, just, you know, maybe it was, um, the jocks were in
one group and it just seemed like they were, you know, they were
always better at sports and stuff, and that's sort of what, in elementary school that's sort of what makes you popular because, you
know like your teacher takes you out for kickball and stuff. And
you pick teams and then they always, the jocks always got picked
first. So it always, maybe it just seemed like they were more popular.

Belten High students look back on the development of social categories at the beginning of junior high school as a sudden loss of innocence and frequently express nostalgia about the simplicity of human
relations in elementary school. They view differences among elementary
school peers as negligible, and their choice of friends as the result of
external circumstances:

We were all the same. We weren't all Jocks but there's no such
thing as Burnouts until junior high. So we were all just friends. . . .
There was probably still little groups, everybody who lived around
each other, but we were all friends.

*   *   *

You know, it was, like I said, when we were young, everything we
did was the same, because—I see that a lot even with younger kids
now. They do the same things not because there isn't more to do,
it's just that that's what everybody else is doing, but their interests
aren't that way. When you get a little older, there's a broader type
of atmosphere where you can just pick what you want to do.
People go their separate ways.

*   *   *

Mentally, you do a lot of growing up, and maybe you realize that
there's different roads to take, you know, so you just got to decide
which one you're going to ride on. Um, you know, elementary,
things are pretty set. You have your teacher, and you go to class,
and go home, play basketball, or something. High school, there
isn't, I mean junior high, there's, you know, there's more choices.
You know, you're just growing up, I guess.

Action and Reaction

The social choices presented in seventh grade were introduced by
the Burnouts who, in their early claims to personal freedom and adult

prerogatives, represented a departure from the relative docility of childhood. At the start, therefore, the Burnouts emerged as rebellious and
precocious in opposition to the obedient mass of seventh graders. Since
this behavior was markedly different from elementary school behavior,
and was based on adult-identified behavior, the Burnouts emerged as
more socially developed and "grown-up" than the rest of the cohort.
The Burnouts' sense of growing up faster, and the others' resentment
of their apparent contempt and their adoption of frightening and "in-
appropriate" behavior, led to polarization. The Jocks, therefore, developed a sense of identity in reaction and opposition to the new Burnouts.

> You know, they [the Burnouts] were on drugs and everything, and
> then the other people were afraid to try them, or drink or any-
> thing like that, and so they became, you know, the Jocks.

This reactive and residual definition of the Jock category at the beginning of junior high is confirmed by non-Burnouts, as illustrated by one
person who considered himself an In-between in high school.

> I'd say at the beginning of junior high I considered myself a Jock.
>
> WHY?
>
> Well, we didn't smoke, we didn't drink, and, you know, we didn't
> do anything [like] that.

The Burnouts emerged, therefore, as a group opposed to an un-
defined mass on the basis of behavior that was seen as a departure from
established childhood patterns. Earlier heterosexual involvement was
another important component of Burnout life, reflecting the general
value that Burnouts placed on adult status.

> It was sort of like, the boys and the girls that were really starting to
> notice each other, you know, they were in one group and then the
> other ones that really didn't care were in another, you know what I
> mean? . . . There was a division, now that I think about it. One of
> the groups that, you know, hung around together [with the oppo-
> site sex], they did turn out to be Burnouts, I don't know why, but
> you know they did, in junior high.

The shift from mixed friendship group to dating was apparently part
of conscious preparation for junior high school, although the nature of
the heterosexual relationships was typically elementary schoolish, as re-

ported by one girl who had hung out with Burnouts in elementary
school.

In about fifth and sixth grade, all our little group that we had, you
know, that I mentioned before, was like, "OK," you know, "we're
getting ready for junior high," you know, "it's time we all have to
get a boyfriend." So I remember, it was funny, Carol, like, there
were two guys who were just the heartthrobs of our class, you
know . . . so, um, I guess it was Carol and Cindy really, they were,
like, sort of the leaders of our group, you know, they were the,
yeah, they were just the leaders, and they got Tim and Joe, each of
those you know. Carol had Tim and Cindy had Joe. And then, you
know, everyone else, then it kind of went down the line, everyone
else found someone. I remember thinking, "Well, who am I gonna
get? I don't even like anybody," you know. I remember, you know,
all sitting around, we were saying, "OK, who can we find for
Sandy?" you know, looking, so finally we decided, you know, we
were trying to decide between Al and Dave and so finally I took
Dave, you know.

WHAT DID YOU HAVE TO DO TO GET HIM?

Oh, I think someone went and delivered him the message that I
like him, you know, that was it. And so I guess the message came
back that, OK, he liked me too, so I guess we were going together,
so he asked me to go with him. So I sent the message back to him,
of course, I wouldn't talk to him, heavens no, you know, you didn't
talk to . . . [laughter].

REALLY, YOU NEVER TALKED TO HIM?

Oh, well, not before then, anyway, you know, so I had someone
else go over and tell him that, yes, I would go with him, you know.
And so, I don't even remember what came of that then. I don't
think anything. I think we would talk, you know, that that was
about it, really.

DID YOU EVER GO PLACES TOGETHER?

No. Oh, one time, yeah. One time, our whole little group, we all,
oh, there must have been about eight of us. Yep. Us four girls and
those four guys. Those four guys you know, they had their own
little group too. So, of course, the boyfriends that we picked had
to be within that group, you know, we couldn't get an outsider. So
the eight of us walked up the Handy Dip. That was it. Big time
stuff, yeah.

During the early part of junior high, the Burnouts enjoyed consid-erable status and were thought of as the "cool" crowd. Their status was based on their relatively precocious behavior—in some sense they were seen as "typical teen-agers" and as "getting more out of life." A number of people were attracted to the Burnouts early in junior high because of this, but later moved on when it became apparent that Burnout activities could lead to trouble.

The adolescent's sense of identity beyond the family is based on the personal autonomy that grows out of a sense of participating as an in-dividual in a social structure beyond the family. For most adolescents, adolescent society provides the only such structure, and the individual adolescent's identity is dependent on the degree of his or her integration into it. To the extent that it is structured around broad cultural values, adolescent society provides the means for the development of an auton-omous identity. Since the issue of separation from the family, which di-vides Jocks and Burnouts, involves just such values within the adolescent context, the development of Jock and Burnout categories enhances the value of adolescent society for its members. The individual's sense of identity is strengthened by participation in the social process of catego-rization both because it provides a separate age-group world in which to participate and because it allows individuals to define themselves in re-lation to global issues.

Expanding Social Networks

Entrance into junior high school represents a great leap into ado-lescence, and the approach of seventh grade brings both anxiety and excitement about teen-age status and the expanded school environ-ment. Although Jocks and Burnouts are opposed in their interpretation of teen-age status, they react similarly to the challenge of the expanded environment. After seven years with the constant and small population of one elementary school, entrance into junior high school is a fright-ening prospect for all. The building and population seem enormous to the newcomer, the secure environment of one teacher and one class is replaced by a variety of teachers and class groups, and the one familiar classroom gives way to the necessity of changing classes. It is probably not fortuitous that social categories, which lend a certain amount of pre-dictability to the behavior of large numbers of people, should arise at this time. Mitchell (1969) observes that this "categorical order" of social relationships is a function of large-scale societies. All the students I spoke with recognized the need to expand their networks to avoid being lost and isolated in the larger environment, and most considered making contacts to be the first priority upon entrance into junior high. The expansion of social networks, furthermore, is an essential aspect of the evolution from the fragmented group society of elementary school into the vast alliances and categories that make up a structured society.

Many students remember being plagued by a need to be "popular" in junior high—a need not simply to get to know people, but to confirm their emerging sense of identity through the recognition of others and a sense of place in the social structure. By and large, the core of each category was made up of people with social ambition and skills, and the categories gained membership and coherence through the networking efforts of their members. Friendship patterns changed drastically between elementary and junior high school, and again between junior high and high school, as the social requirements of the larger school created new differences among friends. Those who lacked the confidence or skills to pursue extended networks were left behind by their more aggressive friends and frequently felt that they were the victims of social ambition.

> Yeah, you see it around, you know, they just—somebody'll, they'll start hanging around with somebody else and they'll just, you know, the rest of their friends or they just—they won't even talk to them anymore, you know? No matter how good of friends they were before.
>
> WHY DO YOU THINK THEY DO THAT?
>
> To be part of the in crowd. Definitely.
>
> *   *   *
>
> You meet a lot more people, but you lose a lot of your old friends, like you never see them any more. Like there's a few guys that you were really close to in Rover that you hardly even say hi to any more. It's different. . . . They just, when they come to Belten, I think it's more that they just don't go out and meet more people or, I don't know, with a littler school they can relate more, or something.

Many friendships broke up over category affiliation, as those who did not want to get into trouble moved away or were left behind by their more daring Burnout friends.

> Once we went to this dance, and, it was me and Janet, and, um, she, she was starting to smoke, she's—you know, she just—it was a

little peer pressure thing, and so she, um, and we went back in the back of the school, and they, like they were bringing out all these little, their pipes and, and filling them up, and I just, I couldn't believe it, drugs, it just, I mean, and so I just, I watched them, and they were smoking it and all this, and then one kid blew it in my face, and I just, oh, that made me so sick, so I, so I finally, I left. Couldn't take it anymore. But, um, that made me feel so un-at-ease. I was just so tensed up with those people. That's when I started branching off and finding my own friends. . . . Janet was my closest friend, and she really was like friends with the rest of the people, and so I always felt like I was the third wheel.

Those Burnouts who appeared the most advanced, and to be having the most fun, became the popular core of the Burnout crowd. They were frequently also the ones who had the most contacts with older Burnouts in the junior high.

They were the ones that had girlfriends and boyfriends first. They were the ones to try out everything new first. They hung around all the junior high kids first.

The Emergence of the Jocks

At the same time that Burnouts were asserting themselves as "partiers" in junior high, others became involved in school sports and the few other school activities available to seventh graders. Among these people, some who had emerged in junior high as athletic and "popular" formed the core of a popular crowd separate from that of the Burnouts. Many of these people had gained visibility and prestige in elementary school through a combination of teacher approval and ability in childhood pursuits. This association of the Jock core with school success introduced the school-based aspect of Jock identity, but also developed into a strong sense of Jock superiority—an aspect of category conflict that remains and even grows through high school and stands in constant contrast to the Burnouts' growing sense of pride in competence in the outside world.

Although the Burnouts viewed the nascent Jock crowd as "goody-goodies" and "teacher's pets," the latter were, in fact, eager to achieve autonomy in junior high school through involvement in peer society. No person who is simply docile toward adults can retain status in adolescent peer society. Those who had gained visibility through being a teacher's pet in elementary school could not retain status in peer society without some indication that they could stand up to teachers and parents. The difference between prestigious Jocks and Burnouts in this regard is the style in which they stood up to adults. In junior high, therefore, two separate popular groups emerged around two crowds of elementary school "stars," defining the center of the Jock and Burnout categories. The popular Burnouts were "rowdy," while the popular Jocks were the athletic and visible achievers from elementary school. By virtue of their reaction to the Burnouts, the Jocks developed an identity based initially on opposition to the Burnouts' rebelliousness. This identity did not remain negative for long—their participation in school activities became a positive trait, reinforced by the more full-blown status of the Jock category in the upper grades of the school.

In early junior high, everyone, including Burnouts, participated in school social activities. Some Burnouts went out for sports and cheerleading; many attended dances, roller skating, and athletic events. The latter events were put on by the school for the students, and Jocks and Burnouts attended them in the same consumer capacity. Both Jocks and Burnouts remember junior high school dances with particular nostalgia, although the Jocks and Burnouts behaved differently at these dances. While Jocks concentrated on the dances themselves, Burnouts organized their private activities around them.

> Well, everybody was there, you know the whole school would go, dance, wow, it was a big thing, you know. I had so much fun at those. Those were just a riot. And, you know, they'd get bands in and you sat around and listened to the band and just had fun. We used to, you know, go out and drink a few beers before we'd get there, and you know, be home by 11 o'clock or you're grounded for life, you know.

Another popular activity was roller skating, organized by the school at a nearby rink. Here, off school territory but not away from school authority, the Burnouts were also eager to pursue their private activities on the fringes of the official activity, which eventually got enough Burnouts banned from school activities that the others stopped going. Thus, as junior high wore on, Burnout involvement in school-organized activities diminished, and, with it, the Burnouts' general prestige. As they became excluded from school activities, Burnouts moved from being simply "rowdy" to adopting a counter-school ideology. Whereas at first being rowdy had been "cool," now participating in school activities was "not cool." One Burnout who had wanted to work on the yearbook in ninth grade explained why she finally didn't.

WHY DIDN'T YOU GO OUT FOR YEARBOOK, AND STUFF LIKE THAT?

In, in, I don't know, you probably know this, you probably heard this from people too. You know, in, um, junior high everybody was stereotype, stereotype. Like, you hung around with the Burnouts. You didn't talk to the Jocks.

YEAH.

You know. The Jocks didn't talk to you. And I talk to so many girls now that I think in ninth grade we didn't talk and stuff because she was a Jock and I was a Burnout, or whatever. And, um, and they were all on all the activities, you know.

YEAH.

So that, sort of—I was the most—. Out, out of everybody, I'd always go, "Come on, you guys, let's go roller skating," or "Let's go to the dance." And we would, but every—, most everybody else was, "Oh, nah, let's go out and walk around instead," you know.

AND WAS IT NOT BECAUSE THEY DIDN'T WANT TO GO TO THE DANCE, BUT BECAUSE THEY FELT THAT IT WASN'T MADE FOR THEM?

Yeah. Right. Perfect. Exactly. . . . Yeah, like, "Well, it's not cool to go to school activities," you know.

The growing conviction that school activities were not cool was based partially on the prohibition against adult behavior at these activities. Those who engaged in illicit adult behavior (such as smoking and drinking) at these activities were banned one by one; thus, those who remained were marked as not engaging in adult behavior, and the school's endorsement of their behavior labelled them as "goody-goodies."

While Burnouts were becoming disaffected from school activities, Jocks were coming into their own. As junior high progressed, the Jocks acquired a new range of roles in the school, which changed their residual status to a more positive one. Whereas as seventh graders the cohort were mere consumers of school activities, when they reached ninth grade the opportunities for active production of these activities increased. Not only were they more apt to play starring roles on athletic and cheerleading teams, but they could also work on such things as yearbook. The opportunity to control certain aspects of the environment, therefore, gave rise to a distinction between producers and consumers. Participation in production, however, was contingent on endorsement by school staff, and such endorsement was forthcoming only to those who stood in good stead with adults. Ultimately, those Jocks involved in production of school activities acquired special status with school staff and began to enjoy heightened visibility and autonomy in the school. At this point, the Jocks' image as "goody-goodies" and "teacher's pets" was transformed into a more cooperative, equal relation with staff.

Whereas Jocks and Burnouts had both been in a subordinate relation to staff, differentiated by docility and rebelliousness, respectively, now the Jocks entered a coordinate relation with staff by virtue of shared interests. The increasingly disciplinary nature of Burnouts' relations with staff kept them subordinate, and the new relation of the Jocks with staff gave them an appearance of ascendency over their Burnout peers. At this point, the possibility of school-endorsed power relations among peers added a new dimension to the opposition between the Jocks and the Burnouts. At the same time, the Burnouts' monopoly on adult behavior weakened as Jocks began to date also, to hang out in heterosexual "crowds," and to enjoy the new exclusive adult prerogative of autonomy within the school. Passage through junior high, with its increasing managerial possibilities for Jocks and the associated exclusion of Burnouts, introduced new and varied material for the opposition between the categories and heightened the need within each category to differentiate itself from the other. As the more clearly class issues of management and subordination entered the category definitions, the initial issue of rebelliousness became symbolic of a more threatening opposition.

Polarization

The development of Jock and Burnout ideology organized the expansion of social networks and united these networks into categories. Behavior originally associated with individual groups became associated with categories, and many aspects of behavior acquired global symbolic status. Category symbols served both to unite disparate groups and networks under the aegis of a category and to promote the differentiation of the two categories. A range of overt behavior was incorporated into a tightly interwoven system of symbolic oppositions that included clothing and other kinds of adornment, demeanor, language, territory, and substance use. As the categories became increasingly distinct on all levels, category affiliation began to dictate individual behavior in all areas of life.

Cigarette smoking at school, the initial issue in the development of the Jock–Burnout split, acquired symbolic status as groups of smokers evolved into a social category. Smoking took on a more general symbolic value, identifying the individual not only as daring and grown-up, but as a member of a social category that was more generally daring, grown-up, and opposed to school norms. Smoking became public group behavior, and other kinds of symbolic behavior were adopted to correspond to the emerging global Burnout image.

> I suppose, like the Burnouts are the people, like they would start, you know, smoking in the johns in Rover, you know, stuff like that. And, you know, like I thought, why can't they wait until they get home if they want to do that, you know, because they're just going to get in trouble here. And people did that, and they started wearing like the, you know, the, the T-shirts that say, you know, "smoke dope," and "Black Sabbath," you know, stuff like that, and um, you know, they would stay, like wearing the same thing day after day. People, you know, thought that was pretty cool, you know, and not washing their hair.

*   *   *

SO HOW DID PEOPLE GET LABELLED AS BURNOUTS?

> Um, they smoked. They wore Levi big bells. The Jocks used to say this in ninth grade, that all the girls that were Burnouts had long hair, scaggly, you know, which none of us really were, you know, and they just—we didn't carry books. We didn't carry big bags, you know, just stuff like that. We didn't get along with the teachers.

SO IT WAS BASICALLY SORT OF—

> Just the way you carried yourself in school, pretty much. How much you got into it.

In this fashion, the two categories drew apart in mutual opposition as experience in junior high fleshed out their differences, and as differences in personal behavior gave way to power differences within the school. As the Jocks' position in the school undermined the Burnouts' prestige, hostility between the two categories became more broad-based and bitter. In addition, the coalescence of Burnout groups into interlocking networks, increasingly defined by an overarching category identity, lent them a new visibility and vulnerability at the hands of the school. The distinctive Burnout clothing and hair styles made them easy to identify, and as the category developed, guilt by association became an increasing danger. Burnouts began to feel that the school stereotyped and discriminated against them.

IS IT HARD NOT TO BE LABELLED?

> Um, back at Rover it was. I mean, no matter what. If you, I mean if you hung around a Burnout crowd, you were considered a Burnout. Even if you didn't, you know. If you hung around a Jock

crowd and you got high and stuff, you were considered a Jock. It's just the way the teachers are, I guess.

THE TEACHERS?

Mm hm. OK, see I hung around the Burnout crowd, but, well, back then, I guess I was, but, but I didn't smoke cigarettes, and you know how everybody used to go in the john and smoke cigarettes, you know, in between classes and that. Well, I had this one teacher, Mr. Gray, and no matter what you said he would not believe you, you know. And I'd walk in class and after being around a bunch of girls smoking, you, you smell like smoke, you know. I walk in and he'd go, "Next time, um don't smoke before my class," or something like that. And I said, "I don't smoke," and he said, "Oh, don't lie to me. I know what you do." He goes, "Do you think I'm stupid or something?" and I go, "Well, you can believe what you want, but I don't smoke, you know." And he goes, "Oh, yes, you do. If you hang around with such and such then you do."

One girl was convinced that she was excluded from a team because of her category affiliation.

I tried out for [the team]. I didn't make it. I made it right down to the last line, but . . . but see, back then you were considered a Burnout, and you didn't make it because of that. . . . The Jocks made it even if they weren't good. Teachers even admit it over there. . . . Mr. Jackson . . . we talked and everything, and he was like, like he would watch the practices and that, and he goes, "Yeah," he goes, "Judy, I think you were one of the better ones." He goes, "I think you should have made it," he goes, "but just because you're labelled a Burnout you didn't make it." And I go, "Right." He's one of the honest teachers, you know. He just tells it like it is. And I go, "Well, you know. Gotta live with it, I guess." And the team sucked all year anyways. So it didn't matter.

According to the reports of virtually all those I spoke with, the salience of social categories peaked during eighth and ninth grades. At that time, students felt the greatest pressure to affiliate and to conform with one or the other category, and at that time hostility between the categories was at its height. This development is no doubt related to statistics showing that the onset of smoking, a key Burnout symbol, peaks in the eighth and ninth grades (Johnston, Bachman, and O'Malley, 1982). Category affiliation, therefore, came to constrain individual choice in areas with lasting consequences:

> But like we got along with everybody and we partied every day and that was the cool thing. And, uh, we'd smoke in school and that was cool. We used to get E's in classes, that was cool.

The rigidity of social categories also seems to have stemmed from a still immature ability to deal with the need for identity. In junior high, social identity was narrowly defined by affiliation with one of the two categories, and the unaffiliated were assigned no status in the oppositional system.

> I was never a Jock and I was never a Burnout. I hung around with most, you know, or like there was the Jocks and the Burnouts who'd sit and give each other dirty looks in the halls, you know. For no reason, you know. And I just thought that was dumb as could be, you know. So I associated with everybody. So that kind of left me right in between everybody else, you know. And so I kind of felt, you know, I was kind of—little bit—I mostly hung around with, I guess you could say the Jocks, because most of my buddies were in that group, you know, or classified there. And uh, but I had some friends that like hung around with the Burnouts too, you know. And kind of left me right in between, you know . . . and so that kind of made me feel like a slight outcast, you know. Somebody left in between the realms, you know.

A girl who eventually came to regard herself as a Burnout gives this account.

> That's, that's where all the Jock–Burn, or the Jock–Jelly thing started, because I didn't hear anything about it in elementary school. But once I hit Rover, you know, that's all you heard was, "She's a Jock," "She's a Jell," you know. And that's all it was. You were either one. You weren't an In-between, which I was.

THE PASSAGE TO HIGH SCHOOL

The cohort's developing ability to categorize and abstract no doubt plays a role in the elevation of previously unstructured personal differ-

ences to more abstract social organizing principles in junior high, but
the still-immature resources lent a special rigidity to these abstractions.
Adherence to a rigid category system is a useful strategy for dealing with
large numbers and a large variety of individuals, as the cohort makes
the enormous leaps in size from elementary to junior high, and from
junior high to high school. Indeed, the social category system serves an
important purpose in the transition from junior high to high school, in
organizing the population's mutual conceptions. The extreme overt differences between the categories provide a way of predicting the behavior of others, and the sense of affiliation with a category that has its
equivalent in the high school decreases some of the anxiety about enter-
ing high school. In fact, the categories facilitate the merger of junior
highs in tenth grade.

> Like the types of groups that [are] at Belten, you find at Finley.
> They come together, and usually those types find each other. And
> then, that's where you get your groups, your cliques, your net-
> works, your gangs, or whatever, you know, things like that . . . it's
> like, they just come together, they fit in, like, just a puzzle, you
> know? The pieces fit in, because you find who's like you and things
> like that.

This process of merger is also facilitated at the entrance into high
school by the specialized mobility and information provided by the Jock
and Burnout networks. A certain amount of high school networking
begins before tenth grade. While Burnouts are still in junior high, they
learn about their counterparts in other schools through their older
peers who have moved into the high school, and Jocks get to know those
from other junior highs through participation in school-run summer
activity camps.

> The summer before I started school here, between ninth and
> tenth grade, I met pretty much my friends that I hang around
> with now.
>
> REALLY. HOW DID YOU MEET THEM?
>
> Basketball clinic. They were there, and I was there. And, I remem-
> ber the last day of the clinic, we sat in the weight room talking for
> about some two-and-a-half hours just about different people from
> our school, different people from their school, and just, you know,
> talking about things we like to do and stuff, and we became really
> close. . . . I only saw them like once or twice after that, but once

the year started, we really were close, and we had things in common.

The power of the category system may be a result not only of the increased size of the cohort, but of the early adolescent's cognitive limitations in functioning in a large group. The strict interpretation of categories, and rigid assignment of individuals to categories, could be said to reflect the kind of black-and-white, right-and-wrong view of the world characteristic of earlier stages of cognitive development. Adelson's (1971) characterization of the early adolescent's view of human motivation corresponds quite closely to what appears to have been the junior high school view of social categories.

> The youngster enters adolescence with a remarkably thin repertoire of motivational and psychological categories available to him. He is like a naive behaviorist; he does not look beneath action to its internal springs. There is little sense of inner complication. Men act as they do because they are what they are. A man acts selfishly because he is selfish; the crime is committed because the man is a criminal. The vocabulary of motives is both impoverished and redundant. Character— character seen simplemindedly—is destiny. (p. 1018)

With maturity, however, the adolescent learns to examine the motivations behind actions and thus to be more relativistic. Furthermore, the older adolescent is less willing to be led by categories set out by others. Adelson (1971) found that older adolescents were less willing than early adolescents to accept either/or alternatives in questions about politics.

> He breaks set—that is, he challenges the assumptions, tacit and otherwise, contained in the inquiry. Should the government do A or do B, we ask. Now he may say "neither," and suggest amendment, or compromise, or some entirely new solution which bypasses or transcends the terms of the question. (p. 1021)

This willingness to "break set" is reflected in the evolution of adolescent social categories as the cohort moves through high school. As their perceptions of social identity develop, adolescents struggle increasingly with the rigid definitions imposed by the categories, and the later evolution of the adolescent social system reflects a changing orientation to social categories. Entrance into, and progress through, high school brings a gradual decrease in the discreteness of the two categories, in individual affiliation, and in simple relations between category opposition and the world. As the cohort advances to high school, the boundaries between the categories soften, and it becomes more respectable to be an In-between. High school students recall the category system of junior high as particularly rigid, and many of them feel that the ability to make judgments independent of category affiliation is a sign of maturity.

Back in Finley, there were the Jocks and then the Burnouts. No In-between, even though we were in-between you weren't classified as In-between.

WHAT WERE YOU CLASSIFIED AS?

Jock. It was just, if you were a Burnout, you're a Burnout; if you weren't, you were a Jock. So I always thought that that's how Belten was, and that I wouldn't be going out in the courtyard. That's not how it is at all.

*   *   *

I think like, in the junior high schools, um, you're not as apt to, like, fall in or out of another group. It's really an oddity if people do that, you know? But here it's, um, a little more accepted, like, you're, you seem to be more of a person here, not just like a, you know, a piece of paper someone shuffles away somewhere. You know, you seem to, it's a little more understandable that you, you want to change.

*   *   *

Throughout junior high, there was a big difference between Jock and Jell. Then all of a sudden you hit, like high school, and, Jells like kind of, back off, you know, and Jocks, you know, Jocks and Jells are mostly, you know, they're friends, you know, you talk to them, you know, and you don't have no grudge, you know, against you know, the Jells. . . . It's like now, once you're into high school, you know, they're all, you know, you're like friends with them all. You know, you leave them alone, and they leave you alone, you know. It's not, no more like the Jellies are hassling the the Jocks, and when you walk by, you know, they don't say, "Oh, you Jock." They just don't say nothing.

Many juniors, and particularly seniors, in high school pride themselves on their ability to transcend the category system and to perceive people as "individuals," as opposed to junior high, when they saw everything "in black and white." They claim impatience with the many people whom they consider to be still bound by these categories.

It's easy to do, yeah, it's easier, it's an easier way to deal with people. Because you don't have to think about them that much. You don't have to think about, well, "I wonder why they're doing that?" you know, it's just, so, "Oh, they're pigeonholed," you know, everybody's nice and compact.

The softening of category boundaries is also due to changes in accepted behavior as the cohort matures. Jocks and Burnouts split in junior high over issues such as smoking and staying out at night: issues of "good" and "bad," "right" and "wrong." Burnouts are seen as trying to grow up too fast. Over the years, as the rest of the cohort catches up with the Burnouts in their claims on adult prerogatives, the apparent differences between Jocks and Burnouts begin to disappear.

Seems like the crowds diminish, I think, a little coming into high school. They still exist, you know, but, uh, some of the Jocks are more into drugs than some of the Jellies. Now that's very true, you know.

But the categories remain long after plenty of Jocks are smoking pot and plenty of Burnouts have given it up. However more sophisticated the population becomes about categories, they remain tied into them. What probably changes more is their way of talking and thinking about categories than their reliance on them in making individual decisions about their own behavior and judgments about others. A wide range of differences remain between Jocks and Burnouts throughout high school, in spite of the many apparent contradictions that indicate strain in the system. And the definitions of the categories retain an important hold on the way that members of the adolescent community view themselves, each other, and the world. Of course, the relative violence of the process of affiliation in junior high school creates divisions that are difficult to overcome and sets up social networks at the point of merger of several elementary schools that make further change of category problematic. By the time the cohort is into high school, the two categories have become separated not only by behavioral differences and hostility, but by sheer isolation.

The ability to see social reality in all its complexity appears to diminish as the cohort becomes larger. The intensity of the alienation between Jocks and Burnouts varies considerably from school to school, and within one school from era to era: Some schools are the scene of violence between the categories; in others, Jocks and Burnouts enjoy a certain amount of mutual respect. School size seems to be an important factor—one principal reported to me that he could observe the opposition between Jocks and Burnouts decreasing as the enrollments in his school declined. Barker and Gump's (1964) report clearly shows that a large proportion of students are excluded from activities in large schools. This would naturally foster alienation from the school, bringing greater separation between students participating and students not participating in the school. Barker and Gump point out that in a smaller school, the greater demand for people to fill roles, and the consequently small number of people without community functions, leads to greater sensitivity to, and closer evaluation of, differences between people. In the larger school, "the person is in the position of a figure against an undifferentiated background, where small differences are clearly seen. Individual differences become important, and the innumerable ways of sorting and classifying people become prominent" (p. 26).

The extent of categorization may also be related to the range of socioeconomic difference among the student body within the school. In one rural community that has recently become an affluent suburb of Detroit the schools have a considerable poor population along with a large body of children of professionals. The difference between these two groups is so great that they know virtually nothing about each other. Both these factors—social estrangement and population size—contribute to the general tendency to stereotype, to respond to the other group on the basis of externals, and in short, to categorize rather than to know personally. In the small school, where most individuals have personal experience of each other, they are less apt to react to each other on the basis of stereotypes, and thus less apt to feel the need to rely on categories either to define themselves or to predict the behavior of others. By the same token, each school staff member, knowing a greater proportion of the student body, is less apt to respond to individuals in this way.

But even in the most personalized schools, differences arise among the student body in their relation to the school, which will be reinforced by the school's mission. The Jock and Burnout categories are no doubt inevitable in our society, where the school dominates so many aspects of the lives of adolescents. The intensity of differentiation between Jocks and Burnouts stems not simply from their differences, nor simply from the fact that the Jocks are favored over the Burnouts in school. The importance of the Jocks' enhanced position in the school is intensified by the fact that the school is hegemonic in American society: So many of the opportunities that the community offers adolescents are funnelled through the school, and failure to conform to school expectations in one realm tends to put the individual in disfavor in other realms. The mechanisms and effects of the hegemony of the high school in adolescent life, which will be discussed at length in the following chapters, represent an important problem in our society, particularly as schools become larger and fewer people are reaping fewer advantages from them.

The persistence of categories through high school is not simply a result of lingering habit or convenience; rather, the social categories "Jocks" and "Burnouts" represent divisions that go far deeper in the community. The following chapters will explore two interacting factors that are responsible for the persistence of social categories right through to graduation day. The first of these is that adolescent social category is the adolescent interpretation of, and to a great extent determined by, parents' socioeconomic class. The second is that the school that houses the adolescent community institutionalizes and thus encourages these categories in its formal and informal political structure.

6

The Corporate Structure of the School

You've heard the expression, "I'm on cloud nine," and we've labelled certain people that are cloud nine people, that are really up people, and then there's us on cloud eight, we're just below them, we gotta work our way up there to be accepted in school and then have a good time on the weekends I guess or whatever, go out with them, and get accepted by them.

Attendance at school takes up 32 percent of the average American adolescent's day, confining activity to one locale within which organizational requirements severely limit the students' personal freedom. The high school has developed ways to compensate for its basic denial of autonomy, particularly by simulating adult social systems through its extracurricular programs. These programs provide a certain amount of self-determination and control over limited aspects of the daily environment. Insofar as there is room for leadership in extracurricular activities, the school provides opportunities to achieve status among one's peers, to exercise managerial skills, and to play adult roles in relation to the adolescent, and to some extent the adult, population of the school. By providing a comprehensive social sphere away from home, school offers the opportunity to play adult-like roles away from parental, if not adult, supervision. Society assumes that parents will cede certain prerogatives to the school and will regard the school's endorsement as sufficient to legitimate their children's activities. It should be noted that this creates problems for many children of immigrant parents, who generally are not willing to cede authority to the school, and who frequently do not acknowledge the social function of the school.

The context for extracurricular activities is a strictly defined corporate structure circumscribed by the school, which effectively limits commitment to communities beyond the school boundaries, at the same time that it fosters intensive involvement and social structure within. The institutions that appropriate student energy and cooperation also socialize participants for a corporate mode of existence. In return for the opportunity to play roles within the school and enjoy the status and freedom associated with them, the student must endorse the corporate norms of the school and the overriding authority of the adults who run it. The school thus strikes a limited bargain with its student population that mitigates, for some, the loss of freedom that attendance imposes.

By and large, this bargain is accepted willingly by those students, particularly the college bound, whose plans for adulthood require the continued sponsorship of adults and adult institutions, and for whom the kinds of corporate roles offered within the school provide preparation for the roles they anticipate playing as adults. As a substitute for participation in the larger community, the school offers mobility within an elaborate internal structure, which is clearly intended as preparation for later participation in an analogous adult structure. The necessity and the adequacy of this preparation for adulthood is a perennial issue in the school, clearly dividing Jocks and Burnouts. It has been shown repeatedly that school caters to middle class norms and career needs, and assigns the vocationally oriented students marginal status. Participation in academic and extracurricular activities is necessary for entrance into a good college, as is the informal sponsorship of school staff, which participation brings. But, as noted in Chapter 3, while the school has a direct role in procuring college entrance for its academic students, it does not play an analogous role for its vocational students in the working class job market. These students do not feel that the activities in the school, with the exception of some vocational courses, provide any kind of training relevant to their future employment; on the contrary, many feel that the kinds of managerial and competitive social skills encouraged in school activities are dysfunctional both in their social realm and in the labor force. The degree of fit between high school activities and anticipated future activities is an important factor in the individual's willingness to accept the school's bargain.

In much the same fashion as Willis's (1977) "Lads," the Burnouts develop a culture that is dominated by the private and opposed to the institutional. Just as, later in life, they will look upon the workplace as a necessity to gain the means to pursue their private life, Burnouts attend school because it is necessary, but focus their attention on relations and activities whose locus is independent from the school. Burnouts do not allow the school to mold their personal relations and pursuits, both because of a surface theme of rebelliousness and because of a deeper belief that the kinds of relations and pursuits that emerge within the school conflict with those adaptive to working class reality and those learned in the working class home and neighborhood. In contrast, the Jocks welcome the opportunity to merge the personal with the institutional. In high school, as in their corporate adulthood, Jocks' personal identity is defined in terms of their institutional roles, and the dynamics of their personal relations come to serve the interests of the corporation that creates those roles.

The causal relation between individual characteristics brought from childhood, and participation and success in the high school corporate structure is complicated. Successful participation in this structure requires a desire for prominence, knowledge of the structure, and the social and instrumental skills demanded in it. It also requires a less tangible element that those at the fringes of the Jock hierarchy would call "luck," because there are too few places in the hierarchy for those who would like to occupy them. The most frequently cited kind of luck is early access to the groups that will later dominate the school hierarchy— an access that is determined to some extent by factors beyond the individual's control, such as placement in elementary school and elementary school classrooms.

> The Morgan [Elementary School] group were the leaders, pretty much. And everybody just, you know, got together. It was bigger . . . it was a good group of people, you know. And they just, we did things fun together, we organized things, you know, and a lot of people.

All of these factors are tightly interwoven, and it cannot be the aim of this study to separate clear causal factors. However, it is obvious that early acquisition of corporate knowledge will predispose the individual to success in the school system, and for many this begins in the home.

Working class family and neighborhood experience instills social values and norms that conflict with those of the high school corporate community. An emphasis on loyalty to tight, supportive social groups and on sharing of resources within these groups works against the kind of competitive relations inherent in hierarchical structures and upward mobility. The age-heterogeneous networks that form in working class neighborhoods, based to a great extent on sibling relations, also work against the commitment to the age cohort that is essential to corporate success in the school. Middle class childhood experience, on the other hand, tends to discourage exclusive friendships and friendships across age groups, emphasizing more extensive task-oriented social contacts. Thus, early training sets social norms and reinforces differentiated social skills, begins the child on a particular course of network building, and, finally, encourages an emotional makeup suited to one or the other kind of social structure. In the course of elementary school, all of these factors can be changed by participation in the school, and by the influence of the school, which encourages the development of middle class patterns. Also, individual experience can lead middle class children to seek closed supportive groups, and working class children to move into more competitive networks. But early social experience predisposes individuals to move in a particular direction as they leave the family and neighborhood and move into broader social contexts.

CAREERS AND THE CORPORATE SETTING

The high school provides a corporate setting through its strict delimitation of the corporate community, its isolation from the outside community, its internal hierarchical structures, its emphasis on role-oriented individual identity, and its task-oriented determination of interpersonal association. The attitudes and orientation of individuals and groups, depending on their place in the corporate structure, closely parallel those found in adult corporate settings.

The corporate organization of the school provides the setting and means for the development of individual student careers. The Jock sees his or her success in the activity structure of the school as a personal career that gives the individual both a place in the history of the school and access to the means to develop an adult career. The latter, preparational aspect of the high school career is well known. Society considers that a successful high school career is evidence of leadership quality and commitment to corporate values. The high school career thus enhances opportunities in middle class employment and is essential to entrance into a good college. In schools across the country, Jocks will readily admit to participating in certain activities because it will look good on their record, but most will insist that their overall participation in school activities is the result of commitment to the school. The development of a corporate ideology of commitment to and identification with the goals of the institution becomes part of the ideology that reifies the opposition between Jocks and Burnouts.

The social-institutional uniformity of public schools across the country is based on common notions of the kinds of civic training that are valuable to the creation of "good citizens." But the particulars of these activities are based also on the commitment of the school staff to their own professional evaluation. School staff look to professional organizations for examples of successful activities, and their own professional success depends on their performance of fairly set tasks. Thus every high school has a student government, sports, and artistic activities; the school itself is evaluated on the basis of set standards of success in these activities. For the student also, the uniformity of school activities serves a purpose analogous to standardized testing: Colleges and prospective employers can measure students' social success on the basis of their level of participation in standardized social roles and institutions. This perceived need for uniformity contributes to the conservatism of the extracurricular activities of the school and to the students' faithful participation in them.

External Boundaries

Kanter (1977) has documented how the success of a corporation depends on the exclusive commitment to the organization on the part of those in discretionary jobs. According to Kanter, upper management ensures this commitment from the outset by limiting the managerial corps, through the recruitment of people of social backgrounds similar to their own, to individuals who feel they share fundamental social values. These recruits must then demonstrate their commitment to the corporation not only through effective participation within, but through renunciation of involvement outside, the corporation.

> Just as long-lived utopian communities build commitment in part by establishing strong boundaries between themselves and the outside world, making it difficult for people to maintain any ties outside the community, so do corporations like Indsco create organizational loyalty by ensuring that for its most highly paid members the corporation represents the only enduring set of social bonds other than the immediate family. (Kanter, 1977, p. 66)

The boundaries of the high school, which serve a function analogous to corporate boundaries, originate with the school's basic mission to serve a given geographic area, and are reinforced through competition with other high schools. This competition encourages school loyalty and the development of a school identity, which is based to a great extent on the students' own perceptions of differences between their school and those around it: differences that are frequently smaller than the differences among the students within the school. The individual who seeks success in the school hierarchy must concentrate his or her efforts on the community in which this hierarchy is based. This is necessitated by practical considerations, because work on school activities is time-consuming, as is the servicing of social networks so necessary to maintaining effective peer relations. Also, identification with outside groups threatens the integrity of the school community, which is necessary for the maintenance of a strong hierarchical organization. Thus there is a strong norm among Jocks of exclusive commitment to the school community.

The emphasis on participating in school activities at the expense of activities outside the school is perhaps one of the most limiting effects of the high school. Community-wide activities that provide opportunities not available in school, or similar activities with a broader range of people, do not "count" for the serious Jock, because they draw his or her energies away from the set of institutions that constitute the high school career, and from servicing the networks so important to maintaining a place in the social structure. The individual who chooses to devote time and energy to activities outside the school does so at the expense of his or her high school career. Where outside groups offer activities similar to those in school, conditions must be exceptional for a Jock to choose them over school activities, as illustrated by one Belten athlete's explanation of why he and his friends left a better independent team to play for the school.

> That was the best team I was on. That was the team I was scoring goals on.
>
> WHEN YOU HAVE A TEAM LIKE THAT, WHY DO YOU GO INTO HIGH SCHOOL SOCCER?
>
> I don't, well, because, you know, you want to play, recognition, I don't know. We should have stayed but when there's high school sports, more people are apt to play that than play another league, you know, because you have the recognition, scholarships, like that.
>
> OH REALLY? YOU MEAN THAT COLLEGES WILL PAY MORE ATTENTION TO SCHOOL SPORTS THAN LEAGUES?
>
> That's the way I see it, because in the independent league you don't get the, you don't really get the recognition.

Some athletes do sacrifice school sports for the better outside teams, but unless they are good enough to attract the attention of the media, they are apt to sacrifice their school status.

While Jocks shun outside activities in general, Burnouts prefer to play sports on independent teams, and those who play organized sports do so in the leagues organized by the local recreation department or sponsored by businesses. By shunning school sports, Burnouts express their unwillingness to be organized by the school and to participate in enhancing the school's corporate identity. In addition, Burnouts refuse to submit to the supervision of personal behavior, particularly "partying," that accompanies school sports.

Social contacts outside the school are discouraged among Jocks. Such contacts take time away from participation in school-based networks and throw the individual's commitment to the school and to those networks into question. In addition, since relations among Jocks are to a great extent a function of roles in the school, individuals not involved in the same role structure can only be anomalous. Jocks who have friends in other schools find it impossible to integrate these friends into their own networks, and encounter resentment on the part of their school friends both if they spend time alone with the outside friends and if they try to include the outside friends in activities with their network. It is taken for granted among Jocks that if a friend moves out of the school district, the friendship will be ended or at least "put on hold." The reason given is generally that people get involved in their own schools and simply don't have time for each other. One Jock, however, clearly perceived the issue more as a matter of commitment, as he told of a dilemma caused by his close friendship with a group of boys from another school. He was striving for popularity in the Belten Jock network and felt that this could be achieved only at the expense of these friendships.

> Well, like last weekend I told them I was sick, you know, and I couldn't go out, because I'm trying to spend less time with them, you know. I don't know, I think if I spend too much time with those guys, the guys at Belten will think I'm a loser.
>
> WHY A LOSER?
>
> Well, maybe not a loser exactly, but they'll like wonder about me always being with guys from Cabot, like I don't care about Belten, and they won't accept me.

Certainly, casual contact with Jocks from other schools can bring prestige, serving as evidence that an individual who can function in the broader context is truly meritorious. Such contacts are frequently made through athletics and various kinds of student activity summer camps such as music, cheerleading, and pompon camp, leadership and journalism conferences, and so forth. However, such contacts must remain casual and strictly instrumental.

Age Boundaries

Seniority plays a role in access to corporate roles, because it takes time to develop experience, contacts, and an image of corporate maturity and commitment. But within these practical time constraints, the corporate adult seeks fast mobility through the levels of the hierarchy. In fact, the individual who remains for too long at a given corporate level, no matter how high (except at the very top), is a failure within the corporate system. The high school, on the other hand, imposes strict age grading, wherein access to certain roles and power depends on school grade. This age grading is, to a certain extent, a function of the status of the school as a training ground and of the significant social, cognitive, and emotional maturation that takes place during the years of high school. To facilitate the learning of social roles and to provide similar opportunities for each cohort, the school limits most competition to age sets. At the same time, the opportunity for broader power in successive years in school helps ensure that the power structure within each cohort will not stagnate and that students will maintain an interest in upward mobility. Within this age-grading framework, the Jock relates to an increasingly large population and increasingly broader and greater responsibilities each year. The Jock's ultimate power, however, depends on his or her position within the hierarchy defined by the age set, and therefore the Jock's attention is focused on the population of the age set. This limitation, like the limitation to the school itself, as discussed in the preceding section, is adaptive for Jocks but maladaptive and unacceptable for those who are not involved in the hierarchy.

No students from other grades are included in the Jock segment of the Belten friendship network, and some are included in In-between segments. The high degree of age-integration of the Burnout segment stands in strong contrast to both. Coleman (1961) reported the same age-specialization in his high school study, in which he found that the leading clique in each grade was composed entirely of people in that grade. In fact, Coleman found that most cliques were within one grade, with the exception of Hoods (in the context of his study, Hoods are the equivalent of Burnouts at Belten) and a religious clique.

Formal age grading begins in the elementary school, where the grades are highly segregated, and many of the cross-age relationships that do survive elementary school are broken up with the passage between elementary and junior high, or junior high and high school, when adjacent grades are separated for a full year. In high school, where there is greater opportunity for the age groups to mix, the structure of extra-curricular activities provides new incentive to age-segregation. At Belten, a yearlong competition between cohorts consists of a series of contests, whose winners are awarded points that accumulate over the year to designate one class as winner of the annual "spirit jug." This formal competition, common in American high schools, is supplemented by a continual underlying drive to be the "best class" in the school and ultimately to leave a greater mark on the school than that left by previous classes. While inter-class rivalry fosters solidarity within each cohort, the political system within each cohort also focuses social interaction within the cohort.

Many extracurricular activities—not simply those that make up the spirit jug competition—are produced by classes. Each class has its own officers, sends delegates to the student government, and raises money for its class treasury through activities such as dances and sales. Competition for roles in these activities, therefore, is limited to the class, encouraging those involved in the competition to focus their social and political activities within the class. Because the primary hierarchy is within the class, the contacts and visibility necessary for vote getting must be within the class constituency. Age grading in the high school, therefore, bears a significant resemblance to that found in age-set societies, insofar as age sets limit competition and control relations among age groups.

The only exception to cross-grade friendships among Jocks is in dating patterns, and even these patterns are not intensive. Dating is an important way to achieve status and visibility and to gain access to opposite-sex networks. The number of "appropriate" dating partners within one's grade may be limited, and the individual may find that he or she can "do better" by raiding another grade. This is often resented by classmates of the opposite sex, particularly in the extreme grades. The taboo against older girls dating younger boys makes cross-grade dating threatening to sophomore boys and to senior girls, since such dating depletes their dating pool. This was brought up fairly frequently by both boys and girls at Belten.

> Well, it always seems that the senior guys are always bored of the senior girls because they've been with them for two years and then new girls come into the school, and they take their shots.
>
> OF COURSE, THE SENIOR GIRLS COULD BE DOING THE SAME THING.
>
> College guys.
>
> OR JUNIOR GUYS.
>
> But that's sort of unlike—

NOT COOL, HUH?

Not for a senior girl. Really, that's—well, I don't know how it is this year. I, I don't even know anyone that's going out with a younger guy.

The age-specialization of Jock networks is not simply subconscious, but it is an important part of Jock ideology. Because of the progressive adoption of adult prerogatives with each grade in secondary school, it is generally assumed that friendship with people in higher grades constitutes a "bad influence," and those who regularly pursue such friendships are frequently judged to be "looking for trouble." This is the common evaluation of Burnout age-heterogeneous friendships, but purely corporate considerations add an entirely different dimension to such friendships among Jocks. In a manner analogous to involvement outside the school, friendships outside the class can throw an individual's commitment to the class into question. Such friendships also threaten the established flow of influence and open the younger participant to the criticism that he or she is "cheating" on the system, by borrowing status from the group currently in power rather than earning it among peers. This sense of appropriate channels applies also to Jocks with older Jock siblings. While it is important to know the Jocks in other cohorts, and siblings are an accepted means for doing this, the line is drawn at actually participating in their friendship networks. Most of Jocks' interaction with Jocks in other grades is task-oriented, and the nature of the relationships generally reflects age differences. The older Jocks guide and instruct the younger ones in school activities and take a somewhat nurturant attitude in personal relationships.

Like there's a lot, a few people in ninth grade that hung around with people in tenth grade, so they'd do stuff with people that go to Belten and stuff, but there weren't many. . . . Um, Joe Forsythe, his brother's older than him, a year older, so he'd hang around with a lot of his brother's friends, but there wasn't that many that I hung around with that would do that, so—I don't know. A lot of people didn't like it, I mean that I know, because they'd all say, "Well, he's—" you know, "just tagging along with his brother," you know and using his brother's name and stuff.

In some ways, this age grading seems to be designed to teach the fundamental lesson that one acquires seniority through simple good-faith participation in the society. During senior year, one actually can sit back and reap the benefits of having worked hard all through school.

The senior year is seen as the culmination of a school career, and the privileges of seniors are particularly sacred. Competitions are frequently felt to be slanted in favor of the senior class: To underclasspeople who worked hard on the competition, this is a lesson in cynicism; to others—particularly the seniors—it is only right that the seniors' "turn" in the limelight should compensate for some lack of quality. The general acceptance of "senior privilege" was illustrated one year at Belten when precedent was broken as the senior class lost important class competitions. A particularly sore point among these losses was that of the important yearly banner competition judged by the school faculty—a loss that was, in my own judgment, clearly justified on aesthetic grounds. One class officer, who felt that the class's status had been undermined, voiced his disapproval of the faculty's action.

> Every year the seniors win everything, the seniors rule, the seniors dominate. I remember when I was a sophomore I was scared to death of seniors. You know, if you walk down the hall, you just jump on the other side of the hall. We don't get that at all. See, we're too nice. I mean, I'm not going to go shove a kid around to get respect. I mean, I know we get respect as being, because we are, you know, pretty cool to other classes, but that does kind of, you know, I, it's, you look up to them for so long and now you're one and then you don't feel like you get their respect. Because I think one reason is because they beat us in everything. And it's like, "Oh, they're no—they're not that great, you know, like they can't even win." And uh, I, I don't, I don't know. I think that they, once, it's been a tradition and Mr. Jones is totally against seniors. Just because it's been the other way for so long. But it's not like it's us as seniors that have won every year. It's different seniors. That's the way the teachers look at it, "Oh, we've voted for seniors for so long, let's, let's pick somebody else," you just, oooh.

The sense of the properness of senior prerogatives extends to other privileges—for instance, one girl during her junior year described her uneasiness about going to the prom when she had friends who were seniors who hadn't been invited.

> Another thing I think that is kind of keeping me too, I have a lot of friends who are seniors. And, like, three, yeah, about three of them who I'm really close to, you know, really good friends with, none of them really, this far anyway, are going to prom, and I

know they'd like to be. And I don't know, I feel awful. . . . I just
don't feel, you know, I feel like, here I am a junior, you know.

Hierarchies

Students and staff cooperate in developing the overall success of the
institution and enhancing its image in relation to other schools. Ultimate
power in the hierarchy resides with the staff, who control the basic resources—materials, space, time, freedom of movement, and sponsorship—necessary to produce all activities and to achieve visibility. Although the ascendancy of staff over students is ascribed within the
system, the individual staff member's position and power depend in fact
on success in dealing with students, who control the important resources
of student labor and participation. The students themselves must arrive
at positions of power through management of contacts with their peers
and with staff. Both groups are aware of the interdependence of their
careers and use their own resources to maintain a balance of power.

Hierarchies are the essence of corporate structure, and career success is a function of upward mobility. Enhanced position in the corporate hierarchy entails not only increased financial rewards, but responsibility for a broader range of aspects of the corporation and greater
discretionary power. The corporate goal of efficient production of goods
or services dictates, under ideal conditions, a liberal definition of power,
as proposed by Kanter (1977):

> The meaning of power here is closer to "mastery" or "autonomy" than
> to domination or control over others. . . . Power is the ability to do, in
> the classic physical usage of power as energy, and thus it means having
> access to whatever is needed for the doing. . . . The powerful are the
> ones who have access to tools for action. (p. 166)

This means that the effective corporate individual must have access not
only to discretionary power (which comes from above) but to a broad
range of skilled and empowered individuals to inform and carry out
decisions (which comes from below). The former is acquired through
cultivation of contacts with one's hierarchical superiors; the latter,
through experience of the workings of the variety of functions under
one's responsibility, and cultivation of contacts with those performing
the functions. All of these depend on length and breadth of experience
within the corporation and on social skill with the individuals that one
encounters and those that one passes on the upward journey. The successful corporate individual focuses, therefore, not simply on the job at

hand, but on the strategic management of his or her career. Credibility and the notice of others depend on the careful management of visibility, which itself depends on choice of job activities.

> For activities to enhance power, they have to be visible, to attract the notice of other people . . . The chance to be noticed is differentially distributed in organizations, especially one that is so large that personal knowledge of everyone in even one's own function is impossible. (p. 179)

Visibility within a large organization is both a means of acquiring contacts and, as evidence of one's position and influence, a means for building credibility both among those one knows personally and those one does not. Access to the public forum and to visible appearances with other visible individuals and groups, therefore, are coveted resources. Visibility is also enhanced by the display of personal qualities desirable in a corporate individual. The corporation provides opportunities for visibility, and clear norms for these personal qualities.

Hierarchies are maintained through the control by a relative few of the resources required for development of the corporate product. At the top of the high school hierarchy are small numbers of staff in relation to students, and even smaller numbers of staff involved in extracurricular activities. These staff can deal directly with only a relatively small number of students, who then serve as brokers between staff and the student body by delivering staff-controlled resources to the students, and student interest and cooperation to the staff. It follows that social and political life among students is dominated by a student hierarchy, and the career of the individual student is developed through upward mobility in this hierarchy.

Position in the Jock hierarchy is defined by a set of formal roles such as class and student body offices, team captainships, offices in a variety of organizations; by a larger set of roles in the production of activities, such as committee and team membership and a range of appointed responsibilities; and by informal influence among those performing and controlling these roles. As in the adult corporation, therefore, the Jock's identity is largely a function of roles defined by the organization, and the individual's power resides in the performance of formal roles and control over subsidiary roles.

Jocks and Burnouts are diametrically opposed in their attitudes toward all aspects of the hierarchical structure of the school. The existence of the student hierarchy puts all who do not participate or succeed in it at a distinct disadvantage, not simply because the hierarchy controls aspects of the environment, but because the freedoms that adolescents covet are incorporated in the reward system of the hierarchy.

JOCKS AND STAFF

The student who can work well with adults is in the best position to become a broker between staff and the student body. As in any hierarchy, working well with one's hierarchical superiors involves not only pleasing them, but being able to "get things" from them. The adolescent who is subservient to adults will have as little success in the high school as the one who is antagonistic toward them. Staff look for student leaders who interact easily but deferentially with adults, who they feel can be "trusted," who are influential among students, and who display a satisfactory level of competence.

In the high school, as in the corporation, trust is based on the perception of the person's commitment to common goals and norms. Kanter (1977) invokes the issue of trust in explaining why corporate owners prefer to appoint members of the family or at least of the same socio-economic and ethnic group to positions involving discretionary power.

> Predictability and trustworthiness, by virtue of membership in the right groups—which themselves could serve control functions—were more likely to be factors in the choice of key managers, since owners and directors appointed those they felt they could "count on," those whose loyalty and obligation to the system could be demonstrated. (pp. 51–52)

Although their interests are clearly different, staff and student leaders must work out a common view of the goals and norms of the school that will allow them to function with a certain amount of mutual trust. This common view includes sharing a definition of the purview of student activities and protecting staff prerogatives in the determination of basic school policies. It also involves a commitment to enhancing the activities and image of the school, sharing an ideal school image, and agreement on the kinds of activities that enhance this image. Finally, it involves sharing norms about the relative power of the staff and students on the issue of personal freedom and autonomy. Membership in the dominant Jock groups, and an obvious middle class upbringing, can be a first indication to staff that the student is committed to these norms and goals, and can provide some assurance that friends and family will exert pressure on the individual to remain committed to them.

Because the entire staff, and particularly the administration, of any school has a strong interest in the success of the school as an institution, an individual staff member's position of responsibility depends to some extent on his or her ability to work well with the students. Although students do not have a direct say in which faculty members control activities, they can affect an individual staff member's image and success by refusing to cooperate, complaining to other staff members, and focusing their efforts on those staff members that they find more acceptable. Staff members, therefore, must work to acquire a balance of power with student leaders that is acceptable to both sides. Staff members may even have to lobby within the staff hierarchy on behalf of the students for greater power.

Since discipline is a perennial problem in schools, and one of the major measures of a school's and an individual staff member's competence, the issue of student autonomy is particularly delicate. At the highest level, autonomy applies to the range of school policies that are open to the student decision-making process; in the middle, it applies to the degree of discretion students have in the selection and execution of extracurricular activities; and at the lowest, it applies to the relative personal freedom of individual students within the school. More negotiation is possible at the lower levels of autonomy, but in all cases, the student body evaluates Jocks' success as leaders on the basis of their ability to procure autonomy. Staff's willingness to accord this autonomy depends to a great extent on their estimation of the Jocks' commitment and trustworthiness, and influence among the entire student body. The latter is inherently limited by the number of students who accept the corporate definition of the school and who are thereby governed by agreements negotiated at higher levels of the hierarchy. By and large, the more generous the staff concessions are concerning the highest level of autonomy, the larger the Jocks' constituency is apt to be.

In Belten, the issue of the closed campus alienated a large number of potential participants, at least in the school political arena. Dating from a period when staff found behavior in the school parking lot to be a problem, the school imposed a closed campus policy—students are not allowed to leave the building during school hours. The closed campus is a matter of concern to all students, and those with the fewest compensatory freedoms are particularly distressed about this restriction on their freedom of movement. The nature of the agreement between staff and student leaders is clearly reflected in the fact that the closed campus never became a legitimate political issue in student government elections. The Burnouts, particularly, refer to the fact that Jocks cannot negotiate on the closed campus as proof that student government is a fictitious and infantilizing enterprise. The leaders, on the other hand, are not willing to press the issue, both because they do not want to compromise their position with the staff, and because they suffer least under the policy. In fact, the general restrictiveness of this policy renders the Jocks' own enhanced freedoms more visible, reinforces their hierarchical position, and lends value to the system that affords them this position. The Jocks' position of trust with staff, along with the practical necessities associated with their administrative responsibilities, renders Jocks visibly more mobile within the school.

Jock mobility at Belten is institutionalized in a variety of ways, the most visible of which is participation in "steering committee," which comprises student leaders who must be approved by the student activities director. Steering committee, run as a class that meets daily, is in charge of the organization of extracurricular activities; participation in it involves a good deal of moving around, hanging posters and making arrangements. Students on steering committee wander in the school more or less at will, and are seen by others as unconditionally free, directly as a result of their status as school leaders. More informal privileges are also awarded on the basis of credibility with staff, with the result that students who are known as leaders in the school generally have sufficient credibility to wander at will. One such student observed:

> I can basically do whatever I want because they just figure I'm
> doing something for the school. And they know me, that I'm not
> going to get in any trouble.

The teachers' assumption that the student who is committed to the corporate view of the school can be trusted results in a certain amount of blind trust. One student pointed out that his Jock status made him virtually immune to faculty suspicion.

> I don't know why I've never had a fear of being caught stoned. I
> don't know why—probably the main reason is because it's the last
> thing anybody—the teachers and everything—expect of me. I
> mean because I've got the image of—you know the image that I
> have and I don't think they suspect . . . you know, if she saw my
> eyes all bloodshot the first thing she'd think—you know—"aller-
> gies"—you know—she wouldn't think I'm high, you know.

Inspiring trust, of course, is only one component of adult handling, since the purpose of handling is to gain concessions as well as cooperation. One boy discussed the importance of his adult-handling skills in his role as student leader.

> If I'm arguing, all right, say Therese and I are arguing for something at Mr. Jones, I'll win every time. Just because I can talk to Mr. Jones, . . . and I know how to get him, you know. And I, that's what I do, I analyze people a lot, and I see how to get them.

These skills are learned from the example of peers, particularly members of immediately preceding cohorts, but they are also learned in certain kinds of family patterns. The student quoted above was quite aware that he had acquired his skill at home.

> My parents have given me this idea too, just, I used to do a lot of things with my parents. See, like until ninth grade I never, like Friday and Saturday, I just, my parents had people over, I would get along great with them, you know. . . . I get along great with adults. If I have a chance to talk to an adult I can do good.

Middle class family ideology, which stresses participation of the child in decision making, parent–child negotiation, mutual trust, and openness, provides valuable training for the Jock role. The issue of authority is facilitated in the American middle class family by the family's acceptance of the hegemony of the school. The average middle class family gives almost automatic permission to participate in school activities: If a school activity runs all night, the child has parental permission to stay out. Parents provide assistance and support when necessary, and limit requirements for participation in family affairs when they conflict with school functions. Because the school's surveillance allows parents to give up some control, they are free to be "buddies" with their children. This, in turn, accords the children a certain amount of adult status and allows them experience at dealing with adults on a more equal level. Jocks make this equality possible by carefully holding up their end. They are fairly careful not to do anything they can't tell their parents, and they are careful to maintain their parents' trust. In this way, they internalize their parents' values; they become their own disciplinarians in order not to disappoint their parents. Many Jocks entertain the notion that their parents are naive and need to be protected—that while they could do things like smoke pot or drink, they don't because their parents "couldn't take it." No trivial enjoyment is important enough to risk hurting their parents.

JOBS AND THE HIERARCHY

The adult corporate career extends over many years, during which the individual performs a large variety of functions filling well over 40 hours a week. By comparison, the high school career is short, and as a result ambition is limited. The conservatism of school politics is one result of this limitation—students in the hierarchy are generally satisfied just to learn and carry out their roles before they graduate. Each class fills the shoes of the preceding one, and most people see their careers as a successive filling of roles, rather than an opportunity to change them. Since no cohort will stay around to benefit from any innovations, no changes are likely to occur that will create significant temporary disruptions. The shortness of the high school career and the limitations of its institutions also limit the depth of the student hierarchy, throwing as great an emphasis on personal influence as on formal roles. Therefore, although there are clear roles that represent importance within the school activities structure, there is considerable opportunity for individuals not occupying formal roles to exert influence. These people, particularly prestigious athletes (frequently called "Jock Jocks"), are part of the hierarchy although they may not run for office—in fact, their disdain for such roles can enhance their status without decreasing the status of the roles themselves.

The importance of the prestigious athlete in the school points out the fact that Jocks are as covetous of their particular kind of autonomy as Burnouts are of theirs, and that the value of "doing real things" is important to both sets of people. The difference lies in the domain in which these things are to be done. Athletic ability is seen as an independent accomplishment that sets the individual off from both adults and peers. Although many feel that places on teams are frequently won through favoritism, athletic ability itself cannot be awarded in exchange for docility or cooperation. The status of varsity athletics derives at least partly from its importance to the school image, and varsity athletes are thus seen as working in the interests of the school. The individual athlete, though, can claim to be playing for his or her own enjoyment—to be "doing a job" that has value in itself. In contrast, the Jock who is primarily involved in nonathletic activities, particularly "spirit" activities, is seen as working directly for the enhancement of the school itself.

Artistic activities can play a role similar to that of athletic activities, but with the reservation imposed by the diminished value that American society places on the arts in comparison with sports. Belten High has an unusually excellent and well-known choir, which gains considerable prestige for the school through competitions and extensive tours. Because of its objective real-world excellence, choir is a prestigious activity, even though its membership is not by any means restricted to Jocks. The excellence of the choir stems not only from the musical ability of its members and its director, but from the director's emphasis on creating the same sort of hierarchy and solidarity within the choir that characterize the high school class. It is not surprising, in view of this, that those in the choir hierarchy are commonly referred to as "Choir Jocks." The choir represents a limited alternative to the wider hierarchical sphere of school activities, and although some individuals participate in both, there is an undercurrent of rivalry between the two.

> Concert Choir is like an individual part of school. Mr. Jones said that, too. That it's so separated from school. It's like they do all their stuff, they have their own president, they have their own secretary. And it's true, they are separated, but you look at that Council and you look at that group of kids, and they get things done.
>
> *   *   *
>
> As far as Concert Choir goes, I like it, and I think it's run really well, but I've never really gotten into it, like gung ho. Never. I feel intimidated in there. Because it's like a reverse situation. There you got the kids that don't do a lot for school, you know, like their class, that are really in there, they're called like Concert Choir Jocks. You know. I've never been one of those. And they're the kind of kids that wear the Belten Concert Choir shirts, and that are always like, they come, instead of going to lunch, they go and eat their lunch down there in the choir room, and they're always singing, and everything, and they're really into choir. . . . They have all the activities that the class has, only they do it with theirself. Yeah, it's too bad that they're separated, but like when I look at him [the choir director] as comparison to us, he's just organized right down, you know, it's professional all the way.

Athletics and art, both requiring objectively judged abilities to do adult tasks in a domain separate from the sociopolitical, can provide alternate roads to autonomy in the school. It is significant, therefore, that some Burnouts do participate in musical activities at Belten. It was also noticeable in all the schools I visited that some Burnouts gravitated to the visual arts departments, where they found a domain in which they could function more or less independently and in which any competition was based on performance of tasks that were valued in themselves.

One could say that, by definition, those working for the adult corporation accept the corporate structure, whereas a large portion of the high school student body do not. Thus, although the school defines the base of the Jocks' operations, their constituency is not as clearly defined as that of adult corporate management. All Jocks agree that ideally the entire student body should be involved in activities, but they do not all agree on the amount of effort that should be spent cultivating a constituency beyond those already actively involved. While those in student government say that they are there to represent the entire school, relatively few advocate serious action to communicate with those outside the Jock network. To a certain extent, again, this is the result of a realistic evaluation of the potential of their short careers, their own limited power, and the degree of hostility of many of the disaffected—particularly the Burnouts.

Nonetheless, school ideology at Belten maintains that student leaders represent the entire school. This ideology led to one project that was intended to benefit the Burnout segment of the population but became a thorn in the Jocks' sides. This project, selling candy in the school to raise money for benches in the courtyard, did not grow out of student interest, but was imposed by staff, and was carried out with little enthusiasm or success. Network distance and hostility prevented such a project from actually involving the intended benefactors, and the paternalistic nature of the project was lost on none. While no Burnouts were involved in the planning, it was obvious to those Jocks who were involved that they should at least make an effort to sell candy in the courtyard. This was enough to limit interest among the Jocks, who were not eager to open themselves to ridicule. Since virtually no Jocks ever go into the courtyard, this aspect of the project created a certain amount of anxiety and was not energetically pursued.

The alienation of the Burnouts prevents serious consideration of efforts to involve them in activities, but there remains a large mass of people who are neither alienated nor involved. In theory, school-sponsored activities, perhaps particularly class activities, are open to all; but there is a limit to the number of people who can actually work on the production of any project—only the actual "consumption" of the product can be open to all. Although everyone in the school is free to attend a dance, no more than a dozen or so can actually work on the dance itself, and although "spirit yell"—a competition to see which class can yell the loudest—requires as large a number of participants as possible, only a few can organize the yell or appear in front of the crowd. The Jocks' attitude toward those outside the Jock network varies among groups and individuals, but also depends on the activity in question. Some activities, such as the "Smoking Committee," which caters to elementary school audiences, and the yearbook and school paper, whose success is judged as much on the basis of interscholastic competition as on sales, rely on a relatively small number of participants. Many others, though—sports events, dances, rallies, artistic performances, class competitions—depend on audience or mass attendance for their success. In these activities the mass of In-betweens, who also constitute a major body of voters in school elections, are viewed as potential consumers, and as such are given serious consideration. Network connections between the Jock hierarchy and the mass of consumers, therefore, are crucial to guaranteeing the success of activities and to securing the interests of those in the hierarchy. Jocks activate these networks cooperatively in the interests of large-scale activities, and competitively in elections and disputes.

The organization of all student activities can be viewed as the production of a corporate product. The means of production is ultimately controlled by the staff, who distribute them through the student leaders, who act as intermediaries. In discussing the flow of power in student activities, it is useful to distinguish three fluid categories of students on the basis of their involvement in school activities: (1) the leaders, or "super Jocks," who gain control of the means of production from staff; (2) the main body of Jocks, and the In-betweens who participate in selected activities, who are involved in production; and (3) the consumers. (To Burnouts, all these people qualify as Jocks by virtue of their participation at any level; the consumers generally do not consider themselves Jocks because they are not involved in production.) These three categories form a hierarchy based on access to resources and on management of the environment. While many people are satisfied to be consumers, most of the main body of Jocks (in category 2) aspire to control the means of production. Although many of them know that they will not reach that level, they acknowledge its desirability. The hierarchy is maintained, particularly in the two Jock categories, by the possibility of upward mobility and by the flow of resources. Each individual's access to resources depends on his or her place in the hierarchy, which must be respected if one wants to do anything but slide downward. Everyone trades the crucial resources of information and jobs downward in the hierarchy, and trades support (labor, skills, and constituencies) upward. Each individual's social mobility depends on the breadth and importance of his or her networks and on skill in exploiting them.

Although there are formal roles in the high school, position in the hierarchy is based also on individual prestige and visibility gained through the performance of a variety of informal roles. Both the election and the success of those in formal roles may depend on the support of those in informal roles. Some of the most coveted positions are elected office, such as student government and class presidencies, which embody formal power. Other formal roles that give some power over a bounded group, such as sports team captains and captains of the cheer-leading and pompon squads, can also bestow influence in the larger sphere by virtue of their prestige and visibility. The same applies to visible members of sports teams and to members of the squads. Finally, a variety of informal roles in the production of activities bestow prestige and visibility.

In describing their social networks, most high school students distinguish between the people that they interact with regularly but only in school, and a smaller group of friends that they see regularly outside of school and go out with on weekends. The former category is particularly large for Jocks, who get to know a variety of people in their different action sets. Conformity to the corporate norm of "well-roundedness" not only has the advantage of indicating the individual's range of interests and competencies, but ensures a broad range of contacts. The visibility of those at the top of the hierarchy can compensate for a certain lack of contact with people outside the hierarchy, and those at the top tend to see a fairly small group of friends outside of school. Their exclusiveness adds to their prestige and visibility, both by making contact with them a rare and thus valuable commodity and by guaranteeing that their visibility will always be enhanced by the prestige of those they are with. Access to these people is also limited by those who surround them, who endeavor to monopolize contact. A small number of people farther down the hierarchy, however, who spend time with the top people in school, divide their time outside of school among several groups. People low in the hierarchy frequently refer to these "intermediate" people as the "truly popular" people, citing the exclusivity of the top group as evidence that they are not friendly and hence not well liked. These "truly popular" people function as brokers between the upper and lower ends of the hierarchy, valuable to those at the top because of their broad contacts, and to those below them because of their contact with the top.

It is in elections that the individual's visibility and social networks become most crucial. The choice of campaign manager for elections is the best example of conscious political alliance in the school and involves the choice of a person whose only formal function is to make a short introductory speech for the candidate at the campaign speech assembly. The real benefit is not in the speech itself but in the networks the manager can bring to the election. Campaign strategies, therefore, involve the careful choice of a manager who commands different networks from the candidate's. The managers, in turn, receive visibility from the post, as well as influence during the candidate's office if the campaign is successful. The managers must be as cautious in their acceptance as the candidates in their selection, for supporting a losing candidate—or one who is running against someone who could be useful in an alliance—can sometimes be risky.

Access to many roles depends on selection by those currently in power. Current members of the cheerleading and pompon squads and the Smoking Committee participate in the selection of new members, people are appointed to roles in the organization of a variety of activities by class and student government officers, and student committees select such things as "acts" for the annual variety show. In all roles, both elected and selectional, skill is supposed to be primary, but in practice, skill alone is rarely sufficient. Furthermore, because many activities do not require a high level of special skill, the number of acceptable candidates can be far greater than the number of positions, and selection generally depends on contacts and visibility among those who do the selecting. Many individuals deprived of opportunities in school activities perceive the lack of powerful social contacts as their main handicap, as illustrated by one very talented but unconnected person who was not selected for the annual Variety Show.

I tried out for the Variety Show this year. I didn't make it.

DO YOU THINK YOU SHOULD HAVE?

Yes. Yes, I should have. Because there's a lot of, there's a lot of these acts that, that are good but . . . some people just—it's just one big popularity contest, you know. Because popularity, there's another part where popularity has a lot to do with it. You know. It's like, if you're not, like, okay, part of it has to do with a good voice. You know, and if you really wow them with a good voice, they don't care if you're popular or not, you know, if you have talent, you're in. You know. But I've been like, every time I come home, I go in my room and I start singing any song, and I think, I think that I have a, a good enough voice to make it. You know. I mean, if they don't like it, that's tough luck. Because I have, I could probably, I could probably sing better than any of those acts. Not that I'm being conceited.

Jobs

High school production events that can accommodate only a small number of people are open only to students who have direct or indirect access to those who run the events, since any individual who participates must be allocated a job or will look and feel superfluous. People who arrive at a production event with few or no contacts are out of place and isolated, not just because people do not know them, but because they are not of sufficient social value to be allocated a job. Individual jobs in the production of each activity are assigned relative status on the basis of their inherent interest and the visibility they afford, and individuals are assigned jobs of increasing status not simply on the basis of skill, but also according to their place in the social hierarchy. Those in control distribute jobs as rewards and incentives to people who can provide hierarchical support—who themselves command sufficient networks to be valuable constituency sources, who are in control of other activities and can be relied on to reciprocate with jobs on other projects, or who simply enjoy sufficient prestige to enhance the visibility of others with whom they work. Student leaders vary considerably in their ability to maximize their job resources so as to accommodate as broad a range of people as possible (thus enlarging their constituency) and to recruit maximally skilled workers for key jobs to ensure the success of the product.

Two annual activities at Belten are frequently described in opposition—both involve the production of a piece of art: a banner and a float. In both cases, each class produces an art object over the period of a week, working after school and late into the evening, "pulling an all-nighter" the last night, and missing part of the school day on the day of the presentation. Both Banner and Float have school spirit themes and are displayed in connection with a sports activity: Floats are the highlight of the homecoming parade associated with a football game, and banners are judged during a "pep" assembly and displayed in the gym during a basketball game. The results of the Banner and Float competitions enter into the yearlong competition among the three classes in the school. The important difference between the two activities is that the banner, measuring approximately 15 by 30 feet, is made indoors and cannot be worked on by more than 10 or 20 people at a time. The float, on the other hand, is made outdoors (in someone's yard) and requires a considerable work force both at the main site and in smaller work groups in people's homes. Although far more people become involved in Float than in Banner, the same social hierarchy controls both activities, and other people's opportunity to participate in production depends on their place in the social network.

In dispensing all resources, leaders have to be careful to achieve a balance between exclusivity and cheapness. If they retain all jobs for themselves and a chosen elite, they will lose (or fail to gain) the support of the wider network and eventually find themselves without backup. If they dispense jobs freely to all who want them, though, they will not

have enough to reward particularly valuable people with, and the resources themselves will be cheapened. Although there are ways to usurp
and to steal power, they normally do not enhance the usurper's position,
and they eventually lead to the failure of the project. Kanter's (1977)
observations about corporate power apply also to the high school activity
situation.

> Power does refer to interpersonal transactions, the ability to mobilize
> other people; but if those others are powerless, their own capacities,
> even when mobilized, are limited. The problems with absolute power,
> a total monopoly on power, lie in the fact that it renders everyone else
> powerless. On the other hand, empowering more people through gen-
> erating more autonomy, more participation in decisions, and more ac-
> cess to resources increases the total capacity for effective action rather
> than increases domination. (p. 166)

The meaning and use of power are continual issues in the high
school, particularly since the high school is a training ground for corporate strategies. In addition, the merger of several junior high schools
into one high school introduces competition not only within but between
hierarchies. Leadership failure, therefore, can be swiftly remedied by a
change in leadership. In the case of Belten High School, one small junior high (Bolder) and two large junior highs (Rover and Finley) feed
into each class, each with its Jock hierarchy, the members of which are
already concerned about their chances of retaining their positions in the
new environment. This caused a power struggle in one graduating class.
Those from Bolder were the hardest pressed to expand their networks
when they arrived at Belten: The Jocks from Rover dominated the scene
from the beginning. One school official suggested that the reason for
the success of what some people resentfully called the "Rover gang" was
that that school had encouraged student participation and solidarity
more than the others had, and that the students were simply more
highly organized when they arrived in the high school. By all reports,
the Rover Jocks had indeed been a large and solitary group in junior
high.

> In ninth grade, we had, I'd say, a group of about 30, and it was, it's
> not just our group, but it was the closest friends. And we'd always
> have, you know, we'd plan parties, get-togethers, dances, we'd al-
> ways go up to the swim club and meet, we'd plan, you know, days
> during the summer, we'd plan, you know, everyone go to the mov-
> ies, everyone go skating, we'd all keep together. . . . And the funny

thing is that Finley people always say that the Rover people are so friendly, that they're the ones that like opened up to them, and introduced them, you know, themselves and got everyone together.

According to general reports, the Jocks at Finley had been less cohesive. One student from Finley accounted for this lack of cohesiveness in the following way:

I think it's because at Rover they have less, um, competition for stuff. . . . Whereas at Finley you've got all these kids, and it's really competitive, and they have some of the best athletes, you know, just do sports, you know, to pick from. So everything is really competitive. You know, you just can't make everything. At Rover, it didn't seem like they had as good, you know, of athletes or whatever, so almost everybody got in everything. So it wasn't so pick and choose. Whereas at Finley there was so much more competition that you had to be, you know, just excel in everything to make anything, so that kind of made everybody just left out, the ones that weren't really good at everything.

The Jocks from Bolder by and large merged with those from Finley. A few people from Finley entered the Rover hierarchy by leaving their old friendship groups, but, by and large, activities in high school were run by a somewhat fragile coalition between the Finley and Rover Jocks. A current of rivalry and resentment between the two groups flowed throughout the entire stay in high school, particularly as the Finley group gradually increased their power during junior and senior years. The issue of power arose continually in this rivalry, the Rover gang accusing some of those in the other group of hoarding power and of sacrificing quality by not involving large enough numbers of the general school population in activities.

There are so many kids out there, you know, in our class that, you know, would really be helpful, like for the Banner and every other event we have, that really are good, that just don't get any recognition for anything because, you know, they're so quiet, or they don't speak up, or they're intimidated, or whatever. But there are so many of them that would be just such an asset to the class and, like I say, I, I fight constantly with Jack. I'm like, "Get them involved," you know, "let's do something," and, you know, he just, he really doesn't want to do it. He's happy with just his friends.

Others farther from the hierarchy and its internal disputes felt that this kind of exclusivity was a property of school hierarchies in general.

> Um, well I think, you know, if people are good at it and everything that they should do it. If they have something to, you know, give to the school. If they have like a contribution to make, like good ideas and stuff like that, but, otherwise, I think a lot of people are there, you know, because they like to jump on the bandwagon, and, you know, have their name up on the wall or whatever, so, I really don't think that they're, you know, a lot of those people, just, they're like bugs, you know, they just hang around, and just, you know, well, "I'll do this." It's a shame too, because I know a lot of people that have, you know, wonderful ideas, and really good, but they're not in that, that group, you know, so those ideas will never get heard, you know. So—

The workings of the rivalry between Rover and Finley were most clearly seen in one yearly Banner competition, which achieved particular attention because what the Rover gang saw as mismanagement by the Finley people in charge resulted ultimately in an inferior product. This led to widespread resentment and became the major end-of-year election issue for that class.

Banner

The creation of the banner takes place every day after school and into the night for a week. Each class is assigned an indoor location (a firehouse or a room in some other school) to make their banner. Since classes compete in the production of banners, secrecy about the design is supposed to be carefully maintained, and spy activities generate amusement, rowdiness, and occasional conflict. The class officers are officially in charge of the banner and supervise the work of a group of "active people." The officers control the activity both through their supervisory capacity and through their control of work hours. They decide whether and when to break for dinner and how late to work, and it is frequently felt that these decisions are based at least partially on whose attendance will be affected by them. The manner of designing the banner is a subject of frequent debate and varies according to who is in charge. Anyone can submit a design: In some cases the ultimate design is the result of group discussion based on submitted designs; in others it is the choice of the few in charge. The latter situation can lead to disagreement about whether the design chosen was the best one or the personal preference of a few, and can ultimately end with the withdrawal of some people from the project. Disagreements of this kind can continue throughout the production process, if it is felt that those in charge are assuming too much power.

Once the design has been chosen, a small model is sketched. The paper for the banner is then taped to the floor and the design is traced out on it. The success of the sketching stages of the project depends on the leading group's access to a skilled artist, and disagreements can arise over whether they have chosen "one of their own" who has less skill than some other person in the class. Once the full-scale design is sketched out, the leaders supervise the painting. It is at this stage that the allocation of jobs becomes particularly controversial, because all painting jobs are considered to require more or less the same degree of skill but carry differential status in the following order: painting detail, outlining, painting lettering, painting background and border. Although the clever class officer will try to recruit the best artist in the class to actually sketch in the picture, the people working on the painting stage will qualify by virtue of their social position. On the last day, a small number of people are authorized by staff to skip morning classes in order to bring the banner to school and hang it in the gym. These are supposed to be the people most closely involved in the production of the banner and are selected by those in charge. Disputes have been known to arise over this selection.

At the beginning of the Banner project in question, there was some confusion about where the banner was to be made. This confusion was beyond the control of the group in charge, but once the school had assigned a work site, the students in charge did not publicize its final location. Many of the students in the class felt that the information had been intentionally withheld, as part of an effort by those in charge to hoard the activity. This criticism was intensified when work actually began and key jobs went to members of the Finley group.

> They, they wanted like, I only went like once, for only about five minutes. I didn't really work on it because they were like, they wanted only a certain group, and, like we heard rumors that people only wanted certain people there to work on it, and it wasn't a class project really, so no one really bothered to go out.

The Rover gang, who had controlled Banner the year before, withdrew their participation altogether, rather than be assigned secondary status:

Oh, they would have put me off, painting something meaningless
maybe or taping it down, or some, some small task, or maybe just
say, "Oh, we're, we're not working right now, just go home for a
few hours."

One person who did participate criticized the leadership because of the
ineffectual operation of the hierarchy in the execution of the project.
This person felt that the drawing could be improved and solicited help
from an older friend.

This is before we did anything—this is why I got really mad at
Banner . . . Judy and I are going, "Please help us, Greg," "Please
help us," you know. And so Greg goes, "Come here, May." So he
drew a little picture for me to make the, to improve the bulldog.
And like we showed John, and John goes, "Well, I don't have the
authority." And he's the president. And it really made us, it really
made us really mad that he wouldn't say, "Go to Al," because like
we can't go to Al and say, "Draw this," "Change it to this," you
know.

WHY NOT?

Just, I mean we could do it, but Al could laugh in our face, you
know. But if, if, um, John did it, then he, he would go, "Okay, I'll
change it." And he didn't. And so, so we showed Al, and Al goes,
"Well, it's kind of too late to do that."

Float

Float is commonly contrasted to Banner, as an activity that allows
the participation of an unlimited number of people.

I'm working on Banner right now. Banner isn't that fun, though,
because it's kind of like, at Float everybody can do something;
Banner, sort of. But it's not like you can have a real, a big group of
people working on it, because it's just, it's, it's more like for the artist. I mean you can paint all solid colors and—but Float, uh, I
really, I like Float, because it brought people together, you know. It
made us more alike, and, you know, I would say two-thirds of
our—you know, at different times, people don't just—there's
maybe a group of 25 that stayed, you know. Or maybe a group of

15, but I would s--, well, maybe, at least one-half. You know, people would stop by, see what's going on, because they knew everybody else would be there, and even if you didn't do any work, there was, you know, people there to see, and talk to, and stuff.

WOULD YOU SAY THAT ANYONE, EVEN IF THEY DIDN'T KNOW ANYBODY, COULD JUST WALK IN AND WORK ON FLOAT OR BANNER?

Hm. Float, I would say, yes. Because, you know, we have to make those flowers. And you can just sit down and start making flowers, and usually people are in their little circle, and you just start talking, and you meet new people and stuff.

Whereas the banner is produced on public property, the float is built at the home of a student, usually a member of the Jock hierarchy who has a large yard and cooperative parents. Certain components of the float are made elsewhere, particularly the tissue rosettes required to cover it, which are made on the outskirts of the float area and at gatherings in girls' homes. A range of networks can be called into service this way, because those who cannot work on the main structure can work on auxiliary aspects of the float. It is in cases like this, where numbers of people must be recruited for low-visibility jobs, that individual Jocks' networks beyond the Jock group come into play. The breadth of the networks used, and the distance of these networks from the actual production of the activity, is exemplified by the case of one person who had been invited to someone's home to make rosettes for the float but did not know where the actual float was being made.

It was at Alice's house. She's one of my good friends . . . they were building, you know, like flowers to it and stuff like that.

WHERE WAS THE FLOAT ITSELF?

I don't know where they keep it. You just, you work at separate houses on different pieces to it, then you put it all together. Probably here [school], I guess.

Status is reflected and enhanced by how close one is to the planning and construction of the main structure. Those who are closer to the main construction get most of the credit and visibility, and many of these people do not know where the rosettes are made. While the expressed ideology of the class leaders is that anyone can work on Float, most people would not agree. For although no one would be sent home because they were not wanted, outsiders would find no place in the work:

While Float is a communal work task, it presupposes its community. As with Banner, an outsider would not be assigned jobs on the float because these jobs are part of the resources allocated to people according to their place in the network. The charge of a particular job on the float brings both visibility and contact with the organizers. The only marginal person who is recruited for an important job is a person with unique skills. Skilled workers in the school are recruited when needed, and a good student leader has access to these people. It is particularly in this area that a person with a true interest in a variety of people can be a valuable leader.

Well under one-half of the class actually attend float construction, and while a Jock may meet new people at Float, a person with no connections would not find it so easy.

> Float, a lot of people like that. There's like a group that will come and help, and it, it's, I don't think a person by theirselves would ever come to, like, Float or Banner if they didn't think they'd know anybody because it would be too, like, scary almost.

The scariness is illustrated by one unconnected girl's description of her one visit to Float.

> I went to one Float. I didn't like it. I hated it. I was just sitting there, and it was really weird. I'm sitting here making flowers . . . and I set my folder on the car, and all of a sudden all these Jocks come there, and they sit there starting inspecting my folder like I'm some kind of alien, you know. And they look at me. And they looked through that folder like, "Wow," you know. Like, "Let's see what this kid does." You know. They did. I don't know why. It was like kind of odd to me. Like, you know how, shoot, you know how people kind of—like, how bears kind of inspect a new person? . . . Two girls and two guys, you know. I never went to any more Float activities because, you know, I don't find myself having a good time there at all.

As with Banner, even those who feel they belong may not be assigned jobs.

> The Float was fun. It's just that it doesn't give you an, I don't know, they say anybody can come over and do it, but, only the main people are doing the main [jobs], you know. You're just there to, that's one thing I don't like about, um, high school is that it's

only the names that are important. You know, I mean like you get a president in there and his name will ring throughout the whole school until he graduates, and he'll be up there, like anybody in sports, that's really good in sports will be up there, and they'll be first pick for everything. Which I think is kind of dumb.

IF SOMEBODY WHO REALLY DIDN'T KNOW ANYBODY, YOU KNOW, DECIDED THEY WANTED TO WORK ON FLOAT OR BANNER AND THEY SHOWED UP—

Well, they'd just say, like, you know, I don't know. Like when we showed up, they'd say like, you know, "you guys can go get some paper and start making the flowers if you want." So they showed us where everything was. And like mainly everyone was like in their own little groups talking and doing stuff.

With Float, as with Banner, certain people get to skip classes on the last day to prepare the product for exhibition. These people are chosen by class leaders—a power that can also cause conflict.

THE CLASS PRESIDENT GETS TO HAND OUT ALL THE JOBS FOR FLOAT?

Well, yeah, the, and then on the day of the parade, he has to pick 10 people, but, not he but the float chairman, I guess, gets to pick 10 people that get out of school, stay out of school, and work on it. Put finishing touches on it and everything. Of course he was there, you know, like . . . and it's like, he said, though, "I get to get out because I'm class president." Oh, no, they ask you if you want to stay. You know, and, that, that's, I had an argument the first night, he goes, "Well, Bill, you know, thanks for the help," but, you know, I'm not going. I go, "But Jim, I worked on this more than you, you know, I'm staying." "No, you're not, well, we decided." There goes "we" again. "Whoever involved you, I'll never know," you know.

INFORMATION

Information is one of the most important commodities traded through networks. Information is essential to participation, and its possession—particularly the possession of exclusive information—is a sign of the individual's place in the social order. The creation and management of information, therefore, is a significant means of maintaining social hierarchies. "The power of a leader (or broker) is dependent upon the degree to which he monopolizes the flow of information, goods and services to and between his followers (or clients)" (Boissevain, 1974, p. 42). Those lower in the hierarchy seek information from above as a means of mobility, and those at the top must keep enough appropriate new information in the system to maintain visibility and their status as producers of information. Those in-between establish and maintain their positions in the hierarchy by acting as information brokers between the people above and below them. These brokers must maintain sufficient access to and control over this information to guarantee their value to the people below them. Certain kinds of information in the high school are considered public: dates and times of tryouts, meetings, auditions and elections, sports events, dances, and so forth. But an entire range of information is disseminated through informal networks. The scarcity of such information makes it highly valuable, and goes a long way toward limiting access to upward mobility.

Most public information is disseminated through the broadcast announcements each morning at the end of third period, and a typed version is posted on a bulletin board in the cafeteria hall. Public information is further channeled according to the audience it is designed to reach. Those events that require a large attendance—concerts, games, dances, fairs, elections—are widely advertised by posters throughout the school. Production events are not posted. There is a notable difference in the wording and delivery of announcements that solicit a large attendance, ("Be sure and come to see the Bulldogs beat . . . !!" "Don't miss the Battle of the Bands!!") and those that convey information needed to participate in production ("Those interested in auditioning for Smoking Committee should . . ." "Cheerleading tryouts will be held . . .").

Announcement and posting do not guarantee the general dissemination of public information. Members of the steering committee read the morning announcements over the public address system just before the close of the third hour. The first lunch period immediately follows, and the beginning of the announcements signals students to gather their things together and to talk. Those who take no interest in the content of the announcements are not the only ones who talk at this time. Those in the Jock network need not listen because they generally have activity information in advance. The pride with which Jocks generally report that they never listen to the announcements is an indication that they recognize that not listening is a clear sign of their prior informal access to information and therefore of their status in the hierarchy. Conversely, any individual who listens to the announcements is in effect signalling his or her lack of informal access to the information. Those students who complained to me about their inability to hear the announcements said that they would not complain to their peers or teachers for fear of appearing ridiculous. These same students would be ashamed to read the posted version, because reading it in the prominent place where it is posted would be a public admission that they had no other access to the information.

A kind of information that is passed only through informal networks enables people to behave appropriately at a wide variety of functions and to interact with other people whom they do not know well. To function in a hierarchy, one must know the important people by name, know their roles and responsibilities, and know who their friends are and who the couples are. This kind of information is important in gaining access to activities and jobs, and its possession and display are important as signs of one's own access to information. Personal information about these people is particularly valuable as an indication of the quality and depth of one's information. Because those trying to gain access to the hierarchy value such information insofar as it brings them "closer" to those at the top, middle members of the hierarchy can trade it downward to strengthen their constituency and to demonstrate their privileged position in relation to those at the top. People can display such information as a sign of their connections, and "newsworthy" individuals can gain visibility by cautiously making such information available. Information about couples' breakups and makeups is used fairly intensively for this purpose and has added value because a far greater proportion of those at the top of the hierarchy have boyfriends or girlfriends than of those below.

Because of its trade value in the Jock hierarchy, personal information must be carefully managed. The Jock with problems at home generally keeps them to himself or herself in order to maintain a carefree image. Whereas Burnouts share their problems and concerns fairly widely, most Jocks told me that they tend to keep everything to themselves. Many Jocks though, have someone outside of their graduating class—preferably someone at another school—that they talk to and confide in. Frequently this is someone who has moved away from Belten, or a neighbor in another graduating class, for whom this information has no trading value.

> Like I'm not in the social circle with Georgia or Debbie. I can just tell them, and I know they're, they're not going to tell anybody. Who are they going to tell? And there's always, they don't go to this school so, you know, there's always that openness, you can just say anything because you're not worried about what's going to happen or who's going to know.

In general these confidential friendships are entirely separate from school life. The friends do not mix with each other's school friends, and they do not spend time together that would detract from servicing school networks. They are, in this sense, purely instrumental relationships.

The cafeteria plays an important role in the dissemination of information. Since there are three lunch periods, friendship groups frequently cannot eat together. This is hard for those whose friendship networks are limited, but it provides an opportunity for the Jocks to service their more extensive networks. There are Jock tables in each lunch period, which seat a range of people in the hierarchy who may not normally spend much time together. The considerable size of the tables allows people in the middle of the hierarchy to eat at the same table as those at the top and to participate in the intensive discussions that produce tradable information.

While people outside of the Jock network may be satisfied simply to know what's happening when and where, those within need also to know such things as which of these things are "worth" going to, what time the "cool" people are planning to arrive, and how to dress. One example of the function of informal information was a school dance, a "Battle of the Bands," featuring a punk band and a rock 'n roll band. Although it was not written on the posters, those in the know knew to dress "punk," and the variety of punk dress displayed by those in the know was considerable. Many people arrived dressed normally. The Jock leaders stood out both by arriving quite late and by displaying a unique style of dress that was more "mod" than "punk."

Participation in the corporate hierarchy of the high school requires and instills a set of social norms and skills that will prove adaptive in adult corporate life. Corporate norms of interaction lead to very specific kinds of social networks, and also to very specific kinds of relationships. Although the external fact of hierarchy and upward mobility is widely recognized in the school, the quality of relationship that it requires and engenders stands in even greater contrast to the quality of relationships that characterize Burnout networks.

7

Life Outside the Corporation

I just think that they're all competing to be better than each other and trying to get as many friends as possible, and they're competing and they're great. And I, I don't, I don't agree with that at all. I think you should be who you are, and do what you want. And not try to impress everybody by being Joe Athlete or Joe Float Builder. I think it's been like that for quite a long time, I don't even know when it—junior high school is really when the first pressure starts. I don't know. Because if you have a lot of friends, and not very many close friends, I think you're cheating yourself, because you don't have anybody to confide in, or anybody to really trust. Because you don't really know, you know, if you just have a broader range of friends.

The previous chapter's focus on Jocks provides a picture not so much of Jocks themselves as of the norms embraced by the school and hence the school's means of evaluation of all students. Within the context of the school, the key word for the Burnouts is alienation, and it is this sense of alienation and of being "in the wrong" that unifies them into a category, just as being "in control" unifies the opposed Jock category. There are more reasons than one could list for an individual to become a Jock—college orientation, competitiveness, need for adult approval, interest in specific Jock-identified activities. By the same token, there are innumerable reasons for becoming a Burnout. Certainly, becoming either is not simply a natural progression from middle or working class family experience—the class-heterogeneity of both categories, as well as the preponderance of unaffiliated students in the school, is adequate evidence of that. The significance of the Jock and Burnout categories is not in any socially deterministic dynamics, but in their function as powerful stereotypes in the school. The most obvious effect of these stereotypes is to lock members of either category into rigid patterns. In addition, the otherwise unmotivated evaluation of Jock and Burnout traits that accompanies categorization serves to justify the domination of productive roles in the school by those who fit the Jock stereotype most closely. Thus it is not only the Burnouts and the Jocks who suffer from the polarization, but the many In-betweens who cannot or will not conform to either stereotype. The previous chapter focused on the norms and behavior of Jocks in relation to the school's corporate structure; this chapter will focus on the norms and behavior of Burnouts in the same relation. The danger of such an approach is in defining a category in negative terms. However, in this context, negativity is an important component of the effect of the school on Burnouts.

This discussion is intended to point to positive interests and values within the Burnout culture that, in the context of the school, force Burnouts into a counter-cultural position. There is, however, an additional factor in the Burnout categorization that must not be ignored. As will be discussed later in this chapter, a number of Burnouts have difficulties that do not stem directly from a conflict of basic norms with the school. The self-sufficiency, solidarity, and supportiveness of Burnout networks is striking and can be connected to a life strategy that is clearly adaptive for any adolescent with blue-collar aspirations. In some cases, Burnouts' social styles and norms correspond to their parents' values and coexist with parental networks in a mutually supportive fashion. At the same time, many—notably some from middle class families—are drawn to Burnout networks by their inability to work out conflicts and problems within the family or with the school. Many find in these networks a way of life that accepts their problems, and that provides alternatives to adult support. For others less inclined to take advantage of the emotional support that it offers, the Burnout category offers excitement and an outlet for rebelliousness. The overall effect is an association of problems and rebelliousness with norms and values that could be seen as virtually unrelated and could be justified on independent grounds. This association leaves little room for a positive evaluation of these norms and values in the school or for an acceptance of individuals' efforts to move forward to productive adulthoods.

NEIGHBORHOOD NETWORKS

Whereas hierarchy and competition within a closed corporate community characterize Jock social structure, Burnout social structure is characterized by egalitarianism and solidarity within a more fluid context. Perhaps the best starting point for a discussion of these aspects of Burnout culture is in the structure of neighborhood networks. In many cases, the neighborhood networks that eventually yield Burnout clusters arise from a family and neighborhood structure that ties children into a network of peer relations that are, in turn, interwoven with those of neighborhood-oriented parents. Elizabeth Bott (1957) documents the difference between family patterns and relations to broader networks in stable working class neighborhoods and in more fluid suburban middle class neighborhoods. Couples who leave their childhood working class neighborhoods, and who thus can no longer rely on established kin and friendship ties, must rely on each other for the help and support that before had a broader base. Their own nuclear families, therefore, develop in relative isolation and become more insular and mutually dependent. Couples remaining in their childhood working class neighborhoods, retaining these ties, are less dependent on each other. It follows that their children, growing up in the same supportive environment, rely in turn on a broader network extending beyond the nuclear family. Neartown, which was developed since World War II, is just the kind of fluid suburb that Bott writes about, where neither the working class nor the lower or upper middle class neighborhoods offer the old and stable networks of a well-established neighborhood. But while many of the parents in the middle class neighborhoods of Neartown have followed an upwardly mobile course and established a suburban middle class way of life, many in the working class neighborhoods have carried their neighborhood orientation with them to Neartown. It is important to note that many of these people moved to Neartown not so much for upward mobility as because their older neighborhoods were becoming the scene of increased racial violence. Thus, although by and large these neighborhoods do not provide the extended family and friendship ties of the traditional working class neighborhood, many of the families recreate some of the interdependence that they have known elsewhere. Children move relatively freely in and out of each other's homes, accepting the supervision of their friends' parents, while at the same time themselves providing supervision of younger children. In this context, children are encouraged to make friends in the neighborhood and to develop cohesive networks based outside of the home.

The encouragement of comprehensive neighborhood networks and their incorporation into parenting patterns can have several effects. First, the networks are likely to be age-heterogeneous, as people take younger siblings in their care into their own friendship groups and gatherings. In addition, the amount of time that children spend outside of the home in a diverse group can make them less reliant on their parents, particularly where some of the parental responsibility lies within the group. This increased reliance on the peer group, in turn, can create an age-group cohesiveness that sets children more clearly apart from the adult age group. Finally, all of these factors foster trust and cohesion not only between small groups of peers and siblings but within the extended neighborhood group. All of the above effects are apparent in a number of Burnout clusters that are traceable to neighborhood networks, and more generally in the norms of friendship espoused in the Burnout category as a whole.

Just as comprehensive neighborhood networks serve a function for the parents who encourage them, by spreading responsibility for the care and supervision of children, they also serve an adaptive function for the children themselves both in childhood and in preparation for working class adulthood. Unlike the Jocks, whose adolescence is preparation for what they expect to be many discrete upward moves, most Burnouts anticipate an adult working life in which advancement is limited and continual, defined primarily by increased earning power through the gradual accumulation of skill and seniority within one job type. Although there is a possibility in blue-collar jobs for movement into the discrete job structure of management, such mobility constitutes a qualitative change in work style, in life-style, and in relations with one's peers. Many workers consider such mobility undesirable and avoid job changes that will put them in a superordinate relation to their peers and separate them from solidary peer networks. The motivations for this avoidance stem from the economic structure of our society and from the working class culture that arises in adaptation to the subordinate position of the working class in this structure.

To the extent that blue-collar jobs are controlled by a white-collar hierarchy preoccupied with minimizing production costs, blue-collar workers assume that their material security depends on mutual support both in the workplace and out. Gains will not be made through the beneficence or even the fairness of the corporate powers, but through solidary action designed to guarantee workers' power in the workplace through the size and cohesiveness of the blue-collar work force. Attempts to secure individual mobility beyond the context of the group can only undermine the power of the group. Working class networks, therefore, acquire strength from the perception that the opportunities for employment mobility are insufficient to warrant the risk of threatening ties through individual competition, and from the unifying effects of efforts to promote and protect the working cohort as a whole. Strength also derives from the relative unification of work groups with friendship and kin groups. Working class jobs are commonly procured in the local area through family and friendship networks, uniting the labor force in any locality through a multiplicity of personal and residential ties. The resulting multiplexity of working class networks favors minimally contradictory roles in a variety of contexts: Where friendship, kin, residential, and work roles overlap, they must remain fundamentally symmetrical if these networks are to endure. Thus pressure in the private sphere contributes to pressure in the work sphere to ensure solidarity and egalitarianism.

Burnout social networks are well on their way toward being adult working class networks. Burnouts' emphasis on interdependence stems from a conviction that they should not, and frequently cannot, rely on parents and other adults for the fulfillment of their every need. Loyalty and solidarity stem not only from interdependence but from a perception of themselves as separate from the more powerful older age group, as well as from a sense that the people who have power over them, particularly in school, are serving separate interests. Finally, multiplexity is almost a natural outgrowth of the above. To the extent that Burnouts feel that their needs are fulfilled by their friendship group, and to the extent that this group is built on loyalty and interdependence, they tend to build their activities and interests jointly rather than forsaking the group for new interests.

Continuity between high school and early adulthood resides in different spheres for Jocks and Burnouts. For Jocks, whose identity is closely associated with their institutional roles, personal networks are discontinuous, while what will remain constant is their relation to institutions. Burnouts, on the other hand, view their personal networks as the continuous element in their lives, and see little relation between school pursuits and those they will be involved in at work later on. Because employment will probably come through local personal contacts, and because lack of resources makes it difficult to move, the Burnout's entry into the work force involves a change in workplace from school to job, but a continuation of high school private life. Many Burnouts, particularly perhaps during the hard times of the early 1980s in Michigan, talked frequently about moving to the Sun Belt after high school. However, the common pattern is for them to remain in their parents' home at least for a while after they leave school, hang out with their current friends, and pursue the same enjoyments as in high school, but with fewer parental constraints. Their assumptions about friendships, therefore, are based on a strong sense of continuity: Burnouts' high school networks derive to a great extent from their neighborhood networks, and they expect their adult networks to be a continuation of their high school networks. It follows that they will begin in high school to develop the very networks that they will need after graduation, extending their local networks to include a wider range of experience and developing close friendships that will provide support in adulthood. In this way, Burnouts' friendship norms stem at least in part from the continuity of their adolescent and adult lives.

FLUIDITY

The Burnouts' fluid orientation to their life stage, interpersonal relations, and community stands in stark contrast to the discrete boundaries encouraged by the school and accepted by the Jocks. The Burnouts' rejection of the school as the center of their lives both stems from and leads to a direct and autonomous relationship with the community and its resources. Interests such as music, cars, and dirt biking serve the same purpose for Burnouts as school activities do for Jocks. The difference is that these interests are most commonly developed and pursued outside of the school—at homes or in public space—in self-recruited groups independent of school boundaries and school supervision. It could be said that all of this stems from a more fluid view of the adolescent life stage, with entrance to adulthood taking place gradually in different arenas. Some Burnouts already have the skills that they will use in the workplace and lack only the formal qualification of a high school diploma. Some, by the time they are seniors, already spend as much time in the workplace as they do in school, and some spend as much time with people who are no longer in school as they do with fellow students. A few are no longer living with their parents, and many rely less and less on their parents as they approach graduation. Romantic involvements are seen as potentially leading to marriage and are pursued with a corresponding seriousness that allows the unashamed discussion of love.

Fluidity of Life Stage

The continuity of adolescence and adulthood is enhanced by the age-heterogeneity of the Burnouts' social contacts. The interlinking of close age groups, by affording regular exposure to other age groups, provides fluidity. The most obvious source of this interlinking is the mixture of close age groups in neighborhood and school networks. Gradually, however, the mobility of adolescence provides a number of other kinds of contact with older age groups. Some Burnouts at Belten report being close to younger siblings of their parents who, as young adults, fit midway between the two generations. These aunts and uncles can act as intermediaries between parents and children, serve as young adult friends and models, and sometimes provide links to their own young adult friends. Many Burnouts who have jobs make older friends in the workplace, bringing them into their own networks and gaining access through them to older networks.

Age-heterogeneity in friendship groups, stigmatized in the school, is frequently invoked as the cause of Burnouts' difficulties with the school. Many people, Burnouts as well as others, point to friendships with older peers as a "troublemaking" influence, because it provides early exposure to the behavior of older children. One Burnout at Belten explained her history in the following way:

> I hung around my brothers, and Don is three years older than me. So when I was in seventh grade, he was in tenth grade. And, um, I was kind of like his assurance policy. "You can go over there, if you don't mind taking Jane." Jane didn't tell on her brother for any-thing. I didn't—you know, I wasn't a little squealer or nothing be-cause they accepted me, and they let me do what they were doing. Um, I was introduced to beer, pretty much, from my brother. And then, that, that is one of the things that leaded me into my other friends and stuff, because it wasn't my first time when it was with them. Okay. My first time was with my brother. And I wouldn't tell. Because I was doing it too, you know. So I think I got intro-duced to it a lot faster, and all that kind of stuff. Because my whole life, I have hung around with older people.

Coleman (1961) attributes the age-heterogeneity of "Hood" networks (equivalent to Burnout networks) in his study to a need to look beyond the grade to find sufficient numbers of people who share their "deviant" interests. It is certainly true that certain kinds of interests may not be adequately represented in one grade to constitute a sizable group, but Burnouts (and probably his Hoods) represent by no means such a mi-nority. The age-heterogeneity of Burnout groups is not a product of deviance but a sign of deviant status within an age-graded system.

Geographic Fluidity

The chronological fluidity of Burnout networks, both in terms of the individual's aging process and his or her contacts with surrounding age groups, is loosely related to geographic fluidity. Once again, whereas the corporate norms of the school sharply define and delimit the locus of Jocks' activities, the Burnouts' life in school is continuous with the metropolitan area outside. To some extent, this is a function, in turn, of the age-heterogeneity of Burnout networks, with older peers providing some of the contact with urban networks. The Burnouts' involvement with the urban area, though, arises gradually and grows to some extent out of an earlier involvement with the local area. The neighborhood locus of friendship networks, and the focus of peer activities outside the home within these networks, leads almost naturally to an association between the network and neighborhood or local geography. Many of the gathering places of Burnout networks go back to elementary school days, centering in school yards or neighborhood parks. Many neighborhoods have a park or a school yard where Burnouts from the area congregate. One girl who did not come from a Burnout neighborhood, but became a Burnout in junior high, followed her shifting friends into their neighborhood parks.

> I used to hang out at this different park, with Joan and Mary, because Mary's older sister did . . . and that used to be, I used to love going up there because it was all older people, you know. And, uh, I got along with the people up there really good. And then, when I quit hanging around Joan and Mary I just quit going up there. And then that's when I started hanging around with Judy and Sue, and I—they went up there all the time [a different park] because that's where they hung out. So I would just go up there and, uh, I knew most of the people, not that I could stand them all. But I used to just go up there and sit around. It was something to do, you know. Better than sitting at home, or whatever.

These designated gathering places serve a clear function in organizing the Burnouts' social lives. The age- and geographic heterogeneity of Burnout networks make it particularly important to have places where people can gather. Many members of a Burnout network may not see their friends in school because the friends may have skipped school or left early, they may have graduated or dropped out of school, or they may go to a different school. The school, therefore, can be an unsatisfactory base of social operations. Neighborhood parks and school yards, on the other hand, can serve as the locus for group activities such as softball games or "serious partying," or as meeting places where people come and go. While parks and school yards are gathering places for a relatively open network of Burnouts, smaller subgroups may have even more local gathering places. A member of one neighborhood-based Burnout group described the group's regular gathering place:

> It's, it's called "The Corner." She lives here, [sketching out a diagram], Don lives here—no, she lives here, Al lives here, and Don

lives here. So everybody parks their car and gets their beer and stuff and sits out there on Friday nights. It's weird—you think, you know, the cops would come and stuff, but they never do. That's what we usually do on a Friday night.

As Brake (1985) points out, working class youngsters' use of streets as a hangout can be attributed to the fact that streets serve as "an adventurous free area . . . in contrast to the antithetical constraining agencies of social control" (p. 36). This does not mean that the youngsters are free of control in the streets, but that they are free of the constraint of an environment created by adults for adolescents. In the streets, their contact with authority is on similar terms to that of adults, that is, they are subject to the same law enforcement as adults rather than to an intermediate supervising power based on age. Although many feel that public law enforcement leans on adolescents, the implications for age status of dealing directly with the police are certainly preferable.

Alienated from the activities planned by adults for adolescents, and lacking in material resources, Burnouts spend a good deal of their time hanging out or walking around. It should be noted that Burnouts' "hanging out" does not have the same status as that of many working class urban groups. The Chicago gangs described by Thrasher (1927) were integrated into adult crime networks, and much of their hanging out accomplished generally accepted purposes within the local community. Today, many in the working class Italian community of Chicago's near west side see the hanging out of adolescent and young adult men as performing a neighborhood service, that is, monitoring the streets and, particularly, keeping out blacks from the nearby projects.[1] Suburban norms everywhere do not allow much hanging out, which is perhaps why many Belten Burnouts walk around as much as they hang out, leaving them less open to harassment and charges of vagrancy.

The integration of network activities with the local area expands as the cohort acquires mobility. Cars allow adolescents to cruise and to frequent gathering places farther from the neighborhood.

If there's nowhere to go, we'll just drive around and if it comes to, it's almost time to run out of gas we'll go, uh, on the other side of Main Street, there's a, uh, what it is is there's a . . . company. Next

---

[1] This observation is based on taped interviews conducted by Dana Raciunas, Kristine Martin, Nida Misiulis, Marcie Reitzug, Anat Stavans, Lei Huang, Patti Trocki, Cindy Wojcziewski, Juan Guerra, Sister Mary Rogers, and Jil Deheeger as part of a research project at the University of Illinois at Chicago.

to that there's a, it's like a . . . school, you know, and there's like a
place to park back there, behind there, called the Gap. Everybody
calls it the Gap. And you can party back there. I don't know, all we
do to have fun is party. Wherever, where—in a car, sitting on the
street, next door, Al's garage, side of my house. We had a keg back
there last weekend.

Burnouts complain that there is little to do around Neartown. Many go
to roller rinks, pool halls, bowling alleys, arcades, and movies. By far the
most outstanding events are rock concerts in such distant places as Detroit, Meadowbrook, and the Pontiac Silverdome. But these are relatively infrequent and expensive. Detroit and, to a lesser extent, Canada
attract Burnouts in large numbers.

That's wild down there [Detroit]. That's the place to go if you want
some excitement, really.

WHAT DO YOU DO?

Uh, go down there, very deep in Detroit, you know, in downtown
Detroit, over by Cobo, you know, and there's lots of things to do
down there. You can get in any bars down there. You can buy
down there. There's always parties going on down there, and
people are pretty friendly down there. Surprisingly.

Cruising is an important aspect of suburban life, and particularly of
Burnout life. Certain large streets that connect Detroit with the suburbs
and that boast sufficient drive-ins and fast-food restaurants serve as regular cruising routes for the suburban population. In general the choice
of cruising route is a function of residence, with people from each suburb using the closest route that connects their town with Detroit. How
far the individual goes into Detroit is an indication of daring and urban
orientation. Many Neartowners cruise Five Mile Road, a main through-
fare running east and west through the suburbs and into Detroit. At the
western end of Detroit, Five Mile intersects Telegraph Avenue, which
serves as a north–south cruising route for the suburbs located along it,
as well as for Detroiters and residents of the western suburbs. One
Burnout who cruised Telegraph regularly pointed out the distinction in
cruising routes.

The ones that are on Five Mile, they're kind of conservative. Telegraph, there's a lot of cool people. I mean, you go from car to car
and pass a joint, at the light.

YOU MEET PEOPLE THAT YOU SEE AGAIN?

Yeah. Cruise around with them.

Another important cruising route is a park that runs through a number of suburbs and into Detroit. This park serves as a gathering place for adolescents throughout the area. People from different parts of the urban-suburban continuum generally frequent different spans of this park, but the spans overlap, providing regular contact with a continuous urban-suburban population. Although Telegraph provides drive-ins for stopping, the park provides ideal areas for hanging out, and many go there not just to cruise but to stop in their designated spots to hang out, party, and play Frisbee.

Geographic mobility is clearly contextualized in a social continuum that corresponds to the urban continuum. Young people living in and near Detroit are considered more autonomous and tougher than those from the suburbs. This impression is confirmed through contacts both with those currently living in Detroit and with Neartowners who have moved from Detroit or the closer suburbs. Two girls who moved to Neartown in late elementary school gave the following accounts:

> I thought they [Neartowners] were pretty sheltered and stuff, you know, because I'd—you know, like I used to tell them that I used to go out, you know, and walk, you know, across Seven Mile and everything. And they couldn't even cross the street and stuff, and like I'm crossing these big main streets, and, you know—

*   *   *

> Well, it was like we were years ahead of these people, it seemed . . . we were much more sophisticated because we, um, you know, we were all into all this stuff—like we, we had the weirdest ideas. Now this is when we were like little kids, like 10 years old. Um, we would sit around and talk about sex and everything, you know, and—and it seems kind of ludicrous now, because 10 years old, that's like—that seems so little. But then—

DID YOU KNOW PRETTY MUCH EVERYTHING?

> Well, you know, we would find out, you know, if we wanted to know. And we had this big group that we all hung around, and we had this club, you know, and it was a real big deal, and I think what was—to get in, you had to wear a bra.

AND HERE THEY WERE ALL LIKE, UH—`

> Yeah, they were—they seemed like, I mean, they were playing on—with dolls, you know, and everything, and I'm going, "Oh, my

god, what did I move into?" That's—that's why my parents wanted to move there, because things were starting to move like a little bit too fast, you know, because they were—if you—if you experience all that too young, what is there to experience when you're older? . . . Some people just try and like amass information and all—all these experiences, like that kind of stuff. And they, um—that—they—it's like they were in a race, you know, and they took every—all the good points out of everything.

Because of their greater autonomy, therefore, Detroiters and people from the more urban suburbs enjoy a certain prestige with Burnouts, and Burnouts are normally eager to get to know them. But just as Belten's Burnouts are ultimately involved in the school, they are also Neartowners, and some of them, while they are drawn to Detroit, consider themselves suburbanites and approach Detroit with caution. Although some Burnouts regularly visit the neighborhoods of their friends (or friends' friends) in Detroit and attend parties in Detroit, others' contact with urban adolescents is through fleeting interactions in public places. Many Burnouts limit their actual participation in urban life to situations that they deem "safe," and recognize that while contact with urban life provides knowledge and experience, it must be approached with caution. Many feel that Neartown has saved them from the unfortunate fate of many of their peers closer to Detroit.

I didn't live in Detroit. I just know people that live out there from—like people that I know up here that went back there, . . . and I go back down there with them to meet their friends.

WHERE IN DETROIT? WHAT HIGH SCHOOL DID THEY GO TO?

Uh, Samuels High. Around Samuels High. Right around the neighborhood right there, too. Kind of a nasty neighborhood, you know.

WHAT'S NASTY ABOUT IT?

Well, you know, busted windows all over the place, boards, you know. You know, Detroit. You know, the way Detroit is. But, uh, you know, it's a lot different in Neartown. And I'm glad I grew up in Neartown instead of Detroit, you know, because I see the way they were and those guys are crazy. . . . They'll stop for nothing.

WHY DO YOU SUPPOSE THAT IS?

Because it was harder to cope with in Detroit, you know. It was a lot harder. It was more of a chance to get involved in crime, too.

And parents were more worried about their making it than they were trying to help their kids out, too. . . . That is one thing you look forward to, getting out of Detroit. I would if I was in there.

However varying the Burnouts' contacts with and attitudes toward Detroit may be, however, they stand in clear contrast to the Jocks, both in their interest in and familiarity with the urban area and in their eagerness to interact with people from there. It is above all through this geographic range that Burnouts participate in a broader world, familiarizing themselves with the metropolitan area, meeting people from other towns, and looking back on Jocks as confined to "make-believe" pursuits in a limited and protected community.

Network Fluidity

Another aspect of Burnout social norms related to fluidity is egalitarianism. It almost follows from their origins that Burnout networks should continue the kind of egalitarianism that they began with in the early years. Such egalitarianism could be expected also from the age-group opposition with adults. In addition, the Burnouts are not engaged in any kinds of activities that would require or yield a hierarchical social structure. While Burnouts enjoy competition in individual endeavors, this competition is not for position in the social order, but is simply a test of the particular skills involved. This egalitarianism makes Burnout networks more open than Jock networks, both in terms of accepting new members and in sharing information and commodities. Where place in the network is not evaluated in terms of distance from a perceived apex, there is no threat in allowing an individual to enter the network at any given point, because that individual will not be distancing others from such a point. Indeed, the effectiveness of the Burnouts' social network depends on its expansion, particularly to people with greater experience. Many people who moved to Neartown after seventh grade told me that they had been befriended at the start by Burnouts and some of them became Burnouts. Very few of them became Jocks. Many Jocks do not recognize this behavior as friendliness or openness, but attribute it to some kind of almost malevolent intent, as might befit a group of outlaws.

They go for the new kids. Like they're trying to recruit, you know?

One of the newcomers who eventually found his way into the Jock network used the same term.

Well, the first people I got to know were Burnouts, because this kid just started talking to me in class, you know, and introducing me to his friends and stuff. He'd try to get me to go out in the courtyard and stuff, trying to recruit me, you know?

Regardless of the Jocks' evaluation of the Burnouts' actions, the latter are clearly more open to newcomers and attract not only those who were drawn to them in the first place but also some who might otherwise have preferred to be Jocks.

I was more of a Jock in the school where I went before, but like when I came here I couldn't get to know any of the Jocks. They weren't friendly, like, and it was like you had to prove yourself. So I stayed with the guys who were friendly to me when I came, so I guess you could say I'm a Burnout now.

DO YOU THINK THAT IF YOU'D STAYED WHERE YOU WERE YOU'D BE A JOCK NOW?

Yeah, I think so, I would, definitely.

DO YOU WISH YOU WERE?

Yeah, I do.

WHY?

I think it was a lot, you know, more fun, you know, being a Jock. You know, there was a lot more to do, you know, and there's a lot more to life than just partying, you know, wasting your mind away.

But if the Burnouts welcome newcomers into their networks, they are not so quick to give up their old friendships. Where the school and the Jocks emphasize shifting task-based friendships, the Burnouts choose their tasks largely in concert with their friends. Mainstream opinion at Belten is that Burnout network loyalty results from laziness and an unwillingness to make new friends. Burnouts are seen as unfriendly and withdrawn. Burnouts are indeed frequently reserved and even hostile toward people whom they have reason to feel look down on them—particularly Jocks and teachers—but they are outgoing in other contexts. Another factor contributing to mainstream opinion that Burnouts are surly is the Burnouts' very different norms of interaction with relative strangers. While Jocks emphasize the importance of "saying hi" to as many people as possible, the Burnouts view the Jock's ready smile and diffuse hall greetings as insincere—as "vote getting." One In-between characterized the Jock demeanor as follows:

Always out meeting people and everything . . . Smiling all the time
and gay, and they're happy and everything.

Since Burnouts have no need for a broad school constituency, they
reserve their greetings for those they know and like. Burnouts also point
out that the person who smiles a lot must either be happy all the time or
phony. And while they are willing to believe that Jocks are happy, they
themselves frequently are not. Phoniness is a common charge against
Jocks, on the part not only of Burnouts but also of In-betweens. Burnouts stress honesty in interaction and relationships, and pride themselves on their outspokenness. Burnouts frequently say that they became
friends with a particular individual because "we're exactly alike." Since
Burnouts view social mobility as an expansion of the friendship network
rather than an individual movement between networks, new friends
must fit in with the old. The resulting uniformity of values facilitates
honesty, and even requires it as an expression of solidarity with the network. The popular Burnout may be the individual who best expresses
the uniform values of the network. For this reason, Burnouts emphasize
the importance of consistency and honesty.

This difference between Jocks' and Burnouts' views of honesty in
social relations turns up in Kohn's (1969) examination of class differences in parental values in regard to their children's behavior. Kohn
found that middle class mothers considered honesty a threat to popularity, since it carried the risk of offending. Working class mothers, on
the other hand, believed that the respect won by honesty would enhance
one's popularity.

Fluidity of Material and Information

The socioeconomic differences that separate Burnouts from Jocks,
and the Burnouts' lack of adult aid, which appears to smooth the Jocks'
way through adolescence, are highly salient aspects of Burnout identity.
Many Burnouts would say that money is what underlies the Jock–Burnout split. It is both adaptive and symbolic of category solidarity, therefore, that fluidity exists also in Burnout networks in the area of material
and informational needs. Burnouts share what they have with their
friends—cars, clothes, money, drugs, alcohol, cigarettes, musical instruments, records, radios. While there are a few individuals who are tolerated in Burnout networks simply because they provide marijuana, such
use of individuals who appear to be better off is not to be confused with
the normal reciprocity that characterizes Burnout friendships.

The most commonly exchanged commodity is cigarettes, and their relatively low monetary and high symbolic value makes such exchange as much a matter of signalling solidarity as fulfilling actual needs. One small incident illustrates this function of cigarette exchange. As I was driving a Burnout home one day, another Burnout pulled up in the lane to our right and called out a greeting. The boy in my car rolled down the window and after the exchange of greetings asked the girl in the other car if she had any "smokes." She handed him a pack containing a few cigarettes and then pulled ahead. It was clearly the giving, rather than what was given, that was the point of this interaction. Without smoking a single one, he left the pack on the dashboard when he got out of my car, and clearly he thought I was unnecessarily fastidious when I brought it to him the next day in school.

What cannot be given is frequently lent or exchanged—and not always returned. Burnouts commonly use borrowed items as their own, and items may be kept for long periods, passed on to another friend, or get damaged or lost. This does not necessarily incur resentment, unless the borrower denies having borrowed the item or does not take responsibility for what happens to it. One friendship suffered a serious setback when one Burnout smashed the car he had borrowed from a friend. But the lender told me that he was angry at the borrower not because of the actual damage to the car but because his friend had denied responsibility and refused to help with the repairs. The lender felt that reckless driving and the resultant accidents were part of the normal use of a car, and while he would not be angry at a friend simply for driving his car recklessly, he would expect the friend to share responsibility just as he had shared the car.

A number of conflicts, in fact, arise over theft and the disposition of borrowed items, but these conflicts are part of a general acceptance of a regular flow of resources. In a questionnaire administered in a Detroit suburban high school similar to Belten, Walker (1982) found that those who identified themselves as Burnouts were more likely than those who identified themselves as Jocks to lend items of small value to intimates, friends, and strangers, and to sell such items to intimates and friends. He also found that Burnouts were more likely to steal items from intimates, friends, and strangers. Walker emphasized that the statistics on stealing had to be interpreted in the light of comments written by the respondents on the last page of the questionnaire. Many who identified themselves on the questionnaire as Burnouts qualified their answers on stealing with comments such as: "When we take a lighter or a joint, we're not stealing, because we all do it and we pay each other back" (p. 20). Burnouts also told Walker informally that they did not necessarily consider it stealing to take something belonging to a friend without asking: Stealing is taking something that the taker knows the owner cannot afford to lend. One Jock, on the other hand, wrote: "I don't loan things—people might break them or not return them."

While a Jock may have access through parents and teachers to a wider adult network with more valuable goods and services, he or she is not on an equal footing but must deal with the adult as gatekeeper, and the flow of resources between parents and children involves the very parental monitoring that Burnouts strive to avoid. Many of the Burnouts' needs are related to activities not condoned by adults, and many of the problems that they face stem from these activities. Thus many Burnouts need to rely heavily on peer networks both because their parents cannot provide them with adequate resources, and because they prefer to keep certain of their needs and behavior from their parents. Peer networks enhance the young individual's access to financial and material means, drugs and alcohol, information, contacts, space (which can be provided by peers who live on their own), and transportation. Network support enabled one Burnout to run away from home on fairly short notice, by helping him accumulate money and camping gear for the trip, marijuana for the long evenings on the trip, and contacts with young adults who would provide living space and job contacts at the other end. The material goods came from age peers, while the contacts came through older siblings in the network. The flow of these resources is not unidirectional as in the Jocks' dealings with parents, but part of a system of sharing and exchange that, in turn, is tied to egalitarian values.

This peer group interdependence is in many ways analogous to the interdependence that Stack (1974) observed in poor black kin groups. Stack's study of reciprocity in "The Flats," a poor black community, uncovers survival strategies that also operate among Burnouts and no doubt among any number of groups whose subordination to mainstream society renders the individual impotent to deal directly with the economy and necessitates the pooling of resources. In The Flats, whose population relies on inadequate public funds, individuals survive through the continual and systematic exchange of money, materials, and services. This pooling requires a total and enduring commitment to the group on the part of all members in order to guarantee the continual reciprocity that spreads sporadic resources throughout the group over time. The departure of any individual for alternative opportunities, such as employment or marriage, creates a break in the flow of goods and services, threatening both the integrity of the system of exchange and the departing individual's chances of reentry into the system later on. Individuals are constrained, therefore, to be cautious in pursuing outside opportunities:

> Those who attempt social mobility must carefully evaluate their job security, even if it is at poverty level, before they risk removing themselves from the collective help of kinsmen. The collective expectations and obligations created by cooperative networks of poverty stricken kinsmen in The Flats result in a stability within the kin group, and the success of these networks of kinsmen depends on this stability. (Stack, 1974, p. 24)

Since the Burnouts derive from their peer networks many of the crucial resources that the Jocks gain from adult sources, separation from these networks constitutes both a loss of access to resources and an abandonment of friends in need. While the Burnouts do not risk survival in pursuing friendships and activities outside the Burnout networks, they do depend on these networks for information, for some material support, and for a good deal of emotional support. There is, therefore, considerable pressure in Burnout networks to remain in the networks and not to pursue interests that would create any significant separation from the networks.

The lasting power of Burnout networks is enhanced by their interdependencies, and the loyalty, trust, and solidarity fostered by these networks become a category hallmark for many Burnouts. Some Burnouts cite longevity as the basis of the closeness of their friendships, saying that they've known each other "forever," know everything about each other, have been through everything together. But not only do Burnouts report close friendships as more trusting than do Jocks; they also are not secretive about personal problems or "transgressions" within the broader Burnout network. Where information is not a tradable commodity and where there is no competition for upward mobility, "negative" information cannot be particularly damaging. Inasmuch as problems with parents, and discussion of these problems, serve to enhance the age-group solidarity that is a keystone of Burnout culture, Burnouts have no external motivation for withholding such discussion. And inasmuch as legal or quasi-legal transgressions are accepted and indeed can enhance the individual's image as independent and adventurous, there is frequently no reason to suppress discussion of these either.

Furthermore, the danger of information reaching people whose knowledge of it might be damaging is minimized by the strong norm of keeping information from adults. The independence of the peer group, and the constant influence of older children on younger, generates, if not conflict with adults, at least circumspection toward adults. Part of the solidarity within the network is in maintaining this circumspection, and it is an affirmation of this solidarity that Burnouts do not generally worry if personal information travels to a number of people in a network. One Burnout who figured that several dozen people had known when he was planning to run away from home never feared that the information would get to his parents before he had a chance to leave. Whereas Jocks are quick to discuss friends' problems or transgressions with their own parents or teachers, on the assumption that they may be helpful (frequently through carrying the news to the transgressor's parents), Burnouts are less likely to share such information about peers with their own parents, and certainly do not share such information with adults in school. It is natural, then, that "narking" should be the ultimate transgression among Burnouts, and a source of constant vigilance.

There's, there's narks in there [the courtyard] too.

REALLY?

I think so.

HAVE YOU SEEN ANY THAT YOU COULD RECOGNIZE AS NARKS, OR DO YOU—^

No. If they were, I'd, I'd beat the shit out of them.

YOU MEAN PEOPLE WHO HANG OUT IN THE COURTYARD?

Yeah, you know, they just look like, you know, they're down there too. But when, uh, Jack Shaw [a student who was suspended for drug use] got taken away the other day, they [school officials] said that they had three kids [who had] seen him too. Whoever that is, nobody knows. . . . I was thinking about going in there and asking them if they need another nark, so maybe I can find out who the other ones are. Because you know, anybody that, that's just like being a, uh, a traitor, you know. And I can't even see it, because you know they, they gotta give them some kind of benefits. Maybe they're going to let them graduate or something, you know, if they nark.

Information, like material goods is freely shared in Burnout networks: drug sources; legal information; sexual, birth control, and abortion information; information about parties, games, and gatherings; personal information about individuals; and knowledge of the urban area all flow in Burnout networks. There is no motivation for the strategic withholding of such information. It is small wonder, then, that Burnouts look upon their network as the ultimate source of support.

Drugs

Drugs are an important Burnout symbol and give rise to the name by which Burnouts refer to themselves. However, drugs must be seen in an appropriate perspective if any understanding of Burnout culture is to be achieved. First of all, Burnouts are by no means the only students at Belten who use drugs. In the course of high school, a number of Jocks take up marijuana and no doubt experiment with other drugs, and there are plenty of In-betweens whose drug use certainly matches that of Burnouts. What is most salient is the Burnouts' public acknowledgment of drug use and their general consensus that they were the only ones to experiment with drugs in the early years of junior high.

Many Burnouts feel that their relatively long experience with drugs has made them wise users. They feel that they know more about the substances themselves and that longer experience has taught them to "handle themselves" and to moderate their use. Those who began using drugs and alcohol in (or before) the early years of junior high distinguish themselves from those who started later and have not yet learned to handle themselves. Many who felt more mature in junior high because they used drugs feel that moderation or abandonment of drugs in high school is a new sign of maturity.

> I've noticed the people that started smoking pot in junior high don't smoke half as much by the time they get to Belten. And then there's kids that just started in ninth grade that are, you know, they're just ruining their high school because—That's why I wish everybody would start early, you know, because then by the time high school rolls around, you pretty much know what you're doing. . . . I, I know that by the time I got to Belten, I matured so much in just that little time, between junior high and high school, compared to elementary school and junior high.
>
> *   *   *
>
> I quit in ninth grade. Before ninth grade. Yeah, I figured, you know, if people are going to like me they're going to like me for who I am, not because I smoke dope or party, or whatever. So I quit.

Many Burnouts say that their drug use, particularly in school, fell off after junior high school, both because the novelty wore off and because they felt that it impaired their functioning.

YOU USED TO AND YOU STOPPED?

Yeah.

WHY?

Um, I kind of got too dependent on it. . . . I started getting high before school, and my grades went down. Because, you know, I'd just be sitting there, and I'd stare straight at the teacher's face and concentrate, and when I left that room, I didn't know what he said, you know. I'd, I'd hear parts here and there because I'd be drifting off somewhere else, I'd be looking at something, or looking out the window, and—. . . I mean you're so tired you don't even want to see anybody's face, you just want to say "Get away from me, I want to go home and sleep," you know, and I slept through half of my classes, I was so tired. And my grades just went down, and—and now, if I were, if I were to smoke pot right now, I don't even think I'd enjoy it. I'd just get tired.

The general association of drugs with the Burnout category results more from the elevation of drugs to the status of category symbol than from anything resembling a concentration of drug use among the category's members. The greater salience of other factors in Burnout affiliation is reflected in one Burnout's distinction between Burnouts and a group of substance users that he had met briefly the previous year.

They had no problems, you know. They didn't get in any trouble except with the, you know, partying and that. They didn't seem like they were real burned out people. . . . They're not like the Burnout type, they're like the rich junkie type.

It is possible, also, that the gradual involvement of other segments of the school population in drugs and alcohol diluted the social significance of drugs and made drug use a less effective or less necessary symbolic behavior. Nevertheless, drug use is the single most important factor in the Burnouts' difficulties in school, both because it interferes directly with schoolwork and because it puts them at extreme odds with school authorities. Some Burnouts, commonly referred to as "burned out Burnouts," get high on a regular basis—in school and out. Some of them say that they couldn't stand school otherwise. Some smoke an occasional joint as a group activity between classes or at lunch; others prefer not to do drugs in school. But whatever the context, most Burnouts think of drugs as an adjunct to group interaction.

WHAT KINDS OF STUFF DO YOU DO TO HAVE A GOOD TIME?

Uh, drink beer, smoke pot. . . . You know, just try and find the party and socialize. Just, that's really where it's at is just socializing and seeing your friends and having a good time.

Most Burnouts regard drug use, like alcohol use, as a legitimate indulgence. Indeed, a few of them have parents who smoke pot.

WHEN DID YOU START TO PARTY [I.E., SMOKE POT]?

Uh, about seventh grade.

WERE YOU TEMPTED IN SIXTH GRADE?

Uh, sort of, yeah, pretty much, because my parents were sort of into it, and I think maybe that's why pretty much I did.

Most of them have clear ideas about their future roles as parents.

I'd let them try it. And if he couldn't handle it I wouldn't, you know, I'd crack down. I—I don't think I'd smoke pot in front of my kids until they were probably 14, 15. And if they weren't smoking by then I wouldn't. At all. You know. It's not something I would force upon them, you know.

While some Burnouts regard drugs as a form of entertainment, others feel that their drug use is intimately tied to personal problems, as articulated by one Burnout who talked of his desire to stop taking drugs. When I asked him how many of his friends also wanted to stop, he said:

All of them. I think every single one of them do, but they just, I don't know. They got problems and they can't. I don't know. That's the way I am anyways.

*   *   *

Well, first I, uh, started doing mescaline in eighth grade. And I didn't do it really heavy till I got here. But when I got here the first semester of tenth grade I don't really remember because I was eating it every day, two and three hits. Me and Don were.

HOW MUCH WERE YOU PAYING FOR IT?

Two bucks a hit. I spent a lot of money on it. Wasn't worth it, though.

WHY NOT?

Uh, well, now I know what it's like, it's not good for you. It messes
your head up. I don't like not being able to remember about three
or four months of my life. It's all sort of a blur. And I quit for, I
don't know, I quit since, oh, winter of last year. I just started up
recently when I broke up with my girlfriend.

Problems

People throughout the school perceive Burnout affiliation as stemming largely from problems at home. This perception, however, is based
largely on a stereotype that is fed not so much by observed facts as by a
societal association of nonconformity with pathology. This perception,
furthermore, seems to add to, rather than mitigate, the stigmatization
of category members. The Burnout perception, however, is not altogether inconsistent with the general view. Some Burnouts point explic-
itly to personal problems as the principal unifying force of the Burnout
category, setting Burnouts off from the apparently problem-free Jocks.

Jocks are the type that they go out and they enjoy life, I guess they
get into sports. They're just, you know, happy people, I guess.
Some Burnouts just get too heavily into drugs and they just sit
around and just bum out.

Indeed it would be a mistake to deny the problems that seem to over-
whelm many Burnouts; many Burnouts have family problems, and
Burnouts perceive themselves, as a group, as having more family problems than the rest of their peers.

A few Burnouts live in homes with virtually no parental presence.
In some cases there are no parents at all in the home, and the responsibility for adolescents falls on older siblings or other relatives. In others,
parents or a single parent is absent for long periods of time or is sufficiently overcome by personal problems to render his or her presence
ineffectual. One Burnout in characterizing his neighborhood as a
"Burnout" neighborhood, gave the following explanation:

No parents. They, uh, none of the parents are ever always around
. . . so that's, that's how they got that way.

The intensive social life in the neighborhood, which provides distraction
and the support of peer interaction, serves for some as a welcome escape
from a difficult life at home. One person who had been a Burnout until

tenth grade reported temporary family problems as an important motivation for hanging out with the Burnouts in his neighborhood.

> You know, they were fun to hang out with. Everybody else was doing nothing at night and everything. And at that time my brother was always fighting with my dad or my mom and dad or something, so I'd, you know, I didn't hang out much at home.

Some Burnout clusters are more problem-oriented than others, and some of the members of these clusters say that they are attracted to each other by the problems they share and that being around people with no problems makes them feel deviant and isolated. It is generally accepted that adolescent peer groups, and particularly "delinquent" groups, take over many of the functions of the family as the adolescent is separating from the parents (Parsons, 1959, pp. 46–47). This function is clear among the Burnouts, many of whom use kin terms and family metaphors in talking about their friends and about the Burnout category in general. Many Burnouts at Belten referred to their friends as a "big family"; some even used kin terms when referring to individual friends. A group of Burnout girls in a school near Detroit explained that they call themselves the "Brothers" because they're like a family. Several Burnouts at Belten routinely referred to certain close friends as their "brother" or "sister."

> Well, he's not my real little brother, but I call him that.
>
> HOW'D HE GET TO BE YOUR LITTLE BROTHER?
>
> I don't—I don't know. He's really close. It's [the group] like one big family.

As with material and informational resources, Burnouts share their familial resources. Those with few or no problems at home provide support and frequently share their parents with their friends.

> ARE MOST OF YOUR FRIENDS CLOSE TO THEIR PARENTS?
>
> No. [laughter]
>
> DO YOU THINK THAT'S IMPORTANT?
>
> I do. Yeah, I definitely do. Because I think, uh, I don't—like when you go through your junior high years, you know, you sort of rebel against your parents, you know. And like I've always been really close with my parents, and then I moved here and, uh, the kids

were different, boy. None of them got along with their parents, or nothing, and then I sort of started getting in some trouble and that. But then—

WHY?

Oh, probably because I was coming home high . . . staying out late, you know, and doing bad things. And, uh, but then, I don't know, I guess I realized what was happening, and I got it together and— then me and my mom became close again—well, we've always been close, but we just had some hard times. . . . I know a lot of people that can't talk to their parents, and they turn to my mom.

It is not uncommon for a Burnout to live temporarily with the family of a friend when things are not so good at home. This is particularly noticeable in schools in lower working class suburbs of Detroit, where Burnouts live with their friends not only when there is trouble at home but when unemployment depletes food resources in the home. Many Burnouts accept that their parents have neither the time nor the resources to be much help, and take pride in their relative independence from their parents—an independence that is facilitated by the possibility of dependence on peers. While a number of Burnouts complain about their parents' shortcomings, some recognize that they, too, have their own problems. One Burnout, attributing his father's abusive behavior to difficulties at work, showed a kind of identification with his father in spite of the fact that he felt that his father made life at home untenable.

It's [the job] a lot of hassles, man. He puts on the years now. It gets to him.

ARE YOU PRETTY CLOSE WITH HIM?

No. Not at all.

BUT YOU DO KNOW WHAT'S GETTING TO HIM.

I can see it. I can see it. He's always pissed, and looks a lot older. But I don't, I don't even talk to him. All he does is yell at me.

DID HE ALWAYS?

Yeah, he always did. He's a short-tempered person. Just like me. . . . You know, he keeps his temper, you know, during work and when he's out with people, then he sort of lets it loose when he gets home. So do I.

Not all Burnouts would agree on the salience of personal problems in their category membership, and indeed a number of problems are as much a result as a cause of category affiliation, because the Burnout way of life can itself create problems where there were none before. Truancy and drug use create problems at school and at home, and keeping the hours that Burnouts must keep to function in their networks creates tensions with their families, with whom they might otherwise be spending time. Some stay out to provide company and support for friends who themselves spend much of their time away from home. And not uncommonly, Burnouts will accompany their friends to make sure they don't get into too much trouble—frequently ending up getting in trouble themselves. One Burnout who enjoys a close relationship with his mother described his difficulty in balancing this with his social activities.

> I'm trying, you know, but that's all I can say to her is I'm trying, you know . . . I am in a way, you know, but . . . it'd have to be solitary, it would have to be inside my house for solitary confinement for—like because every single one of my friends party. Every single one of them. People I've grown up with, you know.

What is salient about problems in the Burnout category is not so much their greater concentration, but the fact that the norms and structure of Burnout networks make it possible to absorb problems. The constraints that keep Jocks from discussing their problems are nonexistent among Burnouts. The Jocks are constrained from discussing family problems with their peers by their hierarchical structure and by the nature of their alliance with adults. Maintaining one's place in the Jock hierarchy depends to some extent on preserving a personal image of control over one's personal life. Therefore, Jocks must keep family problems to themselves as part of their more general information management strategy. Furthermore, the nature of the Jocks' alliance with adults obliges Jocks to preserve adults' positive images as well as their own. As discussed in Chapter 6, Jocks' submission to adult authority is a delicate arrangement that requires that each party appear not to threaten the other's rights. Evidence that the "agreement" between Jocks and adults is not working would threaten the Jocks' claim to autonomy within the adult authority structure. Burnouts do not have the Jocks' need to control personal information. In contrast to Jock norms, discussion of family problems is not felt to detract from the Burnout's personal image, particularly because the individual's identity is based to some extent on the separation of interests from those of the parent generation.

Burnouts also view experience with serious problems as a sign of living in the real world, and for this reason they are as eager to become involved in other people's problems as to share their own. In sharing family problems, Burnouts exercise not only their trust in each other but their independence from the adult authority structure.

If the Burnouts' networks provide many of the resources that Jocks derive from adults, their relative isolation from adult networks also deprives Burnouts of much of the guidance that they need. The experience and resources of a young and powerless age group can be severely limited, and many Burnouts recognize that their networks are inadequate to deal with many of their problems.

> I mean, you think they're helping you out, but really they're not, because they're just getting you farther in the hole, you know.
>
> WHAT DO YOU MEAN?
>
> You know, like partying. I mean, we—we—I talk to Jerry and them guys a lot, you know. But, uh, those guys, they're messed up like I am, you know. We talk about the same thing but it don't go nowhere, you know. I mean, those guys haven't got their shit together yet and I haven't got my shit together.

Alienation from school personnel prevents many Burnouts from obtaining information and advice, for which these adults frequently are the best source. For example, several Burnouts whose parents' inexperience with education prevented them from providing academic guidance, expressed interest in eventually going to college, but were not following a program in high school that could lead to that end and had only a vague idea of what such a program should be. This kind of situation is due not only to a lack of interaction with school personnel, but also to a lack of information within the Burnouts' own peer networks. With the enormous student–counselor ratio in most public schools, academic counseling only supplements information gained elsewhere. Jocks' major access to information about college preparation and entrance comes from their parents and friends. Jocks select courses, sign up for College Board Examinations, and apply to colleges in concert, and may not even be aware that much of their information comes through long discussions with friends as the time for each decision rolls around. Such information does not flow in Burnout peer networks, as it does not flow in many of their families. Thus even if parents are supportive of college aspirations, they may not know how to implement them.

I, I kind of want to be an art teacher, but you have to go through a lot to be something like that.

HAVE YOU EVER THOUGHT OF GOING TO COLLEGE?

Yeah, my parents said, "Well, you know, if you want to go to college we'll pay your way," so why not, you know.

YEAH. DO THEY WANT YOU TO?

Yeah. I'm, I'm pretty, I think, you know, if I really get my stuff together in art, you know, really get into it I, I probably will try to be an art teacher.

UM, ARE YOU TAKING COURSES AND STUFF THAT YOU HAVE TO TAKE TO GO TO COLLEGE?

Um, I re—I'm not really aware of, you know, what I have to do to be in college, but I, I think I've got a low grade, you know, grade average pretty much.

THE CLASH WITH CORPORATE NORMS

Just as the Jocks' social structure and norms are adaptive to the corporate context, the Burnouts' are adaptive to the working class context and to their current orientation to this context. The degree of fit between possible high school careers and anticipated future ones is an important factor in the individual's willingness to accept the school's corporate life. While the school has a direct role in procuring college entrance for its academic students, it does not play an analogous role for its vocational students in the blue-collar job market. The job market, particularly in Detroit, is tough, and many high school students who would like to work cannot find jobs. The closed nature of the school community stands in direct contradiction to the Burnouts' emphasis on dealing in the real world and on the cultivation of social networks in that world; the school's emphasis on age grading challenges the network structure that provides many of the Burnouts' resources. Moreover, the Burnouts' strong norms of commitment to an egalitarian and solidary peer society conflict with the school's and the Jocks' commitment to hierarchical relations within the age group, to the articulation of this hierarchy with the adult authority structure, and to the norm of upward mobility and the social strategies and relations with peers and adults that facilitate this mobility. Just as the Jocks' hierarchical and upwardly mobile culture is adaptive to the place of the middle class in the economy, the Burnouts' egalitarian and cooperative culture is adaptive to that of the working class.

The Jocks and Burnouts who were prominent in junior high are similar in many ways. Popular Burnouts, like popular Jocks, are on the whole physically attractive, friendly, strong and well coordinated, perceptive, and bright. Like many Jocks, many Burnouts are interested in the people and events around them and enjoy a wide range of pursuits. The withdrawal of Burnouts from school activities, therefore, cannot be explained on the grounds of lack of ability or interest. This withdrawal results from a variety of factors, all of which are related to differences in the two categories' fundamental assumptions about their role in society. The fact that many Burnouts find school activities inherently attractive is manifest both in their own testimony and in their early junior high histories. Like Jocks, Burnouts participated on school teams, music groups, and cheerleading and pompon squads; went to dances and other organized events; and developed crushes on teachers. And many of them would have liked to continue. However, Burnouts participated in activities on different terms than did Jocks, particularly insofar as they did not recognize the corporate unity that ties each school activity into a larger structure. Their disaffection from school activities came as a gradual sense of disappointment with the terms on which these activities could be pursued.

Burnouts acquired visibility and status early in junior high through their precocious behavior—smoking, partying, staying out at night, friendships with older people. The excitement of Burnout life was unequivocally greater than that of their peers, and they regarded school activities as something to be pursued along with their other enjoyments. But within school culture, a cheerleader or an athlete is not simply an individual pursuing a pleasurable and rewarding activity, but an agent of the school leadership structure within which each individual is a representative of the school and the embodiment of its values. Thus the cheerleader or athlete is expected to limit his or her enjoyments to those condoned by the school and to engage full time in the pursuit of a school career. Because participation in activities is an important means of acquiring status in the school hierarchy, clean-cut, school-oriented qualities must be requirements for participation if an activity is to retain its value to the school and to the individual member. The presence in an activity of individuals who do not share all the Jock norms of behavior poses a threat to the status of the activity and to its membership. Thus, as one cheerleader told me, personal behavior is carefully monitored by one's peers.

If you smoke in your JV year and the Varsity cheerleaders know about it, it's really hard to make it into Varsity the next year because they judge.

The imposition of school norms of personal behavior weed Burnouts out of activities both by establishing criteria for exclusion and by alienating those who are unwilling to allow the school to monitor their behavior.

Because there were relatively few Burnouts in school activities at Belten, those who participated were excluded from some of their friends' group activities. Some, therefore, dropped activities when they could not persuade their friends to participate with them. But while this alone, particularly if only one activity was involved, did not always create a significant threat to the integrity of the friendship group or to the individual's place in it, other factors did. As the Jocks adjusted their friendship networks to fit their participation in activities, those who did not were gradually excluded. One Burnout who had been on the pompon squad in junior high gave the following account:

> When I—when I joined the pompon squad, you know, when I tried out, none of—none of my other friends made it, so it was just me with, you know, a whole other crowd.

> DID YOU EVER GET FRIENDLY WITH THE OTHER PEOPLE ON POMPON?

> Oh yeah, yeah, but, uh, then you know like in Belten you know I'm still friends with, you know, all those people, but I just . . . um, I don't even remember hardly any of those people's names, I mean I know them all you know, if I see [them] I'll say "that's them," but it's just—

Another aspect of the corporate quality of activities is that as part of career qualification, involvement in activities contributes to the individual's overall status. And while Burnouts are as competitive as Jocks, and have no objection to competing with their friends in individual skills, they are unwilling to participate in competition that sets up the "whole individual" against his or her peers. The most common Burnout (and In-between) criticism of Jocks is that they consider themselves "better" than others. The following Burnout tells how she withdrew from activities to avoid seeming stuck up.

> DID YOU GO OUT FOR CHEERLEADING OR ANYTHING LIKE THAT?

> Now that started in the ninth grade. And that's when I—well, how, [I don't] really know how to explain how I felt—I felt that at that time, I didn't have to do that to be popular. And I thought, mm, cheerleaders, everybody's going to look up at them, and they're going to, you know, they're going to be stuck up, and I don't want

to be known as a stuck up cheerleader, and—so I steered away from that. I wanted to be one though. That's, that's what was, that—I did, you know, because I knew I'd enjoy it. And I thought, well, look at the ones that were last year. All the girls look down on them: "She's a stuck up cheerleader," you know. So—

This quest for overall superiority is the main motivation, according to Burnouts, for Jock participation in certain school activities. While many Burnouts express an interest in activities such as sports, pompon, cheerleading, journalism, photography, art, and music, they express universal contempt for student government. Those other activities are pursued for the pleasure of the activity itself, but student government inherently involves participation in a student hierarchy. Furthermore, because student government does not have the power to affect the running of the school in any significant way, the Burnouts view it as a hierarchy that exists for its own sake. At Belten, they take the fact that Jocks cannot negotiate on the closed campus issue as proof that student government is fictitious and infantilizing—that it is merely a parody of adult roles.

The existence of the student hierarchy puts all who do not participate or succeed in it at a distinct disadvantage, not simply because the hierarchy controls aspects of the school environment, but because the freedoms that adolescents covet are incorporated in its reward system. The articulation of the student with the adult hierarchy makes it additionally distasteful to Burnouts. If hierarchical relations among peers are an anathema, the value of hierarchical status in gaining favor with adults is unspeakable. While Jocks, with the help of the school, negotiate personal freedom with their parents, Burnouts prefer to achieve their more treasured freedoms by stealth or rebellion. This is not because their parents are more restrictive—in fact, Burnouts are free to go out at night at an earlier age than are most Jocks—but because they do not have the same opportunity for extended autonomy through the school. The authoritarian parenting patterns typical of working class families, and indeed of the families of many of Belten's Burnouts, do not develop the kinds of negotiating skills that many Jocks learn in the home and bring to school. Burnouts prefer unambiguous authority, which they can choose to obey or not with clear knowledge of the consequences if they get caught. Burnouts seek freedom in absence of adult supervision and view school activities as one more sphere of adult control. They view the freedoms dispensed within this sphere as vestiges of childhood patterns, because they are acquired at the cost of submission. The kind of self-determination that Burnouts value involves the simple taking, rather than negotiation, of freedom. Negotiation of school freedom, further-more, involves differentiation among students and threatens equality and solidarity among peers. It is not the ultimate authority of adults over behavior in the school that alienates Burnouts; Burnouts accept that the school has to establish and enforce rules to maintain order. What alienates Burnouts is the possibility of exempt status in exchange for relinquishing autonomy in areas of life that they consider private. While Burnouts do not all agree on how much freedom should be their inalienable right, they all agree that rules restricting freedom should apply equally to all students and that violation of these rules should entail guaranteed and uniform sanctions.

Burnouts in general feel that the majority of school staff are incon-sistent in dealing with student behavior. Particularly, Burnouts feel that they are dealt with more severely than Jocks.

> They see who you're hanging around with and, uh, that pretty much if they got suspended then, you know, you'll get suspended pretty soon or they're gonna be watching you. Like this school, um, for instance like me and Ellen. Um, she got suspended for something, then like within—they—they're watching me, I'm pretty sure they were because like the assistant principal used to follow me around.

> SO HAVE YOU EVER BEEN SUSPENDED?

> Yeah.

> FOR WHAT?

> Um, for walking around when I was supposed to be in a class. That's terrible. I just, you know, I was going to go back to class. Like I was late, about 15 minutes late, and I went by study, and I seen someone I knew and I was just talking to them for a second. And, uh, all of a sudden, uh, a teacher came up to me and said, "Where are you supposed to be?" I go, "Well, I'm going to my class right now." He said, "Well, I think you better come to the office with me and I'll check on that," you know. So we went to the office and he just, he suspended me, he said, "There's not—you're sup-posed to be in your class and you're not in there, so I'm going to have to suspend you. If you're lucky you'll get five days." That's what he said. And, uh, I was suspended for a day, though. Because I was talking to the assistant principal, I said, "This is kind of funny, you know. I was late for a class and, uh, I get suspended." He goes, "Well, don't do it again," you know.

DO YOU THINK THAT IF A JOCK WAS LATE TO CLASS AND STANDING AND
TALKING TO SOMEBODY IN THE HALL THEY WOULD GET SUSPENDED FOR IT?

No, I don't. I, I really doubt that more than if I did. Because
they'd think, "Oh, she was outside, uh, smoking pot." Yeah. Or
they'd just say, "Well, they're, you know, this person's pretty nice.
They were probably just talking to a teacher before class or something."

While some Jocks develop part of their sense of power in school
through their ability to influence teachers, Burnouts develop the same
sense through their ability to defy them. Many Burnouts said at one
time or another that the Burnouts "run the school," only to qualify the
statement later to contrast it with the sense in which the Jocks "run the
school." For Burnouts, the school consists of all the people who spend
their days in the building—not the activities that take place within it.
For the Jocks to run the school, the entire school would have to participate in their activities. Some Burnouts pride themselves on the effort
that school staff must expend trying to deal with Burnouts and on the
number of things they can get away with. To the extent that Burnouts
can manipulate school staff in this way, they see themselves as "running"
the school.

I never did like school. I, uh, I never, well, it, it's, to a point it's all
right. It's like a big party, but I don't like the work. Most of the
teachers I don't like, the hassles you get. I always seem to get hassled in this school no matter what I'm doing. Someone will always
come up, "What are you doing? What are you doing? What are
you doing?" I don't like that. I never did like school. . . . Burnouts
get hassled quite a bit. More than the Jocks. . . . They, they don't
like Burnouts in this school because there's quite a few and they
just about run the place. . . . I think they're afraid of us.

WHAT DO YOU MEAN, RUN THE PLACE?

They get away with quite a bit. A lot of things happen that I know
they don't want to happen.

LIKE WHAT?

Lots of vandalism. We're always skipping and getting in trouble
doing this and that. They don't like all the weed in the courtyard
and the drugs. We get away—we don't run the school, but we get
away with a hell of a lot.

The above factors in the Burnouts' abandonment of school activities all derive from the clash between positive value systems, but there is also a negative side. As junior high wears on, Burnouts become increasingly unwilling to compete with Jocks. To some extent this is because the Burnouts perceive the system as unfair and feel that the Jocks have an advantage in the endorsement of the school and in the power of their networks. But one cannot ignore the Burnouts' growing confusion about their own abilities. Because the main group of Belten High Burnouts began junior high as a popular crowd and were gradually edged out by the rival Jock popular crowd, one cannot ignore their sense of failure. Much of the Burnouts' discussion reflects confusion about their own personal worth and indicates that they have internalized at least in part the school's assumption of Jocks' personal superiority. While Burnouts are aware that Jocks' favored position in the school is at least partially due to greater opportunity and discrimination, Burnouts are nonetheless uncertain about their own undeveloped abilities. This, and a more general fear of rejection, no doubt has something to do with withdrawal from competition.

UM, HOW ABOUT POMPON? DID YOU QUIT THAT TOO?

No, I finished it through ninth grade but I didn't—

YOU DIDN'T TRY OUT?

No.

HOW COME?

I don't know. I don't know. They're good. Belten's pompon squad is fantastic and I just—there was a lot too many girls trying out so I just sluffed it off.

YOU DIDN'T LOSE INTEREST THEN, JUST DECIDED THAT—ˆ

Yeah, I—it's fun, I love it, it—it's a blast, but it just—you know, I wasn't in—just wasn't in the mood I guess.

DO YOU GET INVOLVED IN SCHOOL ACTIVITIES?

No, because in ninth grade I was a cheerleader, and then when I came here I tried out for cheerleading and I didn't make it. And after that I just haven't tried out for anything after. That, it really hurt me. So I never tried out for anything.

Contributing to the sense of failure is the Burnouts' performance in the academic sphere. While some Burnouts had academic problems beginning in elementary school, others developed problems in secondary school, when evenings out came into conflict with the homework that was becoming an important part of schoolwork.

> My grades were high and everything. Everybody's, just about everybody's were before they hit junior high. If there was, if there was home studying, none of us would be like this. . . . It's just school that does it. . . . Because you meet people, you know, and they're examples, and you start partying with them. That's junior high. Goes back to they all want to be cool, you know. It always goes back to that, too.

*   *   *

DID YOU CONSIDER YOURSELF A BURNOUT IN SEVENTH GRADE?

> Hell, no. I was a little Jock. . . . I used to get really good grades. I was burning out, what happened to me. I used to be smart. I used to get like B's and—I don't know what happened to my brain.

PROBABLY NOTHING HAPPENED TO YOUR BRAIN.

> It's probably still there, but I don't use it that much.

*   *   *

> Yeah. It changed. The whole scene changed when I hit seventh grade. That's what changed, seventh grade. . . . Came out, went into Rover high graded, you know, good student, came out of Rover all burned out. Three years.

If Burnouts' failure in academics puts them at a disadvantage in school, success in areas that interest them brings little external reward. The vocational arena is clearly isolated in the school. Vocational teachers by and large do not participate in the school's power structure, and the vocational curriculum frequently has low priority and prestige. Many Burnout boys are deeply involved in automobile mechanics and pursue this interest in and out of school with the same intensity with which "Brains" pursue their academic work or Jocks pursue their activities. But the expertise and commitment of those Burnouts, far from earning them recognition in school, stigmatizes them as being "only" interested in cars. The school-sponsored competitions and activities that bring prestige and visibility to sports never extend to cars. Car and motorcycle racing, therefore, is generally pursued under dangerous and illegal conditions in public roads and empty lots.

The school, which restricts adolescents' contact with adults on the outside, is intended specifically as a milieu in which adolescents develop under the guidance of specially trained adults. This guidance, however, is most effective when it involves intensive interaction and cooperation between adolescents and adults, and these are largely restricted to students engaged in corporate pursuits within the school. The Jocks' relationship with school staff in the production of activities serves as an apprenticeship in management and organization. Stinchcombe (1964) has argued that the school denies such an opportunity to the future blue-collar worker. Contrasting the high school vocational curriculum with an apprenticeship, Stinchcombe points out that while an apprenticeship provides a set of positive symbols (identity markers) to help the young person progress to full status as a craftsperson, the school provides such symbols only for academic curriculum.

> The formal rituals so appropriate to symbolize advance toward professional status function badly for symbolizing progression toward the "good working class life." Students destined for the working class are (inadvertently) denied negatively in the formal ritual idiom, as "those left over when the middle class is sorted out." (p. 107)

To the degree that certain high school classes do provide the individual attention, cooperation, and sense of productivity that characterizes an apprenticeship, they are attractive to Burnouts. By and large these classes are vocational, and many of them take their students out of the regimentation of the classroom and into work or work-like settings, where they can perform as more autonomous productive workers. Many Burnouts are also attracted to art classes, which share with vocational courses the opportunity to interact with classmates while working on projects, and to receive individual task-oriented attention from the teacher. Although it would be a mistake to categorize the two sets of teachers, the Burnouts generally regard their vocational teachers as more sympathetic than their academic teachers. They feel that the vocational teachers share their interests and accept them for who they are. Indeed, because Burnouts form an important part of their constituency, these teachers are more likely to regard the Burnouts simply as students rather than as problems. The girls at Belten are particularly fond of a woman teacher in the family life department, whom they say they can talk to about anything.

The blue-collar orientation of many industrial education teachers is also no doubt a source of compatibility. Not only do these teachers endorse Burnouts' interests and aspirations, but many of them are from similar backgrounds and share Burnouts' social norms. Since these teachers are not, by and large, involved in the extracurricular sphere, their relations with students are based on personal contact and issues rather than on political roles. One Burnout, in expressing his preference and admiration for one of his industrial education teachers, pointed in particular to the teacher's disciplinary style, which sets uniform standards for all students and metes out uniform sanctions.

> That guy, he's a mean guy, man. You don't, can't do nothing wrong in his class. He's really strict.
>
> DOES THAT BOTHER YOU?
>
> No, I think of it as a challenge. Makes a lot of people mad, but he don't make me mad because he doesn't do nothing that you don't deserve. He's the kind of guy like if you do something wrong—I screwed up one day and used something without doing something to it first and he—he was pissed off, but all I got was a kick in the ass. He got the message through real good. I don't know, the guy, he's a good teacher.

The mechanisms of the Burnouts' withdrawal from school are in some ways analogous to those discussed by Ogbu (1978) in connection with subordinate minorities. According to Ogbu, racial discrimination in American society imposes a job ceiling on blacks, excluding them from employment mobility through the "normal" channels accepted for the white population, and making them dependent on subordinate strategies. Lifelong expectations stemming from this ceiling lead blacks to develop personal strategies that are stigmatized by mainstream society.

> The reliance on white patronage has encouraged such personal qualities as dependency, compliance, and manipulation, which are quite different from the qualities of personal initiative, competitiveness and perseverance which the white approach to self-betterment encourages them to develop. (pp. 198–199)

Mainstream evaluation of blacks' strategies as evidence of lack of ambition and commitment ignores the adaptive value of such strategies in the mainstream-dominated economy. Although white working class adolescents do not face this racially based job ceiling, their perception of their own limited possibilities is engendered by their view of their parents' limited advancement and by their personal experience throughout primary school, as discussed in Chapter 1. The fact that many Burnouts were not model pupils in elementary school, and hence were not among those who received teachers' positive attention and sanction, undoubtedly led many of them to feel that they could not compete with Jocks. Many Burnouts are overwhelmed by a sense of unfairness, feeling that factors that they could not control led them, at an early age, to a position from which they could not escape. Many students, not just Burnouts, feel that their relative lack of parentally bestowed resources put them at a disadvantage early on in school—a disadvantage that intensified as school status became increasingly tied to having the right clothes, the right friends, and the right interactive style. This feeling was exacerbated for Burnouts through junior high school as their category affiliation itself developed into a basis for discrimination.

Thus Burnouts in general develop lower aspirations than their Jock peers, who have been taught that their potential is virtually limitless. A sense that they can never please the school encourages Burnouts to focus on pleasing themselves and on pursuing private satisfactions separate from their life in the institution. In much the same fashion as Willis's (1977) Lads, the Burnouts develop a culture that is dominated by the private and opposed to the institutional. Just as, in later life, they will look upon the workplace as a necessity to gain the means to pursue private life, Burnouts attend school because it is necessary, but focus their attention on relations and activities whose locus is conceived of as independent from the school. The Burnouts' perception that the institution exists to control and thwart them contrasts strongly with the Jocks' perception that they can share in controlling the institution.

Despite their contempt for Jocks' activities, many Burnouts think of Jocks as "happy people," and see the Jocks' integration into the school as evidence that they "have it together." Some Burnouts who have had academic difficulty since elementary school feel that the Jocks are endowed with superior abilities. But most Burnouts view being a Jock as a luxury that only money, a comfortable home life, and supportive parents can provide. Most Jocks recognize this view, and some consider themselves privileged. But the overwhelming ideology of Jocks and the school remains that the choices and opportunities are open to all, reflecting Kahl's (1964) observation that "the man who has emerged successfully from competition wants to feel that the competitive rules were fair and that he won through superior ability and energy" (p. 197).

CLASS AND BURNOUT AFFILIATION

The association between Burnout and working class cultures needs to be elucidated one step further. To say that the Burnout category embodies many working class norms and constitutes a working class culture for its members is not to say that working class culture is Burnout culture. Burnout culture is, rather, an activation of working class norms within the school situation. There are many working class students in the school who are not Burnouts, just as there are many middle class students who are not Jocks, and it is the polarization of opposing sets of norms within the highly limited and politicized atmosphere of the school that leads each category to become an extreme expression of its class-related norms. But these categories also attract members by their fit with individual adolescent needs that may be, in some cases, independent of class. It is probable that just as some people are attracted to the Jock category by its image of happiness, power, and control, others are attracted to the Burnout category by its image of unhappiness, powerlessness, and rebellion.

The Jock category, because it is endorsed by the school and offers societal rewards, has an apparent independent function in its relation to institutional success that attracts individuals who might not otherwise seek to conform to a stereotype as a means of confirming their identities. The Burnout category, on the other hand, attracts censure that locks its members into an adversarial relationship with the adults who might otherwise provide guidance and support. It is probable, therefore, that the security of category identity plays a greater role for individual Burnouts, while many working class youngsters who share the basic norms and interests of Burnouts but can find security outside of such an identity will join the mass of In-betweens. It is for this reason that Burnout affiliation combines positive working class norms with a problem orientation that is not entirely associated with class. This view was expressed by one working class In-between in characterizing the Jocks, the Burnouts, and people like herself.

> [The Jocks] OK, stuck up. Have to get the good grades. Um, let me see, uh, they push you to a side because like if you get them in a class, uh, they'll hang around with their certain group and then they'll look at you like you're the low class, you know, they won't, they're the ones that have to go to every game. Cheerleaders, they have to be cheerleaders, uh, stuff like that. The Burnouts . . . OK, they—I know a lot of people that study. The Burnouts, OK, they don't really like to work, I'd say. . . . Um, I'm not trying to put them low, but I'm saying the majority do not like, you know, they can move, they can learn, but they just don't want to. Uh, they're the ones that have to go out and party every night, come in stoned, drunk, deal with drugs. Uh, um, and I think that's it. You can tell between the two groups.

AND HOW MANY PEOPLE DO YOU THINK THERE ARE WHO ARE LIKE YOU,
WHO ARE SORT OF—

Not many. Neutral. Not many. . . . They just don't want to seem to
turn to drugs to cope with their problems, and, uh, they want to,
they want to have good grades, you know, but not be stuck up
where you'll look at someone and say, "Well, you are lower than
me," and stuff like that.

Adolescent "class" is based on access to resources that are ultimately
controlled by the middle-aged middle class adult power structure. Jocks'
access to this power structure puts them in a privileged relation to those
who do not have such access. Because of the clear disparity in power
and substance, those who deal with the power structure do so at the cost
of incurring obligation, but this arrangement guarantees them the sponsorship of the power structure and the possibility of access to it and
control of its resources when they themselves become middle-aged.
Those whose parents are part of that power structure not only have
direct access, but have training at home in dealing with it; parents who
are not part of the adult power structure can provide their children with
less information on how it runs and less direct access to it. Unwilling—
some of them unable—to establish trade relations with the power structure, Burnouts work through more egalitarian contacts. The age-
heterogeneity of their networks provides them with access to the
younger adult world. While their young adult contacts are not part of
the middle-aged adult establishment, relations with them incur fewer
obligations. Thus, while the return from these contacts is smaller, the
cost in personal compromise is minimal.

The Jocks' activities in high school and their anticipated further
education are intended to provide them with more power in their jobs
and over their lives. Burnouts, who expect no such later reward, can
find no excuse for doing without this power now. The demand for freedom from adult domination, and the seizing of adventure and real experience, therefore, is at least partly a result of the recognition that
power over one's own person must be seized immediately, for it is not
enhanced through waiting. Waiting until graduation from high school,
or waiting until one's twenty-first birthday, does not change the degree
of power that most Burnouts ultimately expect to get.

8

The Effects of Social Polarization

It's hard to say, you know, it's . . . if there was no goody-goody group or Burnout, I think it'd work out, everyone would all work out. You know, more friends, more activities and stuff.

While curricular tracking has come and gone in the American public schools, adolescent social categories remain as an enduring and uncontrolled social tracking system. Although the choice of curriculum and activities offered by the public schools is intended to provide young people with the opportunity to determine their futures, the social structure of the school, and in particular the social category system, leaves little real choice.

It is largely a result of the polarization between the Jocks and the Burnouts that people are thrown into a choice between two set patterns of behavior on the basis of a variety of unrelated interests and needs. Thus a conspiracy of factors conspires to lead the children of parents of different socioeconomic statuses into strikingly different roles in adolescence, and these roles in time prepare the individuals for their places in adult society. Within the school context, the group that controls the social organization is preparing to control, as adults, the means of production in society. Those who do not participate in school spend their energies developing networks of support and mutual help, which aid them in coping with adolescence and which will help them navigate within a relatively powerless stratum of society as adults.

The Jocks' and Burnouts' roles in school reflect their parents' roles in the adult community. The Jocks, coming from more prosperous families, see their parents more in control of their environment, while many Burnouts watch their parents finding their way in a world that is beyond their control. Parental power is also differentiated in relation to the school. The parents who attend parents' organization meetings tend to be those who themselves enjoyed cooperative relations with the school during their adolescence or who are accustomed to a certain amount of control in their community or place of work. Working class parents tend to carry into adulthood their uncomfortable relations with school when they were adolescents. While Jocks' parents monitor the quality of school programs and of the school's treatment of their children, Burnouts' parents' interactions with the school tend to be limited to the discussion of disciplinary and academic problems. Thus while Jocks' parents exert pressure on the school on behalf of their children, Burnouts see their parents as either aligned with the school against them or as unproductively hostile to the school.

Because it severely restricts choice and vision, polarization is obviously a monster that has been created by a set of institutions that most people perceive as designed to do something very different. Some of the conclusions of the work presented in this book should obviously concern strategies for its elimination. The study of polarization has also led to an examination of social networks and dynamics that point to a number of other serious problems in the current practice and conception of education, and indeed of learning.

THE CONCENTRATION OF RESOURCES

The power that extracurricular activities in the school have to polarize the student body stems from the way in which resources are concentrated within the high school. The segregation of adolescents in an age-graded institution, isolated from the surrounding community, focuses their attention on the population, the activities and the roles that are available within the school. Within this restricted world, recognition and visibility can be achieved only through the accumulation or the vocal rejection of its limited resources. At a life stage when people are seeking a place in the community, trying to define themselves in terms of their relations to peers, and seeking autonomy in meaningful roles, the school's emphasis on a stratified extracurricular program leaves much of its population at loose ends. Although there are rewards to be had in individual activities and classes, there is a single track to community success within the school. To many of those who are preparing for life in corporate institutions, the roles offered by the school are meaningful. To those who are not, school activities are a sham—a caricature of life in the adult community.

Any high school student can look out into the community and see real roles, needs, and opportunities. When school activities come into contact with these, it is always as a vehicle for hierarchical activities. Thus such things as canned food drives, which are intended to benefit the area's needy, are mounted in the school as part of class competitions and are abstracted from the real human needs that justify them. Such activities, put in the hands of Burnouts, would be conducted very differently. The Burnouts' involvement in and eagerness for real roles in the local community alienate them from the kinds of activities sponsored by the school. Opportunities to pursue meaningful activities in the community would give them the kind of outlet that they are denied in school. The high school is a closed youth community watched over by a specialized population of middle-aged adults, who act as gatekeepers to the outside. Community groups wanting to get into contact with adolescents tend to work through the schools, and are in turn dependent on the school to negotiate this contact, and students interested in that contact are dependent on the school's recognition or, more specifically, on the recognition of certain staff members who handle relations with the world beyond the school. The individual's access to outside resources, therefore, depends on his or her access to key staff, and those students with the greatest access are the ones most involved in activities within the framework of the school and thus least interested in involvement outside.

The problem of the current isolation of adolescents in schools is a continual theme in the study of adolescence. Boyer (1983) emphasizes it in his report on the high school, arguing that adolescents need, but have little access to, roles in the community. High schools are not "total institutions" (Goffman, 1961), but they approach such status in their domination of a broad range of adolescent interests. As more responsibilities for the adolescent age group are heaped on the schools (as Boyer, 1983, puts it, "high schools have accumulated purposes like barnacles on a weathered ship," p. 57) adolescents get increasingly trapped. Those who have become alienated from the school become alienated from more and more resources, and as the resources are concentrated in the school, opportunities for adolescents disappear elsewhere in the community.

At a time in the history of the world when human beings need the broadest possible understanding, the school focuses adolescents inward. The school mediates relations not only with the local community, but also with adjacent communities. School attendance carves a coherent geographic continuum into separate units. Where adjacent population segments are demographically similar, this separation creates artificial divisions; where they are not, their differences become emphasized, obfuscated, and institutionalized. Thus schools create boundaries where there is similarity, and impose uniformity where there is dissimilarity. The effects of social polarization are carried out across school boundaries as well as within the school itself.

The concentration of resources for adolescents in the schools and indeed the separation of resources for this age group from those for other age groups is dysfunctional at the same time that it is a burden on the schools. There is no obvious reason why adolescents should pursue their social, musical, dramatic, and athletic interests in the same institution. Furthermore, the association of these activities with a single community status system frequently has the effect of diluting their inherent value, because they become tokens in a cumulative achievement system. People who are truly interested in these activities frequently have to battle for a place with people who are there for political purposes, and who indeed frequently win for political reasons. Perhaps most insidious is the loss of creativity that accompanies the separation of the value of activities from their content. A student engaged in an activity for its token value will be less inclined to contemplate experimentation in that activity, because the risk involved threatens the token value.

The Jock and Burnout categories organize disparate individuals into stereotyped patterns of interaction among themselves and with adults. While this creates problems for all members of the community, there is little question that as a category the Burnouts have the most to lose. Problems that should be dealt with individually are often buried in a mass definition, locking individuals into an adversarial relationship with the very institution that is supposed to free adolescents from the limitations of their childhood environment. It is particularly important today to examine carefully the resources and opportunities to help adolescents work out their social identities.

It is a basic fact of life in our society that children are left increasingly on their own. This enhances the importance of peer influence and the dependence of children on their peers for emotional support and advice. Certain patterns of interaction that are directly adaptive to the absence of parental support are maladaptive in the quest for the kinds of opportunity that only adults can provide. The Joint Commission on Mental Health of Children (1973) has pointed out that "adolescence can provide those lucky enough to have a second chance an opportunity to move away from the malignancies of family pathology, social disorganization, and deprivation" (p. 238). But the Commission stresses that not all children have the luxury of an adolescence and at the moment it is the responsibility of the schools to provide the resources for this adolescence. In reality, those who most need reorientation must rely on their friends for guidance and support, and because friends are normally chosen on the basis of shared needs, it is frequently not within their capacity to provide constructive help.

At the same time that adult society forces many adolescents into mutual dependency, it stigmatizes the strategies that they develop to cope in the absence of alternatives. The overwhelming middle class value that the schools and the Jocks place on changing instrumental friendships stigmatizes the kind of lasting and loyal friendship groups that provide support for Burnouts. Rather than encouraging and helping supportive adolescent networks, society focuses on their potential for delinquency and pressures them to disband. But there are some important educational lessons to be learned from careful consideration of Burnout social interaction. Not only do educators owe it to Burnouts to understand how learning takes place in their social networks, but they owe it to non-Burnouts to offer them some of the Burnouts' strategies.

WHAT STUDENTS LEARN IN SCHOOL

One of the greatest errors in education is to assume that the larger social context of the school is irrelevant or even secondary to learning. The flourishing field of classroom ethnography indicates that educators have begun to take seriously the social interaction in the classroom as part of the educational process. However, the social system that makes up the school as a whole, and the relations among the students and between students and faculty outside the classroom, are still regarded as fairly remote from learning. While it is commonly recognized that these dynamics affect a student's predisposition to learn in school, there is a far more complex relation between social structure and learning. The social structure of the school is not simply the context of learning; it is part of what is learned. What a student learns in the classroom is indeed a very small other part.

One reason that relatively little is learned in classrooms is that didactic methods for the transfer of information are relatively inefficient. For generations, teachers have invented ways to make information "stick" through the use of games and alternative discourse forms. These strategies have worked not simply because they were more fun, but because they embedded learning in real activities. The fact that so much educational research today is focusing on collaborative learning is evidence of the recognition that people learn better when learning is integrated into normal social interaction and when information is shared rather than passed down. The natural conclusion should be, then, that interaction that goes on outside the classroom is crucial to educators, for at least two reasons. First, educators should be able to put the forms of interaction that go on naturally outside the classroom to work in and around the classroom. Second, educators should realize that the social forms and dynamics that students engage in outside the classroom and their strategies for coping with the school are a major part of what they learn in school.

Stinchcombe's (1964) observation that the schools offer an apprenticeship to academic students but not to vocational students is particularly true in the extracurricular sphere. A good deal of attention is currently being given to apprenticeship learning, as a kind of learning that is most natural and that virtually never fails. Lave and Wenger (in press) maintain that it is the possibility for "legitimate peripheral participation" that accounts for this success. Apprentices work their way gradually into the center of activity, first by watching and then trying out simple peripheral tasks with the informal help of those around them, and then by gradually moving in this way toward more central tasks. Extracurricular activities offer just this kind of learning experience in corporate interaction and institutional structure, with faculty and more senior students providing resources for observation and help to more junior students. There is no situation remotely resembling this kind of apprenticeship for Burnouts outside of the vocational classroom.

Learning About Institutional Structure

Movement within society or within an organization requires constant readjustment to new sets of norms, codes, and social groups as one moves between units. The ability to perceive and interpret the differences between these units as one moves rests on, among other things, an overview of the organization that subsumes them and a sufficient understanding of the relations within the organization to grasp the orientation of each unit to the larger organization. The same factors determine the individual's ability to find information within that organization. Organizational knowledge tells people where to go for information, what kinds of information are necessary and available, and how that information fits into a larger structure of information. Understanding the institutional structure of the school, therefore, is essential to the student's ability to get around and to gain access to the informational and other resources of the institution. In turn, this kind of institutional knowledge, and the strategies for acquiring it, carry over into other institutions, including the workplace.

Extracurricular activities provide a means by which students can grasp the institutional structure of the school. These activities combine with the administrative structure of the school to provide a hierarchical organization within which individuals can identify themselves in terms of their roles and their organizational relation to other role holders. For the Jocks, the relative isomorphism between personal networks and institutional structure adds intensity and personal meaning to the institution itself. In the course of their daily interactions, Jocks acquire important institutional information: information about students and school personnel and their roles and responsibilities, the resources they control, their hierarchical relations, and their personal characteristics and relationships. This information allows Jocks to chart relations among people elsewhere in the network, gain access to them and their resources, and call upon their roles as justification for this access. Above all, the Jocks' view of the structure of the institution is essentially the same as the institution's own view of itself, so that their understanding and manipulation of the dynamics within the institution is maximally effective.

Viewed in this way, one must agree that the high school is a very different place for Jocks and Burnouts. Burnouts have the least access to such information in the school, and hence are destined to fail, except in the most fragmentary ways, in their attempts to manipulate the system.

Learning Not to Learn

The strategies that students develop to function in the school environment are part of the knowledge that they take with them into further training or the workplace. Those strategies shape, and are inseparable from, the knowledge that constitutes the school's formal curriculum. What the Burnouts learn in school is how to be marginalized. They look forward to graduation, with the expectation that then they will escape the strictures and limitations of their high school roles. However, the strategies that they have acquired for learning within an institution, whether it be school or the workplace, will marginalize them elsewhere just as in high school. High school, therefore, is not simply a bad experience for these students—it teaches them lessons that threaten to limit them for the rest of their lives.

While class differences in social networks are well known (see, for example, Bott, 1957), these differences have not been connected with class differences in school performance. But it is clear that the network differences between Jocks and Burnouts lead to significant differences in approaches to information.

The most obvious difficulty arising from the Burnouts' age-heterogeneous networks and the consequent speed in development is that their earlier contact with adult experiences and prerogatives creates a need for certain kinds of information earlier than adults are willing to give it to them. Information about such things as drugs, sex, birth control, legal rights, and so forth is generally not openly available from adults until they feel that children "need" (that is, SHOULD need) it. This means that from a fairly early age, Burnouts' most pressing informational needs are met not by adults but, however inadequately, by older members of the peer group. Because of the autonomy of Burnout networks, a whole range of information, not simply stigmatized information, is acquired from friends rather than from adults. And no doubt the peer social context in which this information is imparted and shared has an important influence on attitudes toward that knowledge. With the complexity of peer relations within a heterogeneous extended network, information does not come from a single source, nor does it come from an authority figure who can or would apply norms or strictures on the acquisition and use of information. Indeed, the free-flowing nature of this information no doubt predisposes Burnouts to prefer this kind of learning as available and geared to their needs, and to contrast it with the clearly vertical and one-way acquisition of knowledge from adults.

The middle class children's homogeneous network, on the other hand, leaves its members dependent on adults for information of all kinds. But insofar as these children's developmental timetables correspond more closely (though rarely entirely) to adult norms, they find adults to be more adequate purveyors of relevant information and do not resent the adults' ultimate control of it. In fact, the delivery of information may function in a system of personal rewards. The Jocks' basically hierarchical view of social life, and the intimate place of this hierarchy in the school institution, leads naturally to a hierarchical approach to the acquisition of knowledge and information. The childhood acceptance of adults as sources of information feeds into the structure of the secondary school, where adults also become the sources of social resources and rewards.

In school, the teacher comes to share simultaneously the middle class parent's role as appropriate and major source of adult-controlled information, and the working class parent's role of arbitrary safekeeper and denier of adult information. It follows that the characteristics of Jock and Burnout social networks and the norms governing information embodied in these networks dispose the members of the two categories to different responses to teaching as it is commonly practiced in our schools, and particularly in the academic curriculum. While the Jocks are predisposed to accept information from a single hierarchical source and to compete in its display, the Burnouts are more likely to regard the academic classroom as a center of received knowledge of no great relevance and to prefer cooperative learning and shun both the competitive and the authoritarian aspects of classroom teaching.

Jock social networks and social norms are mapped onto the institutional structure of the school, so that learning in school is integrated to some extent into Jock social activity. Burnout networks and norms, on the other hand, frequently conflict with the structure and norms of the school. In a very real sense, the school is not the same institution for the Jocks and the Burnouts, as the members of each group construct their school community around themselves, according to their experiences, the activities they engage in there, and their information. Jocks' and Burnouts' notions of what is available in the school, the conditions and rewards for using what is available, and the behavior required to gain access to it are as different as their social networks.

The most important skill that students can acquire in school is the skill to learn and to find information on their own. The structure of the school maximizes access to information for students involved in the academic curriculum and extracurricular activities. Jocks, therefore, have the greatest access to information that is controlled within the school. While Burnouts are marginalized in the school, they are more integrated into informal networks in the local area than are Jocks. But the school values the kinds, sources, settings, and conditions of Jock networks, and by and large denigrates those of the Burnout networks. Thus, rather than encouraging Burnouts to use their informational skills, the school forces them underground. It is not preordained that Burnouts will be hostile to education. Although some of them have been unsuccessful in school, or rebellious to adult authority, since early elementary school, it is simplistic to assume that this is true of all Burnouts, or even typical of the category. The Burnout category is above all a working class culture, whose hostility to the school stems from that institution's inability to provide a meaningful experience in relation to the Burnouts' life pattern, and from the dissonance between their patterns of friendship and interaction and those endorsed by the school.

It is time for educators to stop attributing student alienation to forces beyond the control of the school. This is not because all problems originate within the school or can be solved within it, but because such an approach ignores the fundamental relation between learning and social interaction. We need to consider in great detail the kinds of social dynamics that are encouraged within the school, and the interaction between those social dynamics and learning. At the moment, the social institutions of our schools are based on middle class models, as are our didactic methods of teaching and notions of "information transfer." We tend to think of learning as the result of teaching, and of teaching as a simple transfer of knowledge. In fact, most of the learning we do from day to day is collaborative, and most of the knowledge we have is shared. It is only when our status depends on the competitive management of knowledge and information, as in many of the situations created in schools, that we look upon it as something to be accumulated. It is obvious that serious understanding and use of collaborative learning in the curricular sphere is in order. It turns out, in this case, that what's good for the Burnouts is good for America.

Assuming that our society will continue for some time with age-segregated institutions educating its young, the ramifications of this segregation must be recognized and understood. Improving education for the adolescent population depends on the creation of an atmosphere in which all adolescents are equally receptive and equally privy to the resources of the school. This atmosphere does not depend simply on interaction between individual school personnel and individual students or even groups of students, but depends far more on interaction among students. Although an individual may be strongly influenced or even transformed by one teacher at some point in life, the average adolescent probably learns more from peers than from any other category of people. There is a wide gap in our knowledge of the structure of adolescent society, and this gap prevents us from understanding the broader issues in problems that face adolescents. Ignorance about adolescents leads us to trivialize their experience, and our efforts to take them seriously are frequently misguided by our stylized notion of their social relations. It is particularly ironic that, in considering "the youth of today," we seem to translate and apply our own adolescent experience in all the wrong ways. We focus on the surface (although admittedly serious) issues of substance use and abuse, increased pregnancy and childbearing, and alienation, and fail to concentrate on the underlying social processes that are common to at least the current generations.

References

Adelson, J. (1971, Fall). The political imagination of the young adolescent. *Daedalus*, 1013–1050.

Allen, S. (1973). Some theoretical problems in the study of youth. In H. Silverstein (Ed.), *The sociology of youth* (51–62). New York: Macmillan.

Barker, R. G., & Gump, P. V. (1964). *Big school small school*. Stanford: Stanford University Press.

Becker, H. S. (1952). Social class variation in teacher–pupil relationship. *Journal of Educational Sociology, 25*, 451–465.

Berger, B. M. (1971). On the youthfulness of youth culture. In B. Berger, *Looking for America* (pp. 66–86). Englewood Cliffs: Prentice-Hall.

Boissevain, J. (1974). *Friends of friends*. Oxford: Blackwell.

Bott, E. (1957). *Family and social network*. London: Tavistock.

Bowles, S., & Gintis, H. (1976). *Schooling in capitalist America*. New York: Basic Books.

Boyer, E. L. (1983). *High school*. New York: Harper & Row.

Brake, M. (1985). *Comparative youth culture*. London: Routledge and Kegan Paul.

Buff, S. (1970). Greasers, dopers, and hippies: Three responses to the adult world. In L. Howe (Ed.), *The white majority* (pp. 60–70). New York: Random House.

Carnoy, M. (1974). *Education as cultural imperialism*. New York: McKay.

Cicourel, A. V., & Kitsuse, J. I. (1963). *The educational decision-makers*. New York: Bobbs-Merrill.

Clarke, M. (1974). On the concept of subculture. *British Journal of Sociology, XXV*, 428–41.

Clark, B. (1962). *Educating the expert society*. San Francisco: Chandler.

Cohen, A. K. (1955). *Delinquent boys: The subculture of the gang*. London: Collier McMillan.

Cohen, J. (1979). High school subcultures and the adult world. *Adolescence, 14* (55), 491–502.

Coleman, J. S. (1961). *The adolescent society*. New York: The Free Press of Glencoe.

Coleman, J. S. (1966). *Equality of educational opportunity*. Washington DC: U.S. Government Printing Office.

Coster, J. K. (1959). Some characteristics of high school pupils from three income groups. *Journal of Educational Psychology, 50*, 55–62.

Davis, A. (1951). *Social class influences upon learning*. Cambridge: Harvard University Press.

Davis, A., & Havighurst, R. J. (1948). Social class and color differences in child rearing. *American Sociological Review, XI*, 698–710.

Douvan, E., & Adelson, J. (1966). *The adolescent experience*. New York: Wiley.

Eckert, P. (1982). Clothing and geography in a suburban high school. In C. P. Kottak (Ed.), *Researching American culture* (pp. 139–144). Ann Arbor: University of Michigan Press.

Eckert, P. (1983). Beyond the statistics of adolescent smoking. *American Journal of Public Health, 73*, 439–41.

Eckert, P. (1987). Relative values of opposing variables. In K. M. Denning, S. Inkelas, F. C. McNair-Knox, and J. R. Rickford (Eds.), *NWAVE 15 at Stanford*. Stanford University.

Eckert, P. (1988). Sound change and adolescent social structure. *Language in society, 17*, 183–207.

Eckert, P. (in press). Social polarization and the choice of linguistic variants. In P. Eckert (Ed.), *New ways of analyzing sound change*. New York: Academic Press.

Eisenstadt, S. N. (1956). *From generation to generation*. New York: The Free Press of Glencoe.

Erickson, F., & Schulz, J. (1981). *The counselor as gatekeeper: Social interaction in interviews*. New York: Academic Press.

Goffman, E. (1961). *Asylums*. New York: Doubleday.

Gordon, W. C. (1957). *The social system of the high school*. Glencoe, IL: The Free Press.

Heath, S. B. (1983). *Ways with words*. Cambridge and New York: Cambridge University Press.

Hebdige, D. (1976). Reggae, rastas, and rudies. In S. Hall et al. (Eds.), *Resistance through rituals*. London: Hutchinson University Library.

Hebdige, D. (1979). *Subculture: The meaning of style*. London: Methuen.

Henry, J. (1965). *Culture against man*. New York: Vintage Books.

Hiro, D. (1972). *Black British, white British*. Harmondsworth: Penguin.

Hollingshead, A. B. (1949). *Elmtown's youth*. New York: Wiley.

Jenkins, R. (1983). *Lads, citizens, and ordinary kids*. London: Routledge and Kegan Paul.

Johnston, L. D., Bachman, J. G., & O'Malley, P. M., (1982). *Student drug use, attitudes, and beliefs. National Trends 1975–1982*. Rockville, MD: National Institute on Drug Abuse.

Joint Commission on Mental Health of Children. (1973). *Mental Health: From infancy through adolescence*. New York: Harper & Row.

Kahl, J. A. (1964). *The American class structure*. New York: Holt, Rinehart and Winston.

Kanter, R. M. (1977). *Men and women of the corporation*. New York: Basic Books.

Klineberg, O. (1963, February). Life is fun in a smiling, fair-skinned world. *Saturday Review of Literature* (pp. 75–77)

Kohn, M. L. (1969). *Class and conformity: A study in values*. Homewood, IL: Dorsey Press.

Labov, W. (1972a). *Language in the inner city.* Philadelphia: University of Pennsylvania Press.

Labov, W. (1972b). *Sociolinguistic patterns.* Philadelphia: University of Pennsylvania Press.

Labov, W., Yaeger, M., & Steiner, R. (1973). *The quantitative study of sound change in progress.* Philadelphia: U.S. Regional Survey.

Larkin, R. W. (1979). *Suburban youth in cultural crisis.* New York: Oxford University Press.

Larrick, N. (1965, February). The all-white world of children's books. *Saturday Review of Literature,* (pp. 63–65)

Lave, J., & Wenger, E. (1989). Situated learning: Legitimate peripheral participation. Conference on The Place of Knowledge. Jerusalem, Israel.

Leacock, E. B. (1969). *Teaching and learning in city schools.* New York: Basic Books.

Marcus, L. (1961). *The treatment of minorities in secondary school textbooks.* New York: Anti-Defamation League of B'nai B'rith.

Michaels, S. (1981). 'Sharing time:' Children's narrative styles and differential access to literacy. *Language in Society, 10,* 423–42.

Miller, W. B. (1958). Lower class culture as a generating milieu of gang delinquency. *Journal of Social Issues, 14,* 5–19.

Mitchell, C. (1969). *Social networks in urban situations.* Manchester: Manchester University Press.

Mungham, G., & Pearson, G. (1976). *Working class youth culture.* London: Routledge and Kegan Paul.

Murdock, G., & McCron, R. (1976). Youth and class: The career of a confusion. In: G. Mungham & G. Pearson, (Eds.), *Working class youth culture* (pp. 10–26). London: Routledge and Kegan Paul.

Ogbu, J. (1974). *The next generation.* New York: Academic Press.

Ogbu, J. (1978). *Minority education and caste.* New York: Academic Press.

Ortner, S. B. (1973). On key symbols. *American Anthropologist, 75,* 1338–1346.

Parsons, T. (1942). Age and sex in the social structure of the United States. Reprinted in T. Parsons. (1964). *Essays in sociological theory,* (pp. 89–103). New York: Free Press.

Parsons, T. (1959). The school class as a social system, *Harvard Educational Review, 34,* 297–318.

Philips, S. U. (1972). Participation structures and communicative competence: Warm Springs children in community and classroom. In C. Cazden, V. P. John, & D. H. Hymes (Eds.), *Functions of language in the classroom* (pp. 370–394). New York: Teachers College Press.

Rist, R. C. (1970). Student social class and teacher expectations. *Harvard Educational Review, 40,* 411–451.

Rosen, B. C. (1956). The achievement syndrome: A psychocultural dimension of social stratification. *American Sociological Review, 21,* 203–211.

Scollon, R., & Scollon, S. (1981). *Narrative, literacy, and face in interethnic communication.* Norwood, NJ: Ablex.

Sebald, H. (1960). *Adolescence: A sociological analysis.* New York: Appleton-Century Crofts.

Sewell, W. H., & Shah, V. P. (1967). Social class, parental encouragement, and educational aspirations. *American Journal of Sociology, 73,* 559–72.

Smith, E. A. (1962). *American youth culture*. New York: The Free Press of Glencoe.

Stack, C. (1974). *All our kin*. New York: Harper & Row.

Stinchcombe, A. (1964). *Rebellion in a high school*. Chicago: Quadrangle.

Strodtbeck, F. L. (1958). Family interaction, values, and achievement. In A. L. Baldwin, U. Bronfenbrenner, & D. C. McClelland (Eds.), *Talent and society* (pp. 135–194). Princeton: Van Nostrand.

Schwendinger, H., & Schwendinger, J. P. (1976). Marginal youth and social policy. *Social Problems, 24*, 184–191.

Thrasher, F. M. (1927). *The gang*. Chicago: University of Chicago Press.

Varenne, H. (1982). Jocks and freaks: The symbolic structure of the expression of social interaction among American senior high school students. In G. Spindler (Ed.), *Doing the ethnography of schooling* (pp. 210–235). New York: Holt, Rinehart and Winston.

Walker, J. (1982). Unpublished term paper, University of Michigan.

Willis, P. (1977). *Learning to labour*. Westmead, Farnborough, Hants., England: Saxon House.

Willis, P. (1978). *Profane culture*. London: Routledge and Kegan Paul.

Wilson, A. B. (1963). Social stratification and academic achievement. In A. H. Passow (Ed.), *Education in depressed areas* (pp. 217–235). New York: Teachers College Press, Columbia University.

Youniss, J. (1980). *Parents and peers in social development*. Chicago: University of Chicago Press.

Index

189

ABOUT THE AUTHOR

Penelope Eckert received her PhD in linguistics from Columbia University. She is Associate Professor of Linguistics at the University of Illinois at Chicago, and Research Scientist at the Institute for Research on Learning in Palo Alto, California.